Parent Awareness

Positive Parenting for the 1980s

SAF LERMAN

WINSTON PRESS

This book is dedicated to the many parents
who have shared their parenting concerns
with me and with one another.

Library of Congress Catalog Card Number: 81-51159
ISBN: 0-86683-610-1 (previously ISBN 0-89479-071-4)
Printed in the United States of America
5   4   3

Winston Press
430 Oak Grove
Minneapolis, Minnesota 55403

Acknowledgments

I want to thank the people who have helped me form my thinking about children and parents, and those who have shared the writing of this book.

In Parent Awareness, I offer suggestions to parents based on my own thinking and from many other sources. I have developed some of the suggestions in this book using concepts from the published works of the following authors: Stella Chess, Alexander Thomas, and Herbert G. Birch; David Elkind, Adele Faber and Elaine Mazlish, Selma H. Fraiberg, Haim G. Ginott, Thomas Gordon, Frances L. Ilg and Louise Bates Ames (of the Gesell Institute), Susan Isaacs (the pioneer in early childhood education), Joae Graham Selzer, Benjamin Spock, Sara Bonnett Stein, and John E. Valusek. I'd like to thank these authors for contributing so much that is useful to parents. I pass on their suggestions with pride.

I was first introduced to several of these authors by Marjorie Bakken, my friend and mentor. I'd like to thank Marjorie for sharing her knowledge of child development and guiding me to writings that have had significant impact on my ideas. My relationship to Marjorie, her husband, Harald, and their daughter, Martha, has enriched my life over many years.

My other source of ideas has been the parents I've worked with, who, open to exploration and change, have shared their lives and added their insights to the search for positive alternatives. My heartfelt thanks to all of them, and to those agencies and individuals who have been receptive to hosting Parent Awareness groups over the years. Joyce Davis and Sandy Cymerman organized the first one, for the Brandeis Women's Committee of Framingham and Natick. I will always feel grateful to them for giving me and Parent Awareness a good start.

Susan Falkoff, as editor of this book, has given structure to my ideas. Her remarkable organizational ability, her skill with language, her subtle understanding of what I have wished to convey, and her own commitment to positive family life have contributed enormously to this book. Her common sense and humor were ever manifest as we worked together, as they are in her family. I want to thank Susan, her husband, Michael, and their children, Sam and Rebecca, for being the very special people, and friends, they are.

Susan Barron, my dear friend, a professional writer, knowledgeable about child rearing, offered valuable advice on the manuscript. I deeply appreciate her help. Her comments contributed finishing touches, and her positive response to the book's development was a steady source of encouragement. Susan, her husband, Jim, and their daughter, Mia, are important people in my life.

My family has been integral to my work, in many ways. My husband, Dick, has never wavered in his belief and confidence that this is the work I am destined to do. Dick's energy, friendship, love, and intuition inspire me at all times. Sharing child raising with Dick has enhanced my parenting; his belief in positive methods is as deep as my own. Seeing Dick lose his cool at times, as I do mine, helps me accept that we are all truly human.

Without my sons, Joshua and Jesse, this book could not exist. They have taught me how to be a mother and they have shown me what it is to be a child. I love their ability to be so totally involved in what they are doing, playing, acting up at one moment, so reflective and philosophical the next. I want to thank them for the joy they bring to me.

Many of the things I've learned about parenting, I learned long ago, from my mother, Yetta Safran, and my father, Sol. I am grateful to them both for the talks and walks, sharing and thinking we have had all my life, and for their compassion and steady faith in me. They are wonderful parents and grandparents and I love them dearly. My brother, Fred, has contributed valuable insight to this manuscript, and throughout the book the results of our conversations are evident.

Dick's family, too, has meant so much to me. His mother, Anne's, love and active interest were available to us and our children right up until her death. She always urged me on. Dick's father, Phil, a zesty grandfather, and his wife, Sarah, have brought special friendship and affection to all of us. David and Liz, Dick's brother and sister, bring energy and joy to the jobs of uncle and aunt. They are both models of strength and courage to me and my family.

There are special people I'd like to mention: Anita and Andy Harmon, who are bringing word of Parent Awareness to England. Howie Baker and Susan Siroty and their children. Howie has provided a strong example of the positive approaches in a day-care setting. Jerry Grant for his important contribution to the Parent Awareness program itself. My friend Joan for her admirable mothering of four sons. Carol Mann for her guidance. Angela Miller for her deep understanding of this book and her respect and concern for children's welfare. Kendra Crossen for her careful review of the final copy.

My thanks to Gail Bor for typing the final manuscript with care and patience, to Carol Bridges for typing the finishing touches, to Jill Brotman and Heather Barlow for the first drafts, and to all the others who have helped along the way.

Introduction

Six years ago I arrived home late in the evening after leading my first Parent Awareness group. Moved by the sharing and sincerity of the group members, I recorded the situations we had discussed. Since that night, I've led many more Parent Awareness groups and continued to record the issues participants bring up and the suggestions offered by me and other group members on how to handle them. This book is a selection of these discussions together with a summary of Parent Awareness techniques, presented in the hope that they will bring to life the Parent Awareness experience for everyone who reads them.

My interest in children and the way adults treat them began when I was still a child. It concerned me then to see children hurt or mistreated, and I carried this feeling with me into adulthood. My decision to teach kindergarten reflected this interest.

When I had children of my own, I also became aware of the special needs of parents. I saw that a positive way of life is important for the fulfillment and growth of both parent and child. For three years I taught courses in child development and early-childhood education at the college level. As I taught, I reflected on the importance to parents—and future parents—of learning modern theories of child development and child rearing. I was very interested in seeing parents and children get along well together.

At that time, I took a new path in my own road and created the Parent Awareness program to address this need. I am still leading Parent Awareness groups and also training others in Parent Awareness group leadership. It is a joy to me now to see more and more of these groups being formed throughout New England and spreading to other areas of the country.

Parent Awareness groups have evolved a format that meets the needs of parents from widely varied backgrounds and deals with children of all ages. Groups of eight to twelve parents meet for eight to ten weeks, with the possibility of later follow-up sessions. The program teaches positive, creative approaches to child rearing while helping parents to experience personal growth. My goal is for group members to become increasingly aware of their potential as skilled parents. The Parent Awareness structure and content have been developed by combining my experience as a parent, group leader, and teacher with the best from child-rearing and child-development literature.

The first Parent Awareness session begins with a look at the positive side of parenting. We share what we like and appreciate about our children, ourselves as parents, and the job of parenting, and learn a positive attitude toward the ages and stages of children's growth. This leads to an exploration of the balance between finding fulfillment as a parent and as a person. The second session deals with positive methods of discipline, sibling issues, and jealousy. In the third session we share the experiences we've had in the past week applying the positive methods in our families. In each future session we take some time to continue sharing the discipline situations that occur and how we're handling them, so we can keep on learning, absorbing, and using the new methods.

The fourth session deals with our own childhood and how it has influenced our present parenting. We can consciously choose to keep up the good and discard the negative parts of our experience. The following sessions cover sex education, helping children to understand death, children's feelings and fears, building independence, and developing a child's positive self-image. One meeting is devoted to the "difficult issues": what we dislike about our children, ourselves as parents, and parenting in general. We also do "family sculptures," a look at how each family member is relating to the others, in order to appreciate what is good about our family life and identify aspects we'd like to improve.

The sessions combine informal lectures, group discussion, and time for each individual to review the day's theme with the full attention of the group. The search for positive alternatives is combined with the chance to express personal feelings. In some sessions, such as the ones on discipline or self-image, parents learn positive methods and skills. In other areas of child rearing, such as explaining death or providing sex education, parents need the appropriate information to share with their children. This book covers both the information and the skills that parents learn in the Parent Awareness program. I have arranged the topics in this book in a sequence different from that of the discussion groups for easier reading.

I think the greatest benefit of meeting in groups is the opportunity to share family problems and discover together the many helpful ways to resolve them. I encourage parents to build this kind of support system among friends outside the group so that when their series ends, the attitude of helping each other will last.

Group participants have included parents from the city, the suburbs, and rural areas, and from varied ethnic, educational, and economic backgrounds. Group members have lived in nuclear families, been single parents, or lived communally; they have had biological, adopted, or foster children or grandchildren. What has held them all together is the common commitment to relating in positive ways to children. It is a special happiness for me to see grand-parents—who raised children within an older tradition—embracing the new methods.

It isn't always easy to learn new ways, but the satisfaction of a good family life, living in harmony and friendship with our children, is well worth our efforts. Throughout this book you will be seeing how positive approaches *can* be put to work for parents and that they *do* work. The situations you will be reading about are taken from the real-life experiences of the many parents I've known.

The discussions here are not meant as "answers." There is never just one approach to a situation; there are many ways to handle any incident. The key is to learn to choose from the wide variety of *positive* alternatives available to us. As parents, we certainly won't be able to do what is most constructive in every situation, but we can aim for a high percentage! It is my hope that as you read this book, you will be encouraged to use the positive methods I describe and even go on to create some of your own. As you handle a situation with these methods, give it your own special flavor and spice. We can all share the same humane methods, but life is so much more interesting when we do it our own way.

I ask you to join with me and the others who are opting for *a better life for children and those who raise them.*

Saf Lerman, 1980

Contents

ACKNOWLEDGMENTS iii

INTRODUCTION v

CHAPTER 1—The Creative Art of Discipline 1

CHAPTER 2—Daily Life 34

CHAPTER 3—Ages and Stages 52

CHAPTER 4—Sibling Issues 72

CHAPTER 5—Children's Feelings 91

CHAPTER 6—Building a Positive Self-Image 104

CHAPTER 7—Fears 119

CHAPTER 8—Sex Identity and Education 134

CHAPTER 9—Divorce 153

CHAPTER 10—Death 167

CHAPTER 11—Independence and Interdependence 180

CHAPTER 12—Parents' Feelings 196

EPILOGUE 217

SUMMARY OF PARENT AWARENESS TECHNIQUES 219

INDEX 237

CHAPTER 1

The Creative Art of Discipline

Using Positive Approaches with Children

The situations in this chapter demonstrate the process of responding positively at times when limits need to be set or misbehavior corrected. I discuss how parents can give up a punishing attitude in favor of a teaching spirit, and I also give a lot of attention to the reasons why spanking, or hitting of any sort, is harmful, and must be abandoned as a culturally sanctioned way to socialize children. By using constructive, positive teaching methods most of the time, parents create a peaceful and pleasant home environment, based on love, cooperation, and guidance (firm when necessary, but not hurtful). The situations in this chapter are a good introduction to how this can be achieved by every parent in every home across the land.

Parents ask how to handle toddlers who are too young to reason or follow rules.

There are many effective ways to set limits with young children. Even if they can't understand all of our words, toddlers, and even infants, can tell the difference between an approving and a disapproving look. Moreover, their ability to understand speech is usually far ahead of their ability to speak themselves, so it is always worthwhile to state the rule while reinforcing it with looks (and, if necessary, physical removal—gently!—from a dangerous or forbidden activity).

When you set limits in this way, it is very important to take the time and energy to redirect the child from the inappropriate activity to one that is permissible. It's not enough to say, "No, couches aren't for writing on." It is better to say, "No, you can't write on the couch, but you can write on paper," and then set the child up with paper and crayon. If he doesn't want the paper and insists on the couch, then you will need to put the crayons out of reach, repeating the rule letting him know he may draw when he is ready to use the paper. He will be able to understand your actions even if he misses some of the words.

With a two-year-old life can sometimes seem like a series of battles. It s helpful to avoid a confrontation whenever possible. The fewer limits you need to set, the better. Distraction is often the best tool. Instead of commenting on the misbehavior, simply turn the toddler's attention elsewhere. If he is about to pull books off the shelf, swing him over to the window to see what's outside.

Childproofing your home really pays off too. Put any dangerous or valuable items out of the toddler's reach and set up the house as safely as possible so the child can roam and explore freely. It is not appropriate to spank or slap toddlers to keep them from dangers such as cars or a hot stove. The spanking itself hurts and is not a dependable deterrent. The toddler's temptation is great, while his inner control is weak. We protect toddlers better by either supervising them or childproofing thoroughly.

A two-year-old girl scribbled with a pen on an expensive velvet couch. Her mother was not with her to prevent this. When she discovered what the child had done, she spanked her and called her a "bad, bad girl." Was the spanking helpful?

Let's look first at the mother's situation. Being with a two-year-old can be demanding and tiring. Maybe she had just sat down to have a quick cup of tea or close her eyes for a few minutes. Then she walks into the living room and discovers the couch! She is mad at herself for leaving her two-year-old unsupervised, and she is frenzied about the couch.

Now let's look at the two-year-old. Sometimes on her own she does well at finding appropriate things to do, but her world is full of temptations. Toddlers are daily faced with inner struggles: to dump or not to dump the garbage, to draw or not to draw on the wall, to squeeze or not to squeeze the toothpaste on the mirror—all very interesting activities from the child's point of view. Sometimes the child's urge is strong and she gives in to it. At other times she may imagine her parent looking disapprovingly, and this mental picture restrains her. Often, even with this picture there, the temptation is still greater and the child proceeds. Probably she has heard her mother say that walls are not for writing or that garbage is not for dumping. Although she is starting to understand these phrases and rules, she is still lacking one essential ingredient: the emotional self-control that enables her to follow them.

Even adults don't always display self-control. We may say, "I won't eat that piece of cake," and yet we do eat it! Young children are just beginning to develop a conscience. It is common to see a child this age saying "No, no" to herself as she goes on scribbling on the couch or wall. This is the first step. She is registering the rule and even repeating it, but she still needs help to obey it.

Okay, but what is this mother to do now about the writing on the sofa? She feels upset and angry. Even so, spanking her daughter is not appropriate. Spanking or hitting is an injury to a child's body and self-esteem. Calling her a bad girl is just as bad. Parents need to aim their disapproval at the child's behavior, not at her character. Calling a child bad or naughty can make her believe she really is bad, and this is harmful to her self-image. The child is not bad. The *behavior* is unacceptable, but the child herself remains a good person. This is an important difference.

At this time, it is enough for the mother to tell her daughter in an annoyed tone that she is very upset and that "couches are not for writing on." Then she can work off her anger by wiping hard on the stains! The effort that goes into cleaning up will not go unnoticed by the child, and it will help her understand the reason for the rule.

The mother should realize that the girl might write on the couch again tomorrow. This is not because she is stubborn, out to get her mother or mean, but because at her age her self-control is weak. The daughter still cannot be trusted alone with crayons or pens near the sofa, but she is gathering the necessary information to learn the rule. Over a period of days, weeks, or even months, she will develop that self-control (or conscience).

Living with a two-year-old is very hard work. Incidents like this one happen every day. It helps to remember that it is through these very incidents that conscience develops.

A mother said that she had hit her two-year-old with a belt and he had been very frightened. The mother felt terrible about this and resolved not to hit him again in the future. Was there any way to tell the boy about this decision, or was he too young to understand?

Hitting children is not helpful. I believe doubly strongly that children should never be hit with an object such as a belt, hairbrush, or shoe. I was pleased that this mother had made a commitment not to hit her son anymore. Instead of spending our energy feeling bad about the past, we should focus our attention on the future—on using positive methods to create a happier and more relaxed home life.

This mother had felt guilty and bad ever since this incident. Her son was also hurt and afraid. Perhaps he was wondering if his mother would ever do that to him again. It would indeed be wise to talk with him and say something like "Remember when I hit you with the belt? That hurt you a lot and made you feel scared. I feel very sorry about it. I made a big mistake, and I'm never going to do that again." When

several weeks have gone by and the child sees that his mother hasn't
done this again to him, he will become convinced. His emotional hurt
will heal and he will be assured that his mother means what she says.

In fact, the mother did follow this suggestion. Talking about it and
reassuring him that it wouldn't happen again made her feel much
better. She felt that her son had understood her and that his face had
expressed tremendous relief. He gave her a big hug after this talk.
These warm feelings were a big help to her as she stuck to her
commitment.

**A mother described her three-year-old daughter's new tactic. When
Hannah didn't want to hear what her mother was saying, she would
say loudly, "I'm not listening to you, Mommy!" The mother reacted
strongly with an attitude of "I'm your mother and you'd better listen
to me!" How else could this be handled?**

Though what the mother had to say to Hannah was often important,
she realized after we talked that it could usually wait a few minutes.
Several approaches might work well. The mother could let Hannah
know that what she had to tell her was important and that as soon as
she was ready to listen, she should let her know. The mother might
add, "Try to be ready to listen soon." This avoids an on-the-spot
confrontation. With this few moments' leeway, the conflict might be
solved.

Another approach would be to say, "Right now I am a happy
mommy, but if you aren't ready to listen to me soon, I'll be a very angry
mother." This is often effective in winning the child's cooperation, as
she herself concludes that she'd prefer a happy mother.

In either of these cases the mother would be correct to show anger
if Hannah still wouldn't listen. She is right to then say (angrily) that she
expects to be heard, just as Hannah expects attention when *she* has
things to say. Children at times need to be told things like "When you
want to go to the park and ask me to take you, you want me to listen.
You wouldn't like it if I said to you, 'I don't want to listen to you now.'
You'd get very annoyed with me. I want this same kind of
consideration from you. If you don't listen to my important
statements, it will make me angry enough not to want to listen to
yours." Parents can help children learn to respect the thoughts and
feelings of others. Children aren't born with this skill. When parents
let children know how their behavior affects them, it helps children
see that living with others includes learning to regard their feelings as
well as their own. This takes time, of course, but parents can help by
being honest about their feelings from the time the children are
quite young.

A three-year-old was alone in his room and, without his mother's knowledge, had begun to cut his hair. The mother said that before being in the parents' group, she would have spanked the boy and expressed her anger by saying things like "I'll kill you for this." She realized that after using methods like these she did not feel good about herself, and she was eager to change.

This time the mother handled the situation positively and, as a result, felt good about herself. She expressed her anger verbally, saying that she was mad and that this was something he was not allowed to do. She let him know, however, that although he couldn't cut his hair, he could cut other things. She happened to be sewing at the time, and she allowed him to help cut the thread.

The mother verbalized her anger in a helpful way. She did not use her anger to attack her son's character either by calling him bad or by making scary threats. The line between fantasy and reality is thin for a child, and he is never sure whether or not his parent means it when she threatens to kill him. Using positive methods, this woman was able both to express her anger and to redirect her son's energy—and feel good about herself in the process.

A mother and father were concerned about their three-and-one-half-year-old son, who had hit his one-and-one-half-year-old cousin and called her a dummy. Both parents felt that their son had been very bratty and told him so. They wanted to know how to handle this kind of situation.

Many preschool children use hitting to solve their problems until they learn more sophisticated ways of dealing with issues. The son was not bratty; he was simply using a three-year-old's way of solving problems. Labeling children brats and their actions bratty does not help. Very often the children come to believe that they *are* brats, and then they actually fulfill their parents' negative expectations by acting up. No child is a brat and no action is bratty, even though children often do act in ways that adults cannot accept. Adults can help by directing children toward acceptable behavior.

Hitting and name calling among children is not always harmful. There are times when children are equally matched, and neither child is getting hurt either physically or emotionally. The hitting or name calling is just a way to let off steam. At these times parents are wise not to interfere.

In this case the boy did hurt his cousin, and therefore the hitting had to be stopped. Parents can set the limit by saying, for example, "Your cousin is not for hitting; *tell* her if you're mad," or "People aren't for hurting; use words to let her know how you feel." Sometimes a child is just too upset or not yet verbal enough to use words. If so, the parent can help by putting the child's feelings into words, as by saying "I see you're mad at Lauren, but she's not for hitting," and then try to direct them both to an absorbing activity.

If stating the limit doesn't get the child to stop hitting, then the parent can offer something he *can* hit, like a pillow or sofa. The parent can say, "If you still need to hit, come and hit this pillow. It's okay to hit this."

Sometimes a child does not want to hit a pillow and still insists on hitting the other child. In this case, the parent can hold the child (hugging style, but firmly) to restrain him and can say something reassuring like "It's okay to feel like hitting, but people aren't for hitting and I'm not going to let you hit. That's why I'm holding you."

Parents need to be encouraging when they are trying to redirect children. For example, you can get a pillow and *show* the child that it is okay to hit, scratch, or bite it, by doing so yourself. I find it helpful to hold a pillow in front of me and encourage my son to hit it and then I say "Ouch!" as if the pillow were being hurt. Or you can suggest that the child run across the room to the pillow; a running start gives the hitting more power. It helps, too, if the parent says things like "You're so mad. Hit it hard. That feels good, doesn't it!" Usually, after a few hits, the child is relieved and often laughing. If the adult hugs the child afterward, the child will see that his angry feelings are accepted and he is still loved. Children see that their inappropriate behavior (hitting people) will be curbed, but their feelings can have outlets.

It takes time for children to give up their own ways of solving problems. We need to guide them, realizing that in time they will adopt our methods. We must be prepared to repeat our limits and values. When Jesse was two, he had begun to say "People aren't for hitting" and "People aren't for pushing," yet he would still hit and push at times!

Many parents are concerned that if they teach their children that "people aren't for hurting or for hitting," the children will not be able to assert themselves in self-defense if other children hit them.

There are several ways a child can be taught to react when hit by another child. Sometimes, saying to the child who has started the hitting, "I'm not for hitting; if you're mad tell me about it," can be disarming enough to stop the assault. If this doesn't work and if there is a parent or teacher nearby, the child can ask for help. If there isn't anyone around or if the child is older and doesn't want to depend on an adult, he can hit back once or twice to show that he will be assertive in self-defense.

Hitting back just one time shows that the child will not be bullied, and the incident may end. If children keep hitting each other back and forth, one of them may really get hurt, so I think it best to instruct children to strike back only *once or twice* if necessary to show that they won't be bullied. If the other child still keeps on hitting, the first child should repeat something like "People aren't for hurting" or "I don't go for this way of expressing myself and my feelings" or "I don't like to hit or be hit," and try to walk away from the conflict or seek adult help.

At breakfast one morning when Joshua was three, he took a bowl of sliced oranges and dumped it over his head. I told him that he was supposed to be eating the oranges, not putting them on his head, and he informed me that it was really his friend Gabrielle who had done it. Gabrielle was not there at the time!

A young child will often put the responsibility for his unacceptable actions onto friends, teddy bears, or imaginary playmates. One reason for this is that he is very involved in the process of learning what is acceptable behavior and exercising self-control. When he has a lapse, it's hard to own up to it. Parents need to understand that their child is not lying. He's having a hard time developing self-control and doesn't want to admit to having lost any portion of the control he's worked hard to learn.

Parents can help by letting their child know that it's okay to make mistakes and that they will be there to help him remember. Role-play can sometimes be used to good advantage here. I could have had Joshua tell Gabrielle to please stop dumping oranges on his head. This gives him some control in the situation once again. He is not being reprimanded, but is giving the orders himself. Thus the child is really giving *himself* the direction, and this acts as a reinforcer to bring back his self-control.

One morning, when Joshua was three and a half, he was playing in the living room with some very small blocks. Jesse, then one and one half, woke up from his nap and began to cry. I told Joshua that the blocks were too small and dangerous for Jesse to handle. He could continue using them on the kitchen table or in his own room where he could close the door, but he needed to leave the living room now. Joshua said angrily that he wanted to stay where he was. I wanted to help him transfer the blocks to a safe place before I went in to get Jesse, but my attempts were being thwarted by Joshua's intense refusals.

I told Joshua that if we didn't move the blocks now, I'd have to put them into the closet, but that I preferred not to have to do that. Still, he kept on crying that he wanted to use the blocks only in the living room. I was about to put the blocks away when I thought of using role reversal. I said, "You be Mommy and I'll be you." Joshua agreed, so I, playing Joshua, began to cry and say, "I want to stay in the living room with the blocks. I will stay!" As Mommy, Joshua answered, "You can use them in your own room or on the kitchen table. Otherwise Jesse could swallow one." I repeated my refusal, and he repeated the limit. Then, on his own, Joshua ended the role-play and switched back to being himself. He said calmly, no longer in a rage, "I'll have them on the kitchen table." We both went to the kitchen carrying the blocks.

This role reversal scene provided Joshua with extra time to re-evaluate the situation from his safe role as Mommy. He was no longer on the spot and could think things through more clearly. He paid close attention to the limit and the reason for it when he himself was stating it, and he felt powerful now that he was imposing the limit, not I. These factors seemed to lessen that sharp edge children sometimes feel when adults confront them with a limit they want followed immediately. Also, reversing roles was fun. If, after the role-play, Joshua had still insisted on using his blocks in the living room, then I would have had to put them away until he was ready to use them in an appropriate spot. But even if this method had not worked, the limit and the reason for it would still have been sinking better into Joshua's mind as he, playing me, recited it.

A four-year-old boy was putting his feet up at the dinner table. His mother asked him not to do this several times and, not getting any cooperation, threatened that if he continued, she'd spank him. The boy continued, and the mother spanked him. Afterward, he put his feet up on the table again and was threatened with an even harder spanking. The new threat was carried out also, and this time his mother pulled his pants down, put him across her knee, and spanked away still harder. The mother wanted to know what else could have been done to stop his behavior.

The mother did attempt a positive solution before giving in to threats and spankings. She began by setting the limit that tables are not for feet, that floors are for feet. What went wrong?

It's nice to have a variety of positive approaches because we sometimes need to try a few before we find the one that works. Fortunately, the possibilities are numerous for every situation, and as parents we need to keep on thinking creatively. Here are some ideas that might have worked in this situation:

Humor might have helped. The mother might have said dramatically, "I see your feet are up on the table. What an unusual place for them! Well, I am a famous magician, and with the magic words of bluch, bluch, gleech, gluch, your feet will at once return to their proper place on the floor!" Most four-year-olds would find it hard to resist this tactic. They usually appreciate the parent who understands their delight in imaginative play.

Another tack could have been to ignore the behavior. With the attention off him, the child may have his feet down in a few moments!

Yet another approach would be to express disapproval in strong terms: "I see you are still eating with your feet up. That makes me very mad. I expect you to cooperate." When we give children our honest disapproval in ways that are not hurtful, they get the message. Even if this boy doesn't cooperate on the spot (spanking didn't help him to cooperate either), he is getting the information he needs to absorb our standards of correct behavior eventually.

After setting the limit and getting nowhere, the mother might have then tried giving her son a choice. She might have said, "We'd like your company during dinner. But you have a choice. You can go to your room until you're ready to come back and follow the rules, or else stay here and eat with your feet down." If his feet stayed up, she would need to follow through on her choices, insisting he leave, carrying him (gently but firmly) away herself if necessary.

A mother and her five-year-old daughter were sitting next to each other in the back seat of a car. The daughter had an umbrella in her hand and was poking the car floor with it. As she did this, she also wound up poking her mother's foot. The mother asked her a few times to please not poke her foot because it hurt, and then finally threatened to take the umbrella away. Yet the mother felt uncomfortable making the threat.

Some parents set their limits too harshly. Other parents find it difficult to set limits at all. In this incident the mother, realizing the poking could be dangerous, should have set the limit immediately. She could have said, "No poking the umbrella when we're riding this close to each other," with the full intent of carrying through by taking it away if her daughter repeated the action. It so happened that in a few minutes the mother was going to be in the front seat driving and the daughter would have been left alone in the back seat. The mother might have said, "It will be okay to poke the floor once you're alone in the back seat."

In this situation the mother was trying to ask her daughter nicely to stop the poking and then felt bad about needing to threaten to take the umbrella away. Parents need to feel comfortable setting the limits they deem necessary in a straightforward, not wishy-washy, way. Instead of feeling bad about threatening to take the umbrella away, the mother could have felt good about setting a limit and taking the action that was necessary to carry it through.

Frequently, parents fail to set necessary limits because they're afraid their children won't love them anymore. In fact, children continue to love their parents very much even when they take a firm stand. When children are allowed to misbehave too often or at potentially dangerous times, they feel uncomfortable inside. They can't stop themselves, even though they know people don't like what they are doing, and they are reassured when someone stops them. When parents set the necessary limits in nonhurtful, reasonable ways, children feel cared for and protected. Be confident that making your necessary rules will contribute toward your child's sense of security and trust in you.

A mother was concerned about her ability to follow through on her limits. Her daughter was always testing, and the mother felt that she ended up either giving up or spending a lot of energy on little things. For example, if she set the limit on two crackers, her daughter would always want three. To maintain her authority, the mother would try to stick to her limit even though she really didn't care that much about a couple of extra crackers. At other times she'd just give up. For instance, her daughter would go out without a coat and the mother would find herself mumbling, "Oh, forget it, if she's cold, she'll come back for it."

Setting limits does not need to be seen as a confrontation or struggle for power. It is a way to show our standards, not demonstrate our "authority." Some limits matter more than others, and our manner can show this. When something is very important, we might be very angry about it and we can sound very angry. (Sounding angry in a firm way usually works better than shrieking hysterically.) At other times, like the ones above, when the issue is minor, we might be just mildly annoyed and then we can express only irritation, not rage. It will sometimes happen, moreover, that we'll begin to set a certain limit and then not care enough to follow through on it. Somehow, we can't seem to muster enough energy to complete what we've begun. Parents can accept the fact that this will happen occasionally and need not be concerned about it. For the most part, it's wise to set limits we expect to follow up on, but we'll all make some demands that we wind up abandoning, and that's fine.

A large part of our job as parents is to choose the important issues. Many situations can be ignored and the child on her own will stop the inappropriate behavior sooner, with the parent's attention off her. Parents need to determine which situations are really worth their time and effort. If a child wants three crackers and the parent has said she can have two, the parent needs to decide if it's worth everyone's energy to insist on the child's having two. Parents need to find their own balance, learning what to ignore and when to intervene. Each family's balance will differ somewhat. Since not everyone has the same values, you may say yes in a particular instance where someone else would say no. What we can share are the same humane approaches to setting our rules.

One afternoon I had made a rule that Joshua, then almost five years old, did not like. To show me how angry he was, he began to peel the plaster over a spot in the kitchen wall that my husband had been fixing. This was not a case of Joshua's conscience not operating full force; he was intentionally doing wrong to get back at me for my rule.

At times like these, parents are inclined to retaliate and do something the child won't like; but then the parent would be descending to the child's level. Here, I first stopped Joshua from continuing to peel while letting him know I was very angry with him. I told him angrily that I didn't like seeing my things destroyed and that his action made me upset and unhappy, just as he'd be if someone had broken something important to him. I told him he had a right to be mad at the rule and that he could *say* that he didn't like it, but that he wasn't to ruin the wall.

No matter what the cause for a child's misbehavior, a parent can try to respond in positive ways.

Six-year-old Emily didn't want to put her clothes into the laundry bag before bathing. Her mother had asked her about ten times to do this and was getting angry. Finally she slapped the girl. After the slap, Emily announced that she would leave home, and her mother informed her that that would be impossible. A while later, mother and daughter made up and were on good terms again. But the mother realized that slaps made her daughter resentful and wanted to find a better solution for this kind of situation.

Parents like to resolve each conflict that comes between them and their children immediately, but it is not always possible to do so. This mother wanted her daughter to cooperate, but slapping her did not, in fact, get the clothes into the laundry bag. The girl got into the bathtub with resentful thoughts of leaving home.

If the mother was feeling calm, she could have approached the situation humorously. She might have said, "Hasn't that hamper of yours picked its clothes up yet? I'm so tired of waiting for that hamper to do its job!" Humor lightens the mood and creates warm feelings between children and parents. But of course, humor won't work if the parent is seething. If the mother was very angry, she could have said directly: "Now I have to put the clothes in the laundry bag myself. This makes me very mad. I expect you to do this job." Children want parental love and approval. When disapproval is stated in a firm but nonhurtful manner, it tells the child how her behavior makes her parent feel and it allows her to think through the situation more clearly and perhaps resolve to cooperate next time. She may think, "I didn't cooperate. My mother had to do the job and now she's mad. I don't like it when she's mad at me. Maybe next time I should try to cooperate. I'd rather have her approval." At least her thoughts aren't clouded over by resentment, which stops clear thinking. A slap, which is hurtful, causes the child to put her energies into defense—in this case, the fantasy of getting away from the home where she was treated like this.

This parent may need to go one step beyond an expression of disapproval. Perhaps she had planned to read her daughter a story after the bath, but she felt too exhausted by this confrontation to do it. She might say to Emily, "When you don't cooperate with me, it makes me feel like not cooperating with you either. I don't feel like reading you the story now; perhaps I'll feel like it a little later." Such a statement releases the parent's annoyance and gets the point across to the child. The mother could, after all, go ahead and read the story anyway, or she could do it a bit later. If she was still annoyed later, she could say, "I'm a person too. Now that I'm so worn out by our quarrel, I can't really cooperate until I'm feeling more pleasant again. I'll read that book to you tomorrow." This is rarer, but sometimes necessary. There's no point trying to pretend to be cheerful when you are feeling awful. And this way, parents can show their children that cooperation breeds cooperation and that parents are people with feelings and with limited energy.

A mother and her six-and-one-half-year-old son had had quite a hard day together, with several disagreements. The son wanted to go out for dinner, and the mother said she'd take him if he cooper-

ated in the car and made the ride a peaceful one, as she just couldn't take any more hassles that day. The son agreed. In the car, however, he began to make irritating noises. The mother repeated their agreement a few times, to no avail. When the next noise was uttered, the mother announced that she was turning around to go home. The son asked for one more chance. She very angrily told him that he had had his few chances and that she was now too angry to go and enjoy eating out with him. The son continued to fuss in the car, but when they reached home, he stopped his fussing.

In this situation the mother had set the limit that there could be no acting up in the car. She repeated this limit several times (which is always necessary, as children can't be expected to jump to command), but when she did not get the cooperation she expected, she took the action that was necessary to follow through on her limit. The mother felt it would have been wrong to just say, "When you don't cooperate with me, then I don't feel like cooperating with you either," and then go to the restaurant after all. The mother's patience had been spent, and she needed to show her son that since he broke his part of their bargain, she was left feeling so angry and unpleasant that she was no longer up to fulfilling hers. The mother felt good that she followed through on the limit she had set. They ate dinner at home that evening.

A father discovered his seven-year-old daughter lighting matches. In the past, he said, he would have hit her for doing this. This time he used a more positive approach.

The father let his daughter know emphatically that matches were not to be lit or played with in the house or when she was alone, but that when the family next went camping, he would allow her to help start the campfire. In this way, he had set a limit on the use of matches when it could be dangerous, and substituted a time when it would be appropriate, thus handling the situation in a humane and dignified manner.

A mother and father were playing cards, and their seven-year-old son was sitting nearby watching them. The child was being a nuisance, peeking over his parents' shoulders, talking to them, getting in their way. His mother gave him three choices: He could remain there quietly, play with some of his toys in another room, or go to sleep, as it was nearly bedtime. The child continued to bother his parents, so his mother screamed, "Go to bed." The child started chanting, "I won't go to sleep, I won't go to sleep." The

mother couldn't stand the chanting and got a belt and struck her son. How else could the mother or father have proceeded after offering the three choices?

The mother offered her son three choices, but was wishy-washy in helping him to abide by them. After the choices were stated and the son chose to remain and watch his parents play cards, his parents could have taken action verbally and physically to see that their limit would be followed. One of them could have gotten up, saying to the son, "Now I'm very angry. You have continued to bother us. You will not be permitted to watch us play right now." Then the parent could have guided the child into his bedroom to get him ready for bed, or taken him to his own toys and a spot where he could play with them. Parents often need to take a child by the hand and physically guide him to where he should be.

When we set a limit, our tone of voice and attitude should reveal that we really mean what we're saying. We must be confident, reassuring, and firm. When parents are hysterical, shrieking, wishy-washy, and out of control themselves, then it's hard for children to believe the parents are really behind the limit; they instantly pick up that they're unsure of their request. We need to sound confident and calm (angry if need be) and let our manner communicate that we expect to be listened to.

In this case, also, the mother just couldn't stand the sound of her son's chanting. Often the noises children make and the sound of their voices can make their parents feel like whacking them. We should recognize that the sound of a child's voice can affect us to this degree. It is okay to feel this way, but we should avoid actually hitting the child. I suggest that when parents feel like this, they say *to themselves*, "I would love to shut that child up," or "I would love to whack that child." Often this will help to relieve the fury, and they can proceed in a better frame of mind to handle the situation constructively.

Perhaps the very best remedy in this case would have been for the parents to play cards with their son and not just with each other, or to give him some special time, reading to him or talking about his day. They could have been alone together later when their son was asleep.

We can always look for positive methods to correct a misbehavior, but sometimes we need to consider the underlying causes as well. A child may be hungry; we need to stop his whining and shrieking, but we also need to give him dinner. Or he may be tired and we need to let him know that his obnoxious behavior is intolerable, but he needs sleep, too. Often, parents say, "He's just doing that to get attention." We can't allow him to misbehave, but we do need to respond to his legitimate need for attention.

A mother was going out for the evening and had told her seven-year-old daughter, Lucy, that the baby-sitter was coming at seven o'clock. She let Lucy know that she could play outside until seven, but then would have to come in so the baby-sitter wouldn't have to worry about her being outside in the dark. As the daughter was leaving to play outside, her mother heard her muttering, "I don't care what she says, I'm not coming in until seven-thirty." Her mother instantly got furious, grabbed Lucy by the collar, whacked her, and told her she could not go out at all.

The mother's rule was just. She wanted to go out to enjoy a pleasant evening and needed to know her daughter was indoors safe and sound before she left. She also didn't want the baby-sitter to have to be responsible for her daughter out in the dark. Hearing the girl's mumbling certainly made the mother angry. She would have done well to let her know just how angry her comment and intention made her, but without hitting, and in a way that could maintain her own dignity as well as her daughter's. She might have said something like "I heard what you said and it makes me furious. I deserve to have an evening out. When you plan special times, I don't do things to bother you. Hearing you say you intend to come in at seven-thirty makes me feel like telling you not to go out at all because I don't want to be worrying. I want to be enjoying a pleasant evening."

At this point, if the mother felt that she couldn't really trust her daughter that evening, she'd have to say that Lucy must play indoors that night. If, however, at this point the mother felt Lucy was understanding her and was now capable of following her original rule, she might say, "If you now understand better my reasons and feelings and are sure you will be in by seven, then you can go out." This way the mother could take the appropriate action in a nonpunitive fashion. She could use her anger constructively. Both parent and child benefit when limits are set in courteous ways.

If the mother did allow her daughter to go out and she did return by seven as she had been told, it would be important to thank her for cooperating. Parents need to notice and appreciate a child's efforts to correct a misbehavior. The appreciation is positive reinforcement for her continued cooperation.

A seven-year-old boy was waiting for his sneakers to dry in the dryer. He was impatient and began to complain about having to wait. His father asked him to stop groaning, but the boy kept it up. The father then said, "Let me give you something to groan about," and began to slap his son. After striking several times, he stopped, having realized several things. First, he knew he did not want to be hitting his son. Second, he saw that a game had been set up in which he was determined to get his son to stop groaning and the son was determined to get in the last groan. He saw that no matter how long he kept up the hitting, his son would also keep putting in one more groan about his sneakers. Third, the father realized that he didn't care if his son wore his sneakers wet or dry and also that he didn't really care if the child did groan while waiting for the sneakers to dry. So the father stopped hitting his son.

When we're doing something to handle a situation and see that what we are doing is not beneficial, it is good thinking to stop in midstream and change to better tactics. Here the father realized that his son's groaning wasn't really bothering him. But what if the noise really was bothering the father or other members of the family? Then the father would need to set the limit on the groaning, still without hitting. He could have told his son that he understood he was disappointed about having to wait for his sneakers to dry, but that the groaning was bothering him. If the boy felt like groaning, he could go into a room alone where no one would be annoyed by the sound. If necessary, the father could guide the son into another room, away from the rest of the family.

When parents learn of my stand against hitting, they often ask about punishments. One father reported that when his daughter wouldn't listen to him he had her stand in a corner "so she'd know who was the boss." A mother sometimes deprives her son of dinner. A child teased her sister, and her mother wouldn't let her have ice cream. A boy who was riding "no-handed" was deprived of his bike for a week. What do I think of these punishments?

Punishments are humiliating to children and make them resentful. I am against the entire concept of punishment.

Very often, when parents punish children they do so in a spirit of retaliation. The father is angry that his daughter won't listen and wants to get back at her. Punishments given in a spirit of vengeance are not helpful; they cause bad feelings. Having a child stand in a corner, moreover, is demeaning and harmful to her self-image.

Depriving a child of dinner is bad for his health; it is painful and harms his growth. He will be busy feeling resentment for this cruel treatment and not thinking about whatever he was supposed to have done or be doing better.

A child who is teasing her sister will not learn better ways to get along by being denied ice cream. It only shows her that her parent is getting back at her instead of supporting her and helping her forward. Also, if she sees her sister with ice cream, it will only aggravate the sibling jealousy.

Depriving a child of his bike for a week is not very helpful either. The child has usually forgotten the initial incident in a day or two and gets resentful for not being able to use his bike. When a child is showing off on a bike, his parents can keep him off it *until he is ready to use it safely,* whether that is in a few moments or the next day. Whenever a child is deprived of an object or privilege, it should be not for a set length of time, but only until the child is ready to behave appropriately. He sees that he can have a particular privilege when he is able to take the responsibilities that go along with it.

Punishment acts as a barrier between parents and children. When punishments are for a set period of time, when they have nothing to do with what a child has done, or when they are given in retaliation, they are not helpful.

Of course, there will be times when a parent's words are not enough to gain a child's cooperation. Then the alternative to punishments and spankings is *positive action.* When parents take action, they take steps to teach children something specific in the situation at hand. Parents need to set limits and follow through on them, but not with a *punishing* attitude. They can adopt a *teaching* attitude instead.

Our actions should be aimed at protecting our children from danger and helping them learn to do better. Any method of discipline that is damaging to a child's physical or emotional well-being should be discarded. Parents should be guides and teachers, not judges and sentencers. I ask all parents to stop using those old familiar phrases—"I'm going to punish you," "You're on punishment," "You are being punished"—and instead to take steps in a guiding and supportive spirit.

A seven-and-a-half-year-old boy had let the air out of his bicycle's front tire. His mother felt that since he had deliberately done this, he should have to wait until she felt good and ready to go to a gas station and get the tire refilled.

The next morning, which was Sunday, the son and a friend headed for a nearby gas station to fill the tire on their own. The station was closed, however, and the air pump was locked inside. So the boys continued looking for a gas station that was open. This took them to a station quite far away, on the busiest street in their town. They did ask someone to cross the street with them (good thinking here, at least).

The parents discovered from their son's friend's parents where the children had gone and they were furious. When their son came home they sent him up to his room to bed. They called him down to ask him whose idea it was to do this, and he said it was his friend's. The parents then called the friend's parents, who said their son said it wasn't his idea. So the boy's parents called him down again and said, "Your friend said it was your idea, not his." This time the son said it had been his idea, so the parents sent him up to his room again, this time for having lied before. The son was made to stay in bed all day and was also deprived of the use of his bicycle for a week.

This is a good situation to explore for several reasons. First, the mother had been angry because her son had let the air out of his bike tire. She took this act as some kind of stubbornness and mean behavior. I suspect that more likely a boy of this age was just curious about what happens to a tire when the air is let out. He might have done it deliberately, with a bit of experimentation in mind, but not maliciously. The mother had a right to her annoyance, yet she was also motivated by an "I'll show you" attitude. She didn't want to help him fix the tire until she felt "good and ready." I believe the mother should have told her son that she was annoyed because it was an inconvenience to have to go to the gas station. However, I wouldn't make such a big deal over the situation. Perhaps she could have added lightheartedly, "I guess you were experimenting." She might have let her son know she would help him get it fixed in a day or two. Parents need to discriminate between really important situations that deserve their strong annoyance and others that perhaps aren't so important. To make a big thing out of this and to show the child that he'd have to wait good and long till she was ready to help him puts bitterness where it doesn't belong.

However, since the mother did react like this, the son did try to get his tire filled on his own and *then* did something that he really wasn't supposed to do, which was to go far from the house to a very busy street. The parents centered their attention on blame, wanting to know whose idea it had been, and then punished their son for lying. I encourage parents to give up focusing on lying and to stop calling children liars. It would have been wiser to tell their son directly, "We know you and your friend went to the busy street" (without concentrating on whose idea it was) "and that is something we absolutely do not allow." The parents could have sat down with their son and told him how angry and disappointed they were, and they also could have discussed the real danger he had risked. They might have said, "You're allowed to play around the house and to go a few blocks away, but not that far. That was very dangerous. You could have been seriously hurt. We're glad you asked someone to cross with you, but even so, that's a place you're not allowed to go on your own. We're very angry and disappointed. We've trusted you in the past, and need to be able to trust you in the future." The parents then might lean over and affectionately touch their son, saying, "How about it? That made us really upset and angry. No more of that, okay?"

Certainly parents need to take steps to help children learn to do better next time, but these steps should be supporting, not punishing steps. Parents need to stop thinking in terms of punishment. The goal is to be sure the child understands our rule and the reason for it, not to get back at him for doing wrong. The punishments of staying in bed and having no bike for a week were done in a vengeful spirit, were excessive and humiliating, and had no specific learning value for the child. Punishments like these can only cause bitterness. On the other hand, when parents get angry in ways that guide and teach, children know that their parents are still on their side and the relationship is warmer and more trusting all around.

A mother said that whenever her seven-year-old daughter and five-year-old son began to fight or bicker as they played board games together, she would take the game away from them until the next day. She said that in so doing she'd punish herself as well, since the children would spend the afternoon asking for the game back, which was annoying. When she gave them the game back the next day, she'd say, "You'd better not get into fights over this today!" Thus their new day would begin with a reminder of yesterday's fighting.

Punishments like this are not helpful to children. It makes them resentful about not being able to use their game and contributes to animosity between siblings.

After we talked, this mother was able to use a more positive solution the next time. She said, "You have a choice. You can continue to play the game and stop the fighting, or I'll have to put it away, *until you're ready to use it without hassling.*" She left the room. The children squabbled for a few more minutes and then played peacefully. If the children had kept up the squabbling, the mother would have taken the game away, prepared to return it to them as soon as they were ready to play calmly.

This approach works well because it takes into consideration the children's own inner timetable. When we need to remove something from a child, it's best not to take it away for a set time, but let the children know that when they're ready to use it appropriately they can have it back. This shows children that their parents are supportive. When the children are ready and able to cooperate, they'll get the chance to do so.

Sometimes a child says she's ready to use the object correctly and then she starts misusing it again. The parent can say, "I see you're still not ready. I know you will be ready later or else by tomorrow." This leaves room for her to calm down, and when the parent feels she can handle it the right way, the toy can be returned, perhaps with a comment like "I'm glad you're ready to cooperate now." The parent is following up her choice with action, but not punishment.

This mother was pleased to have acted reasonably, to have her children appreciate her methods, and to respond in kind. This incident also taught her the importance of positive expectations. She learned to say, "I expect you to play cooperatively," instead of "You'd better not fight over it anymore today." Parents need to tell children their positive expectations for them and show confidence they will be met. It is good to remember that this need not always be done in a crisis. Parents can make a point of going to their children when they are getting along well and letting them know how good it feels to see them playing well and enjoying each other's company. Even when the children are fighting, parents can focus their attention on the moments before the conflict when they were having fun together. For example, they can say, "You've been having such a good time together. Now let's solve the problem so you can go on playing." This puts the focus where it belongs, on the children's efforts at cooperation and fun. Quarrels need to be resolved quickly; they should not be the focus of family life.

John, who had recently turned nine, was outside playing with some friends when a quarrel broke out among the children. In the heat of anger, John picked up a rock and threw it at another boy. The rock struck this boy in the leg, but fortunately he just got a surface scratch. When John's mother heard about this, she was about to issue one of her old-style punishments, depriving John of either TV or bike privileges for a week, but first she stopped to think. She realized from her parents' group that these punishments had nothing to do with John's misbehavior and would not teach him anything about expressing his anger in better ways. Probably they would only make him very resentful. She therefore did not say, "I'll punish you for this," but turned instead to positive action.

The mother's first step was to sit down with John and talk about the danger of throwing rocks. His friend might have been seriously hurt. She emphasized that even when he gets very, very angry, he needs to express his feelings with words or get a grownup to help. John already felt bad about the incident and listened well. His mother let him know very strongly that this is what she expected from him from now on, and she also expressed appreciation for the fact that in the past he had always been able to handle quarrels in better ways.

The mother told her son that if an incident like this ever happened again, she would feel she could not trust him to play outside on his own, and he would have to limit his outdoor play to times when she was there to supervise. This way, if he got into a heated quarrel, she'd be able to see that it was handled appropriately. When she became confident once again that he was capable of expressing angry feelings to his playmates more appropriately, his outdoor privileges would be reinstated. John understood this condition, and assured his mother that it would not be necessary to limit his privileges, that an incident like the rock throwing would never be repeated.

After quite a time, the mother reported happily to her group that John was true to his word. Nothing like the rock throwing was ever repeated, and she did not need to restrict his outdoor play.

The change in this mother's attitude illustrates well my belief that parents are *teachers*. They are their child's first teachers, and continue to be in a position of guiding and instructing their children for many years. The approach John's mother followed was designed to teach him better ways, and it proved effective. If further action had been required, the temporary change in his outdoor privileges she had mentioned would have been a supportive and educational action that was specifically related to John's misbehavior. Removing TV or bike privileges, on the other hand, would have been a retaliatory measure with no connection to what John had done and no positive learning value.

A father said how good he felt about learning alternatives to punishment when his children misbehave. He described a common scene in his household and told us about his old and new ways of handling it.

His nine-year-old daughter tended to flare up over little things and scream and pick on her brother and sister. Unable to help her calm down, the father used to get angry and say, "I don't like the way you're acting at all. You're going to be punished. Go to your room until I tell you to come down." One time, he had told her to go upstairs to bed, even though it was midafternoon. Her punishment that day also included missing her favorite TV show for two evenings. The father noticed that these punishments did nothing to improve his daughter's mood. In fact, they made her moodier. When he'd come to get her, she'd be irritable and complaining bitterly about her mean, bad father and her terrible home.

Since our group's discussion of punishments, the father was able to take a good look at his responses. He realized that sending his daughter to bed was demeaning, that depriving her of a TV show had nothing to do with her obnoxious behavior, that keeping her in her room for a long time only made her more unpleasant, and that none of these punishments did anything to help her learn better ways to get along.

The next time she was being a nuisance, he tried to divert her to an interesting game. When that failed, he said, "I'd like you to go to another room where you can play alone for a while, and as soon as you feel you are ready to come back and be pleasant, you may join us again. We'd like to be with you, but not when you're acting like this." He guided her into another room. To his surprise, she returned in about two minutes in a much more cheerful mood. After some time had passed, he made a point of telling her how nice it was to be with her when she acted so reasonably.

This man related these incidents with great pride. He feels that the whole tone of his family life has improved, and he likes his new, educative manner "a hundred percent better" than his old punitive approach. He especially liked having given his daughter more responsibility for her behavior. She, not the father, was left to determine when she would rejoin the family. Instead of asking her passively to obey, he felt he was teaching her to be more sensitive to the family's needs.

A mother and father had decided that their eleven-year-old daughter wasn't ready to attend boy-girl parties. Alissa appeared to accept her parents' reasoning and decision. One evening she went to a friend's house to sleep over. There was a boy-girl party going on next door that the girl was not supposed to attend, but she and her friend did go over to the party for a few minutes. In casual conversation with another mother, Alissa's mother learned that her daughter had gone to the party. The mother became very upset and confronted her daughter. She told her not to lie, but to tell her if she really went to the party. At first the daughter said no, and then admitted that she had gone. The mother punished her daughter by having her go to bed at six-thirty each night for a week. She also decided that her daughter should not sleep over at any friend's house for another year. Now she realizes that these punishments were inappropriate, but she isn't sure what the best response would have been.

First of all, when we know that a child has done something wrong, it is best *not* to create a confrontation by asking the child to "tell the truth and not lie." When this mother learned that her daughter had been at the party, she could have spoken directly to her. She might have said, "I learned that you did go to the party, and I'm very disappointed and angry. We had an agreement. If you had wanted to go very badly, I would have expected you to come to me so we could rethink the issue together. We had a deal and now I'm really disappointed; I want to be able to trust you." Punishing with an early bedtime for a week will not teach the child to follow the rule about parties and will not help her to develop self-control. It will just breed resentment and possibly retaliatory actions.

Alissa needed to hear her mother's honest disappointment and anger. This would have made her feel bad, which works toward helping her follow the rules, as she really would prefer approval. The mother could have let her daughter know she expects to be able to trust her and that if the daughter is ever dissatisfied with a rule, the mother is willing to discuss it with her again to explain its rationale, or consider revising it.

When the mother said that Alissa couldn't sleep over at anyone's house for a year, she showed that she had lost faith in her daughter and no longer considered her trustworthy. Parents need to give children chances to develop their trustworthiness. By allowing Alissa to continue having some sleep-over visits, the mother would express confidence that the child will follow the rules from now on. On the other hand, it is realistic to expect an eleven-year-old to have some lapses in self-control and to need adult supervision. Since the mother felt so strongly on this issue, I suggested that she speak to the parent whose house her daughter is sleeping at to find out what the children will be doing that evening and state her expectations. This should be done with the daughter's knowledge. Otherwise the child might feel that her mother didn't really trust her, even though she had pretended to. The daughter should know that the adults in her life will act together to protect her and help her learn.

This approach treats children with respect and allows them the chances they need and the support from their parents to develop and nurture their trustworthiness. Parental disapproval expressed in nonpunitive ways helps to guide children without judging them. When children have lapses in control, they aren't helped by being deprived of all opportunities to develop control. They are helped by their parents' continued faith in them and opportunities to live up to that faith.

A minister had taken some teenagers from his parish on a retreat and they had used the facilities at a camp. Upon returning home, two of the young people told him that some others had stolen $150 worth of sweatshirts from the camp's supply. The minister was very upset because the teenagers had done something that was clearly wrong, had caused a breach of trust in the good relationship they had built with him, and had jeopardized his relationship with the camp. A parent involved advised him to deprive them of more retreats as a punishment, but the minister decided to try problem solving instead. He called a meeting of the people who had been on the trip. He told the group that he knew about the theft and told them how upset and disappointed he felt. He said that he wanted this group to come up with a workable solution to the problem. After leaving them to talk, a spokesperson for the young people said that they would like the minister to call the camp and tell the administrators there what had happened, and say that they would work to repay the money. The minister agreed to this, and then they had a moving discussion about theology, forgiveness, and trust.

Turning to problem solving was an excellent choice. The minister wanted to teach his young parishioners to be responsible citizens. What better way than to give the teenagers the opportunity to take responsibility for their behavior and make amends? This taught them so much more than any punishment could have done.

Parents are often quite surprised at how well problem solving works, even with children much younger than these. Children usually come up with creative and original responses, and they cooperate much better when they've had a part in forming the solution to a problem. Parents and children become allies, working together toward a suitable solution, rather than opponents, focusing on blame. The more parents use problem solving with their children, the more they will see them turning to this technique on their own as a way to resolve conflicts with others.

One evening a father asked me to go over all of the reasons to give up hitting children. He wanted to know exactly why it was bad, not only for the child, but also for the parent. Many fathers and mothers have wanted to understand this to help them give up hitting and also so they could pass this information along to other adults.

Hitting is bad for children and for parents. Children have the right to have their bodies respected and protected. When children are hit by adults, their bodies are being violated. They are hurt physically and also emotionally. They begin to wonder about their self-worth when they are being treated like this, and they can develop negative feelings about their bodies. Many adults who were hit as children have told me that they felt as if their parents were trying to tell them they were really stupid, since all they could understand was a slap. This damaged their self-esteem. Positive methods show our children we consider them intelligent and capable of responding to more reasonable methods.

Body language should be used to enhance a child's self-image, not lower it. Children need lots of positive body language: hugs, kisses, back rubs, a hand on a shoulder, holding hands, stroking hair. Parents should eliminate all body communication that is hurtful, like pinching, slapping, pulling hair, spanking, squeezing, and shaking.

When children are hit, they wish they could hit back, but they can't. They are in a powerless position. Let's put ourselves in their place. Imagine an adult being hit by another adult, a boss, spouse, or friend. Most adults would feel furious and insulted, and would want to hit back, and many would. Children feel the same fury and insult, but they can't hit back. They register pain, resentment, fear, and humiliation. And they learn that it is okay for people to hit other people—or, more specifically, that it is okay for bigger people to hit smaller people. When these children grow up, they finally can get back and relieve some of their built-up resentment by hitting their own children. So often parents hit children to vent their pent-up feelings against their own parents for hitting them. Better to stop this cycle right now! It takes a concentrated effort to contradict these old feelings of rage, but there is no need to pass the angry and powerless feelings on to the next generation.

Many parents enjoy the feeling of power they get from hitting children. Again, this can be a holdover from feeling powerless as a child, or it can be a reaction to feeling powerless in other areas of their lives right now, such as job or relationships. We adults do need to feel important, but we should not get our sense of power from hitting children.

Hitting is not necessary to teach correct standards to children. When parents want a child to learn to do or not to do a certain thing, and they hit the child to teach him, very often what happens is that the child is not at all thinking about what he's supposed to be learning. His energy is being focused on his painful and resentful feelings. Even if the rule is stated along with the slap, very little energy is left over to concentrate on the rule. In fact, when parents think back to their own childhoods, they often remember *that* they were hit, *how hard* they were hit, and *with what* they were hit—but they rarely remember *why* they were hit or *what* they were supposed to be learning to do better!

Parents say that in some instances nothing positive *or* negative works with a child. This is true. In these cases, the best thing parents can do is to give their strong verbal disapproval to the child's behavior or, in an actually dangerous situation, to physically remove him from the danger.

Some parents say that at times it seems a child is just asking to be hit. These parents need a better interpretation of what is going on. The child is not asking to be hit and doesn't want or need to be, but he *is* asking for the limit to be set. If the child is used to having limits set by being hit, it seems as if he is asking to be hit. Children feel protected when parents set limits and do want this. When parents learn and use constructive methods to set their limits, children will be thankful. Children love their parents. When parents hurt children, some hate and bitterness gets mixed in along with the child's love toward the parents. This isn't helpful. Children actually listen to and regard better a parent who treats them with respect.

Sometimes parents say that if nothing works except a slap, they should use the slap. The slap may appear to work at that moment, but it is only because the child doesn't want to be hit anymore; the child obeys out of fear of another slap. It is our job, however, to teach inner control. The slap teaches the child to look to the parent (an outside force) to stop him. Often when a child is hit, he feels his debt has been paid for what he's done and then actually feels free to go ahead and repeat the misbehavior. Sometimes, out of resentment for being hit, a child will repeat what he did or do something else that is inappropriate, to get back at the parent.

When you use positive methods, you are teaching the child to know, on his own, what is right, and not to depend on an outside force to guide him. Eventually, you will have helped him to build a strong conscience that will guide him in all the situations of his life.

Some parents say that they do not ever really hit their children, they merely threaten to hit and the threat gets the child to do whatever the parent was indicating. So often we hear parents say in public, "I'll beat your butt for this," or "Stop it or I'll hit you hard," or "You'll get a good spanking." These violent expressions have no place in family life. In a similar way, parents sometimes threaten children with "Wait till Daddy/Mommy comes home and then you'll get it!" It is not helpful for one parent to turn the other parent into the "heavy." The parent who is there should deal with the situation in the best way possible.

I encourage parents to give up hitting, threatening, and all other discipline methods that are based on fear. Children should not experience the grownups in their lives as frightening creatures with great power to do them harm.

Hitting does emotional damage. Some parents say they see their children compensating for having been hit: A child has trouble falling asleep that night or gets clingy, asking for love and reassurance. Parents have reported that when they are not even about to hit a child, but are just going to tell him they are mad, the child starts to defend himself. He cowers, covers his face, puts up his hands to protect his body. Parents admit this makes them feel bad. If children are used to being hit, however, they do need to defend themselves from attack. Parents don't like to see their children needing to defend themselves. If they give up hitting for good, then children will not need these protective reactions.

Other parents say that they want their children to cry when they hit them and that it makes them mad when their children act defiant, as if they didn't care they were being hurt. Let's give children the credit for at least wanting to be brave against attack, but let's stop seeing parents and children as enemies at war.

When children hurtfully hit each other, parents go to stop them. Hitting is not the way to stop them. We really need to think about how we teach. To teach a child not to hurt by hurting him is contradicting our lesson. Parents need to be positive models for children. Adults usually do not hit their own parents, sisters, brothers, friends, or spouses when they are angry at them, and they should not hit their children either. Children need to learn from us the acceptable and positive ways to deal with interpersonal conflicts. If we use humane methods in our attempts to humanize children, then our means justify our end. If we use methods that invoke pain, resentment, and humiliation, then even if we do achieve the desired result at the moment, what an inhuman way to humanize!

The entire family atmosphere suffers when one child is hit or beaten. Siblings feel scared and threatened, and parents may feel guilty or drained of energy or still angry. Often parents admit they feel like bullies when they hit their children. Many say, "It hurts me more than it hurts my child." What does this mean? It means that deep down, parents feel bad for hurting children, knowing they are doing something that is not right. Hitting children does nothing positive for the parents' own character development or for their own growth and potential.

Many parents admit they feel bad when they see other parents hitting their children; they sympathize with the children. And yet, they turn around and hit their own children. They ask, "Why do I then hit my own?" The main reason they resort to hitting is that they have no other tools available to stop the inappropriate behavior. Once they learn other tools, they no longer resort to hitting.

Sometimes parents discuss feeling terrified at losing control, hitting their child much harder or longer than they had expected. Parents who may have intended to spank a child's bottom three times or to strike a child twice with a belt instead wind up spanking nine times or striking twelve times with the belt. They get caught in the momentum of the hitting; it overtakes them. Their anger seems to keep on flowing as they hit, and they just can't stop. It is scary to be hitting so hard and so long, and some parents have found the only way to end this is to stop hitting altogether. Once they have made the commitment, they find it much less likely for their anger to go out of control.

The term "spanking" itself can often act as a cover-up for what is really going on. The word has a cute ring to it. It sounds more pleasing to say "Do you want a spanking?" than to say "Do you want to get hurt?" But this is what a spanking really is. Spanking is the hurting of children by adults, and this is not cute at all.

Often adults will say, "Well, I was hit when I was a kid and I turned out okay." When children turn out okay, it is because of the love, not the spankings, they receive. Fortunately, most of us do turn out okay. But what about the child's inner feelings, the powerlessness, resentment, and fear? And what about the living, day-to-day process of being a parent and being a child? Childhood should be a good experience for children, and parenting should be a rewarding experience for parents. When children are in the process of being hit and parents are in the process of hitting, it is not pleasant or beneficial to either.

We live in an age of liberation movements: the civil rights movement, the women's liberation movement, national liberation groups, and now children's liberation. The children's rights movement is a natural part of the political and social enlightenment of our times. In 1979, Sweden passed a law making it illegal for parents to hit children or discipline them in a humiliating manner—an important step forward. It is my hope that the United States and other countries will soon follow Sweden's lead. Children deserve freedom from injury—in their schools (where shockingly often policies of corporal punishment persist) and in their homes.

The law protects grownups from assault. If you were walking down the street and a stranger hit you on the back or arm, you would have solid grounds for an assault and battery charge. If, in that same instant, you hit your own child anywhere on his body, this would not be recognized by most people as equal cause for a lawsuit. This double standard is appalling. The law of our land applies to people. Children are people, too. Please remember this and tell your friends. *Children are people!* They should not be hit with belts, shoes, cords, paddles, or hands. They should not be hit with their clothes on or their bottoms bared! They need protection from all slaps, all spankings, all beating. Children cannot lobby for themselves to ensure that the laws are enforced, so we must protect them. Let each of us take a stand and abide by this law in our own homes, and spread it throughout the land.

Quite often parents, and also professionals who work with parents, are disconcerted by what they call my "radical" stand on hitting. One mother put it this way: "Child abuse is one thing, but surely you'll admit that a light slap can't hurt, and there are times when a 'good spanking' is an invaluable disciplinary tool!"

It should be clear by now that in my opinion there is no such thing as a "good" spanking or a slap that doesn't hurt. These are myths! Children can respond to reasonable methods, and even when they are too young to reason, there are numerous constructive alternatives from which to choose.

Calling spanking a disciplinary tool is incorrect. Discipline is teaching children, not hurting them. Under the name of discipline, parents slap, spank, even beat children. Let us grasp the fact that when we hit children, we are hurting them, and this has nothing at all to do with true discipline. Parents ask me to draw the line between discipline and child abuse. Certainly, there is a big difference between severe and repeated beatings and an occasional spanking, but even so, I believe that *all* degrees of hitting are wrong, and *no* hitting has disciplinary value.

Too many of us currently feel that only child abuse needs correction, but it is wrong to isolate only a certain segment of society as needing help in this area. The fact is that the great majority of parents in our country use hitting to one degree or another. One father said that several weeks before the group met, had he been asked at the end of a typical day if he had slapped his son at all that day, he would very likely have responded, "No" or "Maybe once." Yet now, giving this careful thought, he realized that, in fact, he often had given his son a short, quick slap here and there throughout the day, for this and that reason, and would not even have taken these into account. This man is hardly unusual. His group members readily agreed that this slapping pattern could be called a national habit. It is a habit that needs to be broken! No matter where an individual is on the spectrum (hitting children a lot or a little, often or seldom, with hard or light strokes), he or she needs to recognize harmful methods for what they are and do away with them entirely. This is not a radical viewpoint; it is the only fair and sensible alternative before us.

Parents express their concerns about changing to positive methods. They are afraid it will be very hard to make the switch. Some parents ask if it is appropriate to tell their children that they will no longer be hitting them. Other parents ask, "How can I take the first step to stop my hitting?"

Learning positive parenting does take time initially, just like learning any new skill. If you were learning to bake bread, drive, type, or play the piano, you would need to practice. At your second piano lesson, you would not be ready to give a concert. You would keep on studying and practicing, and soon you would be able to play a piece from memory. The positive methods for parenting also become second nature after a while. The more you use them, the more used to them you will become, and soon you will be responding constructively out of habit.

The first step is to make the commitment never to hit a child again. Then you need to keep reminding yourself of this until it becomes automatic. Many parents tell me they have gone home and thrown away their belts or sticks and without those objects around they weren't tempted to use them. Others have trained themselves to stop at times of intense anger before plunging in and doing something they're certain to regret later. They learn to wait a moment, even close their eyes, and think: "What is my goal here? What would be a positive response?"

One mother told her group that she went home after our discussion on hitting and told her children (ages four and almost three) that she had learned something new: that "people are not for hitting." She told them she was not going to spank them anymore and that, instead, she would use better ways to teach them to act appropriately and solve problems that came up. Many other parents have followed her example.

Children will take time getting used to the new ways. They might test us, acting up to see if we really mean we won't hit them. After a while, they will learn that we really won't hit, but we *will* set and follow through on limits. When anger is expressed constructively and we let our children know verbally what we are feeling, why, and what we expect of them, then the tone of our homes is still pleasant. It is only anger expressed in hurtful ways that takes away from family happiness.

When learning any new skill, it is good to have a goal before us. I urge parents to strive for the goal of choosing positive methods over negative ones in all the daily situations they face. Certainly, we will make mistakes, but having a goal before us helps keep us on the right path and can fill us with inspiration.

A mother reported happily that she had not hit her children for one and a half months. Yet she wanted to know what to do with her feeling of wanting to hit.

When this mother felt like slapping or spanking, she needed an outlet for her feelings. She found that she did not need to hit and did not really want to. How can the feelings find expression?

There are several positive ways to handle angry feelings. The mother can say her feelings to herself or even aloud, too quietly for the kids to hear, before she approaches the children to resolve the situation. This way her urge to hit won't be "on the tip of her tongue," as she had put it, but would have already been given expression. Saying to herself, "Oh, I could wallop those kids," or "I'd sure like to slap them," with the intensity with which she felt these feelings would give her some relief.

Most parents also experience stronger thoughts like "I feel like killing her" or "I'd sure like to wring his neck" during moments of intense anger. These thoughts are normal to have, but it is never appropriate to utter them to our children. Saying them to ourselves in our own mind, mumbling quietly out of earshot, and sharing with other adults are helpful ways to handle these feelings.

I also suggested to the mother above that if she gets so mad that she needs to hit, she can hit a pillow or a sofa or a punching bag a few times to work off the intense momentary anger. Then she can take care of her children and the situation in a positive way.

Some parents fear that stating their angry feelings verbally will not give them the relief that hitting does, and their anger will grow and grow. This is not true. In fact, we feel more relieved when we handle our anger constructively. When we hit, we feel ashamed and guilty later, but when we use methods that guide and teach, we feel good about ourselves, proud of having used mature and humane approaches.

It isn't easy changing old patterns and ways of handling things. However, we do live in a world of change. Many of us would gladly trade in an old-fashioned refrigerator for a newer one. It's not as easy to give up older methods of child rearing for the newer approaches. I strongly encourage parents to make the effort and commitment to do so. Let's embrace the opportunities and knowledge of child rearing our new age offers to us.

From the time a Parent Awareness group gets under way, and increasingly as it nears the final sessions, parents share with enthusiasm their successes using the positive methods. They discuss how much easier it is to handle the conflicts that arise with their children, and they say they can now enjoy their children so much more. They become more relaxed about those times that don't work out so well, recognizing that even with the aid of positive approaches, they will not be able to resolve every conflict in ways that will immediately succeed. This realization brings parents considerable peace of mind. They no longer feel that their authority is on the line in every situation, and their expectations become more realistic.

I am pleased when Parent Awareness helps parents feel more relaxed about their parenting. Sometimes children comply readily with adult requests. At other times, they comply after we take a firm stand. And there are yet other times when children just won't comply at all, no matter what we do. There is always some nonhurtful way to express displeasure at this last possibility. As parents, we need to remember that every situation may not be as important as it seems (providing nothing dangerous is going on that we absolutely must stop) and that our real job is to instill our standards and values *over a long period of time.* We're helping to build consciences, and that job is just not completed overnight. It helps if we don't view each situation as a struggle between parent and child. If we see parenting as a long-range process, then we won't get so caught up in every single incident. We need to tune ourselves in to the important situations and let some of the others go.

Sometimes (even pretty often) we adults do things that aren't so terrific, and we're probably glad when no one's there to make us turn around and act acceptably on the spot. Often we're harder on our children than we are on ourselves. I'm sure parents would even agree that all children need some chances to get away with some of the things that they do. (Or are we that far away from our own childhoods?)

This doesn't mean we should ignore our children and leave them alone. But we can learn to be discriminating, realizing that we're not essential in every situation and that some actions, even disruptive ones (but not dangerous ones), are best ignored. We can also learn that in some situations the child isn't going to comply, but that doesn't mean our anger has been ineffective. The child may have registered our anger and rules very well, but just not be ready to put them into immediate practice. Adults sometimes change in their attitude about something, too, yet there's a lag until the behavior can change to meet the attitude. A man may have decided to quit smoking, but finds himself still taking some cigarettes. So, too, with children.

There is, nonetheless, reason to be optimistic about the wonders of time. Certainly, four-years-olds have more self-control than do two-year-olds, and five-year-olds have better control than most three-year-olds. Conscience develops steadily in time, but everyone has occasional lapses in self-control. These lapses do not signify stubbornness or meanness on the child's part. Many adults say to children at these times, "How many times have I told you not to do that?" These kinds of remarks aren't helpful. Children's consciences are not yet completely stabilized. They will backslide. If we discover a four-year-old scribbling on the wall, something the child hasn't done in months or even in years, we should remember that these lapses will occur, and handle the situation in a helpful, positive way.

Our patience is very often rewarded in an unexpected way. We have tried to get a point across to our child, and getting no apparent results, we feel disappointed. Several days later, however, we overhear our child repeating our information to his friend or sibling. Our child not only has registered the rule, but has joined the forces of those who perpetuate it!

CHAPTER 2

Daily Life

Dealing with the Full Variety of Life with Children

In Chapter 1, I discussed some common areas of confrontation between parents and children, the times when intervention is needed to enforce parental rules and standards. But it is the everyday events, the eating and sleeping routines, getting dressed, and going out to play, that compose the major parts of our lives, and set the tone of family life. In this chapter, I explore the use of positive techniques to make our daily lives more pleasant, and thereby reduce the number of discipline situations that arise.

A mother left to answer the telephone during dinner, and as soon as she was gone her children started throwing spaghetti at each other. When she came back, she was so angry that she dumped the whole plate of spaghetti on their heads! Though the Marx Brothers might have appreciated this scene, it was not the harmonious dinner hour we like to imagine!

Actually, parents report that many battles with children occur over eating issues. Aside from the kind of horseplay above, parents complain of children who don't seem to want to eat at all, and those who say they are starving but then hardly touch what's on their plate, and others who will only eat a few favorite foods. How can these parents make mealtime more enjoyable?

Some children are just not very interested in eating, certainly not three times a day. It is not wise to force them to eat a lot of food. Parents might encourage them to eat half the sandwich or half of the half, but if they don't want more, it is best to concur. Sometimes a piece of fruit or cheese will satisfy a child instead of a full meal.

At times, a child will eat a good breakfast and then won't want too much for lunch. Then at around three or four o'clock, she is hungry for dinner. Parents wonder if they should give the child her dinner right then or make her wait until the family's dinnertime.

If a child is hungry, she should get something to eat. Some parents wouldn't mind giving the child an early dinner, while other parents would rather offer a carrot or a piece of cheese to tide her over until the regular dinnertime. Either way is perfectly reasonable.

Some parents insist that children eat everything on their plates before they leave the table or eat dessert. Understandably, parents do not like to see food being wasted. I recommend giving a small portion first, and if the child wants more when that's done, she can have it. Even so, it is common to see a small amount of food left after a meal. We shouldn't expect an absolutely clean plate. Some parents hover over their children to see that every bit of food is eaten. This can make children nervous and not enjoy eating.

Sometimes a child will skip lunch and then ask for candy or ice cream in the afternoon. Generally I feel that nutritious food should precede sweets, but occasional exceptions aren't harmful. Some children really eat only one large meal, breakfast, and if it is a healthful one, an afternoon snack can be their dessert. Naturally sweet snacks like fresh fruit or raisins can be substituted as much as possible for nonnutritious sugary ones. Sweet desserts do not have to be served at every meal; perhaps once or twice a week is better for everyone in the family.

Often children don't like what their parents are eating. Should the parents go to the trouble of preparing something different for the child? Or would that be spoiling the child? Well, when parents plan to cook a certain meal for themselves, they are pleasing themselves. Children also deserve some choice in their meals. This doesn't mean fixing two elaborate dinners, but offering easy substitutes, such as a sandwich or yogurt, is certainly not overindulgence. Adults and children both enjoy eating what they're in the mood for. The children can help to plan menus sometimes, too, so that their interests are taken into consideration.

Many young children prefer diets limited to just a few foods. They should be allowed to eat the foods they like, providing they are nutritious. Children can be encouraged to try new foods, but it's nothing to worry about if they resist. Many youngsters won't like a great variety of foods until they are much older.

How important is it for young children to eat dinner with their parents? Certainly, a pleasant and relaxing mealtime is lovely for the family, but many young children are just not that interested in sitting still for a meal. They do not look forward to eating the way adults often do. A one-and-a-half-year-old may be finished eating in one minute. A three-year-old may prefer to eat a sandwich and then be off to play. If dinnertime with the children will be frantic, it is better to feed them earlier. Then the adults can enjoy a peaceful meal together later. There will be many years for the family to eat together when the children are older.

When the family *is* eating with a young child, there's no point in forcing her to sit too long. A parent can help her to concentrate on eating her dinner (sometimes using humor and a game approach) and then allow her to take off to play. While she is there, focus on subjects of conversation that include her, not on how much she is eating. Mealtimes should be pleasant times, as hassle-free as possible.

When there are two or more children in a family, there is often teasing at dinnertime. Parents hear statements such as "I'm winning," or "I have the big spoon—na, na na," or "Look at you, spaghetti-head." I find with my own two boys that it's wise to ignore some of the teasing. This helps to get it out of their systems. At other times I say things like "When people eat, it's not a race," or "Put your energy into concentrating on eating and not into who has the bigger spoon," or "Spaghetti is for eating, not for throwing." This usually settles everyone into eating more quietly.

During dinner a father began playing with his daughter's toy train. The parents suddenly realized that if their duaghter had done this, they would have asked her to leave the room until she was ready to eat her dinner without fooling around. So the mother turned to her daughter and playfully asked her what they should do about Daddy's dinnertime behavior. "Send him to his room," she said. Her father went upstairs, pretending to cry as he did so. Then the mother said, "What should we do now?" Her daughter replied, "Tell him to come down when he's ready to eat without playing!"

Here, spontaneously using role reversal, the family was able to handle a situation in a humorous way. The daughter had a chance to enforce a limit that was usually imposed on her. This delighted her and gave her some feeling of parental power. It makes it easier to accept being on the receiving end of limits when she gets a turn to make sure they are imposed equally on the whole family!

A mother was having a recurring conflict with her three-year-old daughter. The mother thought it was important for the girl to drink at least one glass of milk each day. The daughter preferred apple juice. Each day, the mother punished her daughter, sending her to her room until she came down to drink her milk. The daughter would go to her room and cry but then finally return and drink the milk. Her mother wondered if there was any easier way to get the girl to drink her milk.

If the girl is getting some dairy products—puddings, cheese, or yogurt—her mother need not insist that she drink milk at all. Most children like some cheeses and puddings, and put milk on their morning cereal. Nutritionists stress the importance of four food groups: (1) dairy products, (2) fruits and vegetables, (3) grains, and (4) protein foods such as meat, fish, and nuts. It's important to get some food from each group every day, but no one particular food is indispensable. A child who doesn't like chicken can get protein from peanut butter, and unsweetened applesauce can substitute for a particularly despised vegetable.

It's important for children to see eating as a pleasurable activity. If a child eats from fear of being punished, she will get the nutrition, but at the cost of emotional calm and a positive attitude toward eating.

One morning, Joshua, then five years old, asked to have dry cereal for breakfast. After I prepared it, he changed his mind and asked for oatmeal. I hadn't yet added milk to the cereal, so I said that I'd make oatmeal. Just as I combined the oatmeal and water to cook it, Joshua said that he wanted dry cereal. At this point, I felt he should eat the oatmeal. He began to cry and fuss that he really wanted cereal. I was tired and couldn't stand his crying. I said to him, "This makes me mad. I didn't mind switching the cereal because I hadn't added the milk yet. But I don't want to waste the oatmeal. Also, I can't listen to your crying right now." That would have been the end of it, except that now Joshua took a juice glass, went over to the sink, and threw it in, saying, "Then I'll break this glass." This happened so fast there wasn't time to grab the glass away. I shouted, "You can be mad, but glasses aren't for breaking." Since he was still screaming and quite excited, I led him to his room and said, "Stay in here until you're ready to come out and eat the oatmeal and have a peaceful breakfast." He stayed in his room for a few minutes. I didn't hear a sound. Then he came out, actually cheerfully, and ate his oatmeal calmly. All was well after this.

I felt good. I had set my limit in a clear, positive way, had stuck to it, and had regarded my own feelings.

Later, I thought, "What if Joshua had come out after several moments, more calm, but still insisting on dry cereal?" At this point, I would have given him the cereal he wanted, but I also would have let him know that I don't like to waste food. I would have added that he was having a hard time deciding what to eat this morning, and the next time he should think more carefully first, before stating his preference. If I had done something like make Joshua wait all morning until he would eat the oatmeal, the eating issue would have gotten too tense. A peaceful breakfast and a good start to the day is even more important to me than the little bit of wasted oatmeal. As parents, we want to aim toward keeping our limits, but we need to be flexible too, and realize when to bend in getting our points across.

A mother believed that a five-year-old should dress himself, but she was concerned about a tense morning routine that was developing in her household. Each morning she would sit on the stairway threatening her son that he wouldn't be allowed down for breakfast until he was dressed. Every morning there was some rebellion. The mother was uncomfortable about the conflict, but asked, "Shouldn't a five-year-old dress himself?"

The issue is not whether a five-year-old is able to dress himself alone. Even if he can dress himself competently, a specific child may prefer help and attention while he does. If a child is happy dressing alone, he should be allowed to, but it is not a good issue to battle. Slightly older children as well—six-, seven-, or eight-year-olds—often want extra attention while dressing. The important thing is to have a *pleasant* morning experience. With his mother entrenched on the stairs demanding that he dress before daring to come down, the morning routine was tense rather than welcoming for this child. Most children enjoy and need some loving attention in the morning, to remind them that this world is a nice place to wake up to.

Gayle, a four-year-old, was invited to eat lunch at her friend Kathy's house. In the car on the way over, Gayle said to Kathy's mother, "I don't want to eat at your house." Kathy's mother was about to say sarcastically to her daughter's friend, "So don't eat!" but she caught herself midsentence and said instead, "If you want to eat at our house, you're welcome to. If you don't want to eat, you can just play, and if you would rather go home, I'll take you home." Then Gayle said, "I guess I will eat over at your house after all."

Had Kathy's mother been sarcastic, Gayle probably would have cried and wanted to go home. Sarcasm builds resentment. It puts children down and hurts emotionally. Bravo to this mother for cutting off the sarcastic response and substituting one that led to an enjoyable afternoon for her and the two girls.

A mother was disturbed when she heard her six-year-old son swearing loudly in the yard with a friend. What should she do about this?

I suggested to this mother that she tell the children not to talk like that in the yard because it could offend the neighbors. If they wanted to say those words, they could do so in the son's room, with the door closed, as she didn't want to hear it either. This way, the limit is set on swearing where others can be offended by it, yet the children are given some leeway to work it out of their systems.

When children are allowed to experiment with swearing, the fascination disappears much sooner than when it's forbidden and the parent gets upset over it. Certainly parents should *not* wash a child's mouth out with soap or put pepper in his mouth. These old-fashioned methods are humiliating, demeaning, and physically hurtful.

Attitudes toward swearing vary in different households. Some parents bang a foot and say, "Oh, shit!" Children learn to use swear words in contexts like this from their parents, and should be allowed to do so if their parents do. If the parents don't use or allow swear words in the house, then children need to follow house standards. When a child uses swear words to call someone else a name, the parent does need to step in, as this kind of swearing hurts feelings and self-esteem. Parents can set an example in this regard and never use swearing to call others names, not their children or anyone else.

Swearing often peaks between the ages of three and five. Children this age especially love to play around with bathroom words and rhyme and chant them, though parents tire of the choruses of "caca," "doodoo," and "bumbum." Their children's enchantment comes from their interest in the human body and their attention to toilet functions. They are either just over toilet training or still involved in it, and often struggling to stay dry at night.

It is quite common to see older children, six and up, still fascinated with swear words. We need to allow for some of this experimentation. If it really bothers parents, they can say something simple like "That's enough right now." Other parents are not so offended by bathroom talk and may on occasion turn to humor, making a joke of it and chanting along. Young children enjoy a good laugh seeing their parents enter their world every now and then. With that laugh, their repetitive chanting will often end more quickly and on a lighter note.

A six-year-old girl was having trouble playing well when she invited a friend to her house after school. She would call her friend names and say she didn't want to play with her or be her friend, yet she still wanted her to come over. Her mother was quite upset

by this and told her daughter she couldn't stand seeing her act so mean and nasty to her friend.

First of all, the mother needs to be very careful not to say things to her daughter in a humiliating way in front of others. This can make her even less comfortable with friends. If the mother is annoyed, of course she can let her daughter know, and state her positive expectations. "I expect you to play nicely when you have your friends over. I know you can find interesting things to do together." The focus should be on helping the girl deal better with the situation, not on identifying her behavior as mean.

It can also be helpful to appreciate the child's successes. If the mother said, after even five minutes of good playtime, "I appreciate that you and your friend are getting along and enjoying yourselves. It's nice to see both of you play like that," the daughter would be encouraged to keep it up. Children change and learn when we build upon their accomplishments, not when we keep telling them about their failures.

Several approaches that work with sibling quarrels might work to get these children playing well together. It is possible the children need more adult supervision. The mother can help them get started and even play with them for a time, or she could do her own work while the children play nearby. Once they are getting along, then she can withdraw. Just being around, showing occasional interest in what they're doing, can help, and stopping to play with them for a while can have a very calming effect. Also, a snack at the right time can sometimes relieve tension and refresh the children for playing again cooperatively.

If none of this is working, the mother can ask the children to take a short break from each other. One can play indoors and the other outdoors, or they can be in different rooms. This can be viewed as a positive alternative. It can remove pressure when they know they're not expected to spend every minute together.

If a temporary separation doesn't help, probably the children have reached their limit with each other for the day. Then the playtime can be ended. The friend can go home, but the mother can still stress the ways in which they did well.

Leroy was reluctant to play at other children's homes unless his parent stayed for the entire visit. He felt comfortable when his friends came to his house, but he wouldn't play at their houses. His father wondered how strongly to insist that Leroy be more independent.

I would not recommend forcing a child. One approach that can help is for Leroy's father to go to the friend's house and stay long enough to ease his child into the visit. When he feels that Leroy is managing well, he can let him know that he's leaving, and even if the child starts to fuss, he can still leave, saying something supportive as he does, like "You've been having fun already and I know you'll keep on having a good time. I'll be back at four o'clock." The friend's parent can help at this time by guiding the children back to interesting play.

Having Leroy bring along a special toy, a game, or his bike may help make him feel more comfortable away from home. His visits can be brief ones at first and get longer each subsequent time. After the child does successfully visit a friend alone, the parent should be sure to appreciate his efforts, saying, "I'm glad you decided to stay. You really enjoyed playing there today." If none of these methods are too effective, I recommend backing off, not making it a big issue, and waiting until he seems ready before giving it another try.

Four-year-old Amy returned home from Nicole's house with a toy blue car, which she said was a present from Nicole. A little later, Nicole's mother called to ask if Amy had come home with a blue car, as it was missing and was currently her daughter's favorite toy. Amy's mother apologized to Nicole's mother and then confronted Amy, saying, "You stole this from Nicole and you lied to me before!"

Young children walk a fine line between fantasy and reality. Amy wanted to take the blue car home so badly that she probably convinced herself Nicole had given it to her. Parents need to help young children sort out what is pretend from what is real, but accusations don't help. Amy's mother might instead have said, "You wanted this blue car so much that you wished Nicole had given it to you. Really, Nicole would like to keep it and we need to return it to her."

Sometimes young children take something from a friend or from school to ease a separation. They would like to have a part of their friend or school at home with them. Parents can teach their children to ask to borrow things they want. They need to let them know they disapprove of just taking things, but it is better to tell them in a teaching than in a blaming way.

As for lying, we can stress the benefits of telling the truth, instead of dwelling on the falsehood. When a parent already knows a child has done a certain thing, it is better to say out front that she knows it was done and focus on a solution than to get caught on a "Did you do it? Yes you did!" merry-go-round. When a parent suspects something has happened but isn't sure of the details, a supportive attitude is the most likely way to get a straight story. A statement like "I want you to tell me what happened" or "There's something I need to know" or "If you find it difficult to talk with me now, then I expect you to discuss it with me as soon as you are ready" work better than threatening confrontations. Treated in this manner, our children will be more willing and able to come to us with information and they do not build up a negative image of themselves as liars.

Parents often confuse storytelling and lying. Children, especially from three to six, will come home with fantastic stories. We want to encourage their creativity while helping them distinguish real from pretend. The parent can say, "I bet you wish your teacher let you walk all the way to the ice-cream store by yourself during school-time, but I trust Mrs. Forte to be with you and keep you busy in school," or "What a wonderful story; I love your imagination!" It's fun for parents, too, to join in the pretend world, as long as they let the children see they know it's not real.

A number of mothers of four- to six-year-olds were having the same problem. Their children "pestered" them constantly and wouldn't play alone for long. The mothers felt they were screaming things like "Leave me alone" and "Get out of here" far too often.

This situation can occur for any of several reasons, and each one suggests a different approach.

The parent's attitude is very important. If a mother is tense, letting her children know she can't stand their hanging on to her and complaining there is nothing to do, but nonetheless sits there while they do so, the children will most likely continue to whine and cling. A more positive stance is to say, "It's sometimes hard for you to decide what to play with, but now it's your time to play alone and my time to do my own work," and back up this statement by actually doing something else. If the parent can refrain from being tense or hysterical, staying reassuring and lighthearted, the children will pick up the attitude that they are expected to play on their own at times.

On the other hand, sometimes a continual clamor for attention can reflect a child's need for more high-quality, special time alone with the parent than she has recently been getting. It is not a parent's role to entertain all day long, as some of these mothers felt pressured to do, but it is essential to give each child some individual time every day. This actually makes it easier for her to go off and play on her own at other times.

The boredom may be in part legitimate. Children need playmates. When there are few neighborhood agemates, parents can help by structuring events for their children, as by inviting a school friend over to play one afternoon a week and having the child visit a friend on another day. Other planned activities like trips to the library or swimming lessons make the child's life more interesting. Children need exercise, too, and a walk to the park might make it easier to settle down and play. Children benefit from a variety of play materials for their use and exploration. Simple materials like paper and crayons, paste and old magazines, can encourage creative use of time. If a child seems bored with the toys she has, a simple change might make a big difference. Moving the blocks from the floor to the kitchen table might renew her interest. For other suggestions, the book *What to Do "When There's Nothing to Do"* by Elizabeth M. Gregg and Boston Children's Medical Center Staff (Dell) is a treasurehouse of everyday play activities for young children.

Sometimes, especially when it's too cold to go outside, children act frantic from having too much energy. Parents can play the same "pillow game" they use to help a child express anger, even though the child isn't upset about anything in particular. A child can pinch, scratch, and hit a pillow as a way to let off tension. The parent can stay with the child to encourage her to do this and even join in punching.

So children may be pestering because they are bored or because they are getting too little attention, or too much attention of the wrong kind. Each mother will need to evaluate for herself the situation in her home and choose the best combination of approaches to help her child play happily.

A four-year-old boy had been used to playing at the dining room table. Now that he was four, it was no longer as convenient for the family to have him working in the dining room and insisting, for example, that his elaborate block constructions remain set up there overnight. The mother was worried about asking the child to move his toys, however. She felt that he was very attached to the table and would only be happy if he could play there.

Sometimes the problem is with the parent, not the child. Children pick up parental concerns very readily. If the mother's attitude shows she feels her son can only be happy playing in the dining room on a certain table, then, in fact, he'll be miserable playing anywhere else. Parents can help children change. As a transition, the mother might suggest that there are times it is okay for him to use the table and other times it is not. Perhaps the parents can construct a simple cardboard table that he can use in his own room. This might make it easier for him to play in his room, since he was so used to working on a table. The parents have to realize that the child is flexible. He can learn to play in other rooms and on other spaces, and their attitude should let him know this.

A mother was shopping with her son. When he said in a loud voice, "Look at that fat lady," she was so embarrassed that she fled the store without making her purchases. She wondered how to handle this kind of situation more constructively.

I encourage the parent, if possible, to apologize to the person who was insulted. Afterward, it is important to talk with the child about the fact that everyone looks different and people feel bad when they are called names. Children need to become sensitive to the feelings of others. Often, their comments stem from fear. They are being faced with the unfamiliar, and they may worry that they will become that way. Explaining differences to our children helps them understand that even though people look all different ways, they are very much the same inside.

An inquisitive five-year-old boy would plague his mother with questions at the supermarket. The mother, following her notions of a "good mother," would answer his many questions, only to find that by the end of the shopping she had become quite irritable. She couldn't concentrate on her grocery list and at the same time be interested in her son's questions. Yet she was terribly afraid that to ignore him would hinder his healthy interest in the world around him. What should she do?

This mother needs to face the fact that the supermarket is not the place for her to be so concerned about her child's curiosity and growth. There are more suitable occasions for her to offer her son attention. It would be helpful for both mother and son if she talked with him about her needs and explained to him that in the supermarket she needs to concentrate on shopping. Perhaps the son could sit in the cart and look at a book, or help his mother wheel the groceries. If they discussed it together, I'm sure they would be able to come up with something interesting for the child to do which would not involve asking so many questions. Perhaps they could reserve the time riding to and from the supermarket for questions. Whatever they decide, the mother has the right to respect and care for her own needs. Working this out with her son allows him to share in the process of finding a solution that will please them both.

We make life much easier when we are true to our real feelings and our facial expressions and body language match our verbal messages. This mother had been pretending to be interested in her son's questions, but since they were really so annoying to her, no doubt her impatience came through in her face and tone of voice. Children often detect these indirect messages and then become confused. Her son may not really have known if she liked answering his questions or not. By giving our children clear messages, we avoid this kind of confusion, as well as our own frustration.

A mother reported what an ordeal it was to take her two-year-old shopping with her. The child was fascinated by escalators and other such things, and the mother couldn't shop in peace. How could she handle her daughter's behavior?
I believe the supermarket is the one store parents can enjoy with young children. They are usually happy if they have a box of crackers to eat or some fruit to munch, and they like the motion of being wheeled in a cart. In other stores, it's usually not appropriate to bring toddlers and preschoolers along, for their sake as well as the parent's. Young children are explorers. They learn by touching. So often we see children getting slapped or threatened for touching things in stores. Parents wind up screaming, being nervous, and having an unpleasant trip. Is it worth our energy to set limits on young children in a store and to be worried about their behavior? I don't think so. In general, it's better to leave them at home with a baby-sitter or friend and to shop in peace. Young children are much better off in a playing space they can be encouraged to explore.
If, on occasion, you cannot avoid bringing a young child shopping, then you can at least be understanding of her predicament and set any necessary limits in nonhurtful ways. Perhaps bringing along a snack or a favorite toy can help to keep her appropriately occupied.

A mother commented that before she had children, she had decided never to bribe them. Now she found that when her two-year-old son didn't want to get into his car seat, something like raisins helped him to cooperate. She hated to go back on her resolution, but the raisins didn't seem to be doing any harm. She wondered what I thought about this.
When a snack or toy is used in this manner to help a child ease into a situation, I call them "adjusters," not bribes. If the mother had said, "If you get into your car seat and stop having your tantrum, I'll give you these raisins," this would be a bribe. An adjuster is different. The mother was giving the child raisins to help him get into the car seat and compensate for having to sit still in the car. It

is uncomfortable for him to have to sit still, and there is nothing wrong with using raisins to make this transition more pleasant.

Unlike this mother, I believe that bribes, too, have their place. As parents, we are human and sometimes just need to make a certain situation easier for ourselves. Certainly, we don't want to be bribing children constantly, but I have nothing against an occasional bribe to lighten our load.

Parents are troubled by children's disruptive behavior during car trips. One mother said she had occasionally threatened her five-year-old son that she would stop the car and he'd have to wait outside it until he was ready to get in again and ride cooperatively. The mother wanted to know if this was a good way to handle this problem.

The answer to this mother's question is no. It is not wise to threaten a child that he will have to remain alone, out of the car, until he is ready to get in and behave. This could be very frightening. He might well worry that his parents will drive off and leave him there, even if they have told him they never would. Also, it could be dangerous for a child to wait on the side of any road.

Sometimes, if parents tell their children how the wild car behavior makes them feel, children stop being so unruly out of appreciation for their parents' feelings. A parent might say, "I can't drive with all this noise. It's very unpleasant and dangerous, as it makes it hard to concentrate on driving. I'll have to pull the car over and wait a while before driving on." Often this will work.

Parents also need to realize that long car trips are quite hard for children. Parents should come as well prepared as possible, by bringing along snacks and suitable toys and inventing games and singing songs along the way. Planning extra time for stopping to stretch and run around is essential, too, and makes it easier to settle down again after.

A couple had taken their four-year-old son to an amusement park. When it was time to leave, the child kept asking for more rides and for one more this and that. Finally, he threw an embarrassing full-scale tantrum. How could his parents have handled his requests for "one more" without letting things get so far out of hand?

The parents could have let their son know ahead of time that there would be about fifteen minutes left to enjoy themselves and then it would be time to leave. If the son protested, the parents could support his feelings, but keep to their limit: "You'd like to stay, we know, but it's almost time to go. We had a lot of fun."

If the protests continued, they could say, "Instead of hearing that you don't want to go home, we would like to hear a thank-you for the nice day we've spent together." When it is finally time to go, the parents need to take their son and decisively leave the park.

A father was having a hard time getting his four-year-old daughter to brush her teeth each night. He would say, "It's time to brush your teeth," but she wasn't interested. A mother was experiencing this same difficulty with her thirteen-year-old son, highlighting the fact that toothbrushing and other personal-care routines are often an issue with children of all ages.

To gain children's cooperation, try including them in the decision-making process. The father might talk with his daughter about the necessity for brushing and then say, "When would be a good time for you to brush each evening? Would you like to do it before I read you a story, or after?" It is often easier for children to follow through on decisions they have helped to make.

The mother above found that humor did the trick with her son. Nagging reminders and similar approaches weren't helping. One day when he walked into the living room, she went up to him, getting close to his face, and said, "Can you just smile a little wider? It looks like something interesting is growing in your mouth." He got the message and raced upstairs to brush his teeth. She also found that humor and other gentle, low-keyed reminders were more effective in getting him to do his chores than yelling and nagging had ever been.

For a couple of weeks in a row, Dick and I were having a hard time getting Joshua and Jesse to bed. Dick would let them know it was pajama time and they would shout, "Not yet!" and disappear. It was wearing us out to chase after them each evening.

One night, Dick got a flash. Both boys were interested in dinosaurs lately, and as they were just beginning to give Dick the usual hard time, he said, "I'm the Pajamalasaurus, relative of the Brontasaurus and Allasaurus, and I'm here to get your pajamas on." They ran to their rooms giggling as the Pajamalasaurus chased them, and they quickly got themselves ready for bed. This worked so well and was such fun that Dick repeated the dinosaur act for a couple of weeks. The boys looked forward to this game each night.

Children of all ages appreciate humor. Fun and games and humor so often get things moving much faster than a sterner approach ever could.

Three-year-old Rachel had come home excited from her aunt's wedding. She was tired and her mother wanted her to take off her fancy dress and get into her pajamas. She began to cry and scream about sleeping in the dress. The mother felt that the dress was much too delicate to sleep in, and she really did want her daughter to put on nightclothes.

The tantrum was continuing, so the mother left the room for a few moments, put on her own nightgown, and then came back to Rachel, saying, "I'm ready for bed. Now you need to get ready. Would you like to wear one of my nightgowns tonight?" Rachel replied, "Yes, the yellow one." The mother brought in a yellow one and Rachel said, "No, the other yellow one." So her mother gritted her teeth, tried to remain cheerful, and brought back the other yellow nightgown. Rachel changed and went to bed.

The mother was wise to leave the room for a few moments when she saw herself about to get into a major conflict with her daughter. Then the mother thought creatively and came up with a surprising suggestion that Rachel wasn't expecting. This mother deserves credit. To stay detached and take a few moments to think positively and creatively are steps that can help us all out in tight situations. Leaving the room and coming back for a fresh start can put a new beginning on a situation that is headed in a bad direction.

Each evening a mother set a different bedtime for her five-year-old daughter. Some nights the mother enjoyed her daughter's company until late hours (eleven P.M. or midnight), while on other nights she wanted the child to go to sleep much earlier and couldn't tolerate having her awake. The mother realized she was being inconsistent, but hated to be tied down to a routine herself. Yet she was aware that she'd get very angry at her daughter for not being able to comply on the evenings she wanted her to go to bed early.

In general, I encourage flexibility. We needn't be slaves to arbitrary rules and follow routines just for the sake of being consistent. It's good to act according to how we're feeling and follow our intuition in a given situation. Here, however, the parent's inconsistency was not helping her out. It was hard for her to deal with her daughter on the nights she would decide on an early bedtime. It was hard for the child to get used to going to bed early on some nights when she didn't have to on others. At times one must weigh which need is more valid. Was the mother's dislike of routines more important than a five-year-old's need for a reasonable bedtime hour? I would say not. Though the girl loved to go to bed very late (what five-year-old doesn't!), it is better to provide her with a bedtime appropriate to her age and health needs. There could be special nights to stay up late every once in a while. When late nights occur too frequently, they become a norm that is hard to give up on the other nights. A more structured routine would eliminate the daughter's rebellion and the mother's anger.

When we find that too much flexibility isn't working, then it's best to make the rules more fixed for our own comfort. It's not good to be a slave to inconsistency, either!

A mother was having a problem with her four-year-old son, Seth. Each night she'd tell him it was time for bed and cover him. Then for quite a long time, he would cry and fuss and want her to come into his room and read a story or give him juice. The mother was afraid that if she did, he'd become dependent on her and always demand lots of time before he went to sleep. Yet each night he did take up a lot of her time with his long tantrums. The mother said she just wanted to have peaceful evenings and didn't want to have to give Seth too much attention at night. Yet she wound up giving him lots of negative attention by going into his room to yell at him to go to sleep.

It's true that bedtime can be rough on parents. Many children go on and on, never wanting to end the day. Certainly there are times it is appropriate to yell, "Get to bed now!" after a long period of protest. In general, however, this is not a good way to end a child's day. Positive routines can help. When it comes to bedtime, the more approaches available to us, the better.

Many children love ending their day by hearing a story or playing a game with their parents. My own children often like to listen to a record with me and then for us to lie down together for a while. Cuddling close and giving a back massage sets a restful tone and is pleasant for me as well as the boys. If a child can fall asleep easily or doesn't seem to care about special time before bedtime, that's fine, but many children do benefit from having time with a parent before falling asleep. It helps them to relax, unwind, and sleep more easily.

This mother certainly would have done better to give her son fifteen minutes of happy, positive attention than to spend more than an hour fighting with him. Seth was in a pattern of crying and having long tantrums to get attention. His mother could help him to break his pattern. It might take several weeks of effort, but it would certainly be worth it.

During the day, Seth's mother could explain to him that she realizes the evenings have been unpleasant for both of them, and from now on she will read him a story or play a game with him before bed, and after this time together she will expect him to go to sleep. She could even let him know that she realizes he is used to fussing to get her attention, but now she will be giving him time, so his fussing won't be necessary anymore.

Seth's mother can also explain the reasons for a good night's sleep, for him and for her. If he doesn't get to bed on time and get enough sleep, then he will be tired and probably crabby in the morning. She won't want to do anything special, like going to the park or having his friend over, if she has a tired child. Seth himself will not be able to enjoy nursery school or playing if he is too tired. Sleep, he needs to know, is a way to take good care of his mind and body. It helps him to feel creative, energetic, and happy the next day.

His mother might want to write a bedtime book about this situation. She could draw Seth and picture him having tantrums, and also draw herself, a yelling mother coming in to tell him to get to bed. Then she could draw the new scene, with her reading a story and watching him fall asleep peacefully. The book could conclude by saying, "Now Mommy and Seth have a good bedtime routine!" Such a book can be made in ten minutes, with quick drawings. Children love these homemade books about themselves.

Some children like to play on their own for a while before going to bed. If Seth is not being disruptive, his mother could allow him to play quietly alone after hearing the story. A planned bedtime snack may also relax him and prevent requests for one more glass of juice far into the night.

Seth will no doubt continue to fuss and have tantrums after hearing a bedtime story the first few nights or even weeks. Then his mother can tell him firmly that she is busy elsewhere, she has given him time when she read to him, and tomorrow night she will read to him again. If she stays calm, it will be helpful. If she yells, he will continue to believe he can get her attention by fussing. Staying detached will show him she intends to relax herself and she will not get involved in battles with him anymore.

For parents as well as children, bedtime can be an intimate and meaningful part of the day. Older children (teenagers included) as well as younger children appreciate a parent's attention at the end of the day. Often they will share feelings about school, a movie they've seen, or their special interests most readily at this time. Parents can sometimes recall at bedtime pleasant events of the child's day, sharing happy memories: "Today you really enjoyed listening to your record" or "I enjoyed seeing how much fun you and Justin had making that fort" or "We had a great time making the vegetable soup together." This is so much better than ending the child's day by criticizing him in any way.

Sometimes parents and children can talk over something they will do together the next day, like playing a chess game or coloring. That way children can fall asleep happily looking forward to the day ahead.

CHAPTER 3

Ages and Stages

Relating Positively to Children
As They Grow and Change

Childhood, as every parent knows, is not an unbroken line of increasingly agreeable behavior. On the contrary, the childhood years alternate between calmer times and stormier stages that involve a great deal of turmoil and stress. Every age has its positive qualities, nonetheless, and even the negative aspects are signs of growing that can be handled in positive ways. Parents who have an idea of what kinds of behavior to expect, and when, have a very useful tool as they search for appropriate responses to the situations they face. This chapter attempts to meet the need for information by describing typical year-by-year behavior patterns for children, from birth to age sixteen. In addition, I offer practical advice to parents as they face the challenges each age and stage present.

A father was concerned about the change in his daughter's personality. He and his wife had been sharing work and child-rearing responsibilities. He spent several mornings a week watching their child while his wife went out to work, and in the afternoons she would be with their daughter while he went out to his job.

The father felt that he had gotten along easily with his daughter during her infancy and early toddlerhood, but since she had turned two, he had found their time together more difficult. What was happening to his once-easygoing daughter? She was now often defiant and moody. He didn't know whether she was reacting to some trauma he wasn't even aware of, or the changes he was seeing were normal.

Children do go through different ages and stages, and each stage has its special tendencies and characteristics. I gave this man some basic information about ages and stages to help him understand the changes he was seeing, and would continue to face, in his daughter.

Erik Erikson, in his book *Childhood and Society* (W. W. Norton), presents each stage in terms of a basic issue. A successful resolution of each issue in turn leads to the formation of a healthy personality.

According to Erikson, infancy is the time when a person establishes a fundamental trust in his environment. The infant needs to learn that the world is a nurturing place where his needs will be met. When he is hungry and gets fed, is lonely and gets held, he begins to experience his caretakers and the world they represent as trustworthy. In order for an individual to partake in and contribute to the world in a healthy way, he needs to be able to see that world as a basically kind, friendly, and supportive place.

During toddlerhood, ages one to three, the child strives to establish a sense of autonomy and individuality. He needs to begin doing things on his own, like feeding himself and climbing stairs, and to dispute some of his parents' requests. By doing so, the toddler begins to see himself as a person in his own right. The sense of self is developing, and we need to provide opportunities for it to emerge securely and be strengthened.

The preschool child, from three to six years old, enters the phase of initiative and flowering imagination. Creative play is an important part of his world at this time, and many opportunities to initiate ideas and see them carried out enhance his growth. Not every idea the child has will be appropriate and we will need to censor some of them, but we do need to show sincere respect for his creative thinking, offer recognition when his ideas are good ones, and help him to see them implemented. Ideas like building a train or playing the role of parent while his friend plays baby are important steps in learning to influence and control the world.

During the ages from six to eleven, children become more involved in the real world than in pretend and magic. They realize that they will need real tools to participate in the adult world that lies ahead, and they build skills in many areas: language, math, art, science. Children, for the most part, are eager to learn what they will need to know to be competent adults.

Adolescence brings questioning: Who am I really? What will my values and goals be? What kind of world do I want to see and lend my energies to create? The adolescent is seeking his own identity, and this soul-searching can involve upheaval and anxiety.

Erikson describes the life cycle past adolescence. The young adult years are a time for seeking intimacy through close friendship, marriage, or affiliation with ideas. The mature adult has a great attachment to the world and wants to benefit it in meaningful ways, by caring for the next generation of children and/or by pursuing a career that contributes to society. The close of a person's life is a time of evaluation and integration during which the healthy individual will come to see himself positively, accepting the life he has lived as worthwhile. He can accept the strengths and limitations of those around him, appreciating the totality of all life with its value and imperfections.

Each of the issues in Erikson's scheme (trust, autonomy, initiative, industry, identity, intimacy, generativity, ego integrity) is confronted throughout life, but each has a time to hold center stage. If that element is resolved positively at its designated time, the individual is freer to deal with the key issue of the succeeding stage.

Erikson provides a basic overview of life stages, but the everyday behavior of children at each age has also been described in detail, beginning in the 1940s with the classic Gesell Institute works *Infant and Child in the Culture of Today* by Gesell and Ilg (Harper & Row) and *The Child from Five to Ten* by Gesell, Ilg, and Ames with Glenna E. Bullis (Harper & Row), and in the later useful volume *Child Behavior from Birth to Ten* by Ilg and Ames (Harper & Row). A different discussion of childhood, year by year, is found in David Elkind's *A Sympathetic Understanding of the Child: Birth to Sixteen* (Allyn & Bacon). Elkind goes into detail about physical, social, emotional, and mental development, with valuable emphasis on the child's self-concept and school adjustment.

The age guidelines in all of these books are extremely valuable, but do keep in mind that not all children go through the stages exactly on time. A child may begin any stage up to six months earlier or later than the age that is given, and some children will stay in a particular stage for longer than others.

Parents soon learn that each stage of childhood has its positive and negative aspects. Some years (generally the ages of one, three, and five) are calmer times when the child seems more at ease with himself and the world. Other ages (roughly two, four, and six years old) involve more turmoil and stress. The child is changing more rapidly at these times and struggling to get his physical, emotional, and mental sides in balance. Negative behavior isn't confined to any specific age, but is often more pronounced at ages two, four, and six, though the intensity of the behavior varies. All children go through the stages and express the characteristics appropriate for their age, but some children do this more deeply and dramatically than others. Though two, four, and six are harder ages for parents to live through, some two-, four-, and six-year-olds are easier to live with than others.

As parents, we need to accept matter-of-factly the negative behavior that goes along with a certain stage. The stage will pass.

We need to learn to deal in positive ways with any negative, unpleasant behavior that goes along with a certain phase. These negative characteristics are signs of growth. We can appreciate that the more difficult ages are not easy for the child to live through either.

It also helps to remember that the negative behavior that goes with certain stages is just a part of the total child. Every stage also has its delightful aspects. The two- to two-and-one-half-year-old may be demanding, but he is also becoming a conversationalist, is making sense of how the world works, and is often cuddly and affectionate. The four-year-old has a wonderful imagination, can make up fantastic stories, is socially inclined and becoming more interested in his friends. The six-year-old has valuable new accomplishments, like learning to read and riding a two-wheeler, and is becoming a good companion for serious conversations. Along with this, each child still has his specific, wonderful personal qualities. This beautiful side of each of our children is more constant than the temporary, hard-to-live-with stage characteristics. Each child possesses and demonstrates his own personal good qualities during every stage of life.

The key, then, is for parents to search out and focus on the enjoyable aspects of each stage and on the specific good qualities unique to their child, while dealing positively with the negative stage characteristics. Parents need to let their children know what they appreciate and like about them during every stage they go through. This attitude will be taking the age/stage considerations in proper perspective.

A one-and-a-half-year-old was described by her mother as very sweet, except when she had tantrums. The mother got very upset during her daughter's tantrums and sometimes found herself yelling at her older child to let out tension.

Most one-and-a-half-year-olds have tantrums. They are just beginning to see themselves as people. Often they reject our proposals and say no simply in order to establish their own autonomy in the situation. So if we say, "It's time to get ready to go out now," the child might say no and run away or even have a tantrum. This is normal. It's hard for children of this age to make up their minds about things, and they are struggling for some control.

This mother was unusually tense about tantrums. She missed her daughter's sweetness so much that I wondered if she was overemphasizing this quality. I suggested she try to accept her daughter along with her varied moods. It wouldn't be good for the child to feel that her mother only felt comfortable when she was very well behaved. The daughter needed freedom to be a person of many moods and feelings.

Several approaches toward the tantrum itself are helpful. At times it is appropriate to reflect the child's feeling by saying, "It's so hard for you to decide whether you want to get ready that you just need to fuss about it. That's okay." This can be reassuring. After saying this, allow the child to continue her tantrum until it's over, staying calm and detached. At times, of course, the parent must proceed to put the child's shoes on because the two of them have to go somewhere right away. Then she can hold the child firmly to do so, at the same time understanding her feelings by saying, "You don't want your shoes on yet, but I have to put them on." Not always, but sometimes, it will work to hug, comfort, or humor a child out of a tantrum. At other times, offering a cracker or some other distraction, like looking at cars out the window, can help. These tactics are usually most effective when the tantrum is beginning to fade out.

Sometimes a parent can use role reversal, taking on the child's role and imitating the tantrum. The child may instantly snap out of the tantrum on her own, finding it hilarious to see the parent acting up as she had been doing (but don't keep it up if she's not amused). An older child confronted by a hysterical parent may stop her tantrum and pretend to be the parent, offering comfort to the parent who is having the pretend tantrum. This can be fun for parent and child.

At times parents can't help getting angry. When this happens, a statement like "It's really unpleasant for me to have to hold you like this," or "It would be helpful if you would cooperate," can express the angry feelings in a nonhurtful way. But in general, if a parent can be accepting rather than angry during a child's tantrum, it helps by keeping her from getting upset about her parent's being upset.

It is certainly not pleasant to be confronted with a kicking, screaming, wailing child, but it helps to know that tantrums are normal for one- and two-year-olds and that they are part of a stage that will pass, with patience and positive methods. As the child gets older, she can go on to think creatively and express her mind in better and more interesting ways than by merely taking a stand opposite to her mother's views and requests.

One father asked what the biting and hitting of his one-and-a-half-year-old meant. Was it misbehavior or just exploration?

One- and two-year-olds are constantly exploring the physical environment, including the people in it. Often the bites and hits are playful, the child's way of reaching out to explore. Initially, he doesn't even realize that these actions can hurt. It is inaccurate to call this misbehavior. It is actually behavior that is appropriate for his age, though it is no fun for the parent.

When no one is getting hurt by the child's actions, there's no need to call attention to them by saying, "Don't bite" or "Don't hit." If the biting or hitting is hurting someone, then the parent does need to step in and say, "Biting like that hurts, and you must stop it right now." Then it is helpful to redirect the child to a toy or game. The main thrust of the parent's intervention should be to get the toddler happily and busily involved in an appropriate activity, being sure to notice and appreciate it when he is, so that his better behavior is reinforced.

Toddlers also bite and hit when they are angry. The parent might say, "Are you hitting her because she has the toy you want? Let's ask her for a turn with it instead," or "I see you're mad, and it's okay to be mad at your friend, but you may not hurt him." If he needs to hit a pillow to discharge his anger, the parent can help him to do so. Parents should not call their toddlers bad for hitting, and they should never hit or bite their toddlers back as a way of reprimanding them or showing them how it feels. Toddlers may believe it's fine to hit or bite if they see their own parents doing it to them.

It is not worthwhile to invest too much emotional energy in this behavior. If the child gets a lot of attention for hitting and biting, it is more likely to increase their incidence than to reduce it.

Parents want to know how to handle the tempers of their one-year-olds when they don't want to get their diapers changed, and why toddlers begin to rebel against being changed.

When infants begin to walk and to stand, they have a strong physical urge to be erect. Lying down is against their need to get up and go. They do need to be changed, however. Some parents become quite skilled at diapering a child who is standing. If he won't stand still, the parent will have to just hold him down and try to get the diapering done as fast as possible.

While we change toddlers, it is good to talk with them about what we are doing so they will begin to understand the toileting process. We can say, "I'm giving you a fresh diaper because you made a B.M." It is not helpful to make disparaging remarks like "Let Daddy change your yucky diaper," or "I need to clean up your messy pants." Comments like these do not help the toddler to develop a good body image. They contribute to his feeling that certain aspects of the body or body functions are to be considered with disgust. We human beings are physical as well as mental and emotional. Our emotions and self-image are closely tied to how we feel about our physical selves. The process of elimination is a healthy process and needs to be viewed as such.

As children get slightly older, it is also important to give them information about their body wastes. It is wise to indicate that the food and liquid we eat and drink is used by our bodies to create the energy we need to live, play, and think. The part of the food and liquid the body can't use comes out as body wastes, urine, and bowel movements. Children need this information. Their bodies are important to them, and they should understand how they function.

Disappointed that her older child was not toilet-trained until age three, a mother decided that she would train her younger one much earlier. She sounded quite determined.

Most parents are eager for their children to be toilet-trained well before the children themselves are ready. There needs to be a balance between the child's readiness and the parent's encouragement. Toilet-training should be the child's achievement.

Actually, more children are ready for toilet-training closer to age three than age two. Each child is unique, and parents are wise to follow their child's indications for readiness. Some signs of readiness are the child's interest in his productions, wanting to see the soiled diaper, a vocabulary to discuss toileting, staying dry for longer spells, and interest in the potty. Parents can help prepare him by letting him see them or older siblings using the toilet. Children often want to be able to imitate more grown-up ways of doing things.

Most important is to be encouraging in a relaxed way, not anxious and pressuring. When parents are determined to train a child without his cooperation, toilet-training becomes an unnecessary battleground. When they remain calm and gently supportive, training usually occurs easily, when the child is ready. Parents should also remember that complete training comes about gradually over a period of months for most children, and parents should remain accepting and relaxed about the accidents and backsliding that are likely to occur.

Parents ask when children should give up their bottles.

Each child is different. Some children never drink from a bottle. They go right from breast to cup. Others become quite attached to a bottle and derive great comfort from sucking. Some children give up their bottles at around age one, others at two. Many three-year-olds enjoy bottles and even quite a few four-year-olds enjoy them occasionally. The same is true of a pacifier.

I would not pressure a child to give up a bottle, but would gently encourage him, being attuned to his specific needs and pace. There's no reason to rush this step; it will surely happen sooner or later. Not too many fifteen-year-olds walk around with bottles!

Many parents fret that their young children find it hard to share their toys and belongings. How much can parents expect young children to share?

One- and two-year-olds are just forming a sense of self. Often they want to hold on to a special belonging, almost believing that that object is part of themselves. "It's mine" and "It's me," or "What is mine" and "What is me," are interconnected. As a child's personal identity gets stronger, he begins to reach out to other people around him. At a certain point, children begin to view other children as more important than their toys, and they will share to win a friend, but it is still hard to do. Calling children selfish when they won't share is dangerous, for they are liable to believe us. It's better to accept the fact that sharing can be difficult for children at times and express confidence that they will learn to do so.

If a certain toy is particularly special at a given time, the parent can help by saying something like "This toy is special to Jessica now," and then help Jessica to find something the friend or sibling can use. Sometimes it's encouraging to add, "She'll share the special toy when she's ready." It happens that a child won't share a certain toy and then is dismayed that the friend or sibling will not share one of his toys with her. At these times the parent might say, "When you won't share your toy with Joey, it makes him feel like not sharing his toy with you." Parents can also assist by supervising children in taking turns.

Many parents forget how hard it is for adults to share—not only their special items but other less important things as well. Parents need to help children with their sharing problems, and should not put them down for struggling for a quality that is so difficult to learn.

A two-year-old boy was out playing in his fenced-in backyard. His mother, who was watching him from a window, called him in for lunch. He refused to come, so his mother went out and spanked him and then brought him in to eat. She was concerned about being so furious at her son's rebelliousness so much of the time.

Two-year-olds often resist adult requests. If you ask a toddler a question, he will usually respond with a loud "No!" He is trying to assert his newly forming sense of self and show that he has a mind of his own. Also, many two-year-olds have trouble making smooth transitions, as from playing to lunchtime. It's best to avoid head-on clashes with them when possible. Rather than asking questions like "Do you want to eat now?" or "Do you want to go to bed now?" it is better to present things affirmatively by saying, "It's time for lunch now," while walking the toddler to the table, or "It's time for bed now," and beginning to undress him.

When we do need to intervene, we can set limits and express annoyance using the many positive techniques described throughout this book. Keeping it light, with a humorous and gamelike approach (pretending to chase him indoors—the enjoyable "I'm going to get you" game—or carrying him in airplane-style, for example), is an especially helpful method to remember with a two-year-old. Focusing on the delicious sandwich waiting inside instead of on his refusal to eat, giving him a few minutes' notice before lunch, and going outside to tell him to come in (all children respond better when we are facing them than when we shout across rooms or from inside to outside) are techniques that could have been useful in this instance.

Two-year-olds *can* be very trying, and many parents are often angry. Nonetheless, it's important to deal with negative stage characteristics in positive ways. All too many parents get too involved emotionally with the qualities of being two. The tantrums and refusals can be so intense that the parents forget that it will all pass in time. I urge parents to try to stay detached and remember that their child is only two, and quite new to the universe. Naturally he still has much to learn about reasonable behavior!

When parents get stuck focusing on the negative aspects of any stage, there is a tendency to want to rush through that stage and get to the next. This saddens me. Let's not rush through life; let's take time living it. Stubborn refusals, after all, are not all there is to being two; two-year-olds are wonderful people, too. They are often joyous, bubbling over with life, beginning to bloom in language skills, interested in the world around them, and very loving. Let's appreciate the good side of two-year-olds!

Many parents of two-year-olds find it difficult to be with their child all day long. They wonder if it is appropriate to send such a young child to a preschool classroom. Many parents feel guilty, assuming that two-year-olds belong at home, yet they realize that parent and child get bored with each other at times and cannot always sustain an entirely pleasant day together.

Two-year-olds are usually quite active. I agree that it's difficult to keep up with them all day long, day in and day out. They are ready to enjoy many activities a preschool can provide, like playing with modeling dough, block building, water play, and painting. They also enjoy spending time with other children and with adults outside of their family. Children of all ages need chances to be with adults of both sexes for a variety of role models.

More and more children at two, and even younger, are having preschool group experiences. Some parents arrange home-centered play groups where two or more parents take turns watching the children. Other parents band together and hire a teacher for a few mornings a week; the group may meet in one child's home. Other children are in more formal settings, like day-care centers and nursery schools.

I am a wholehearted believer in this kind of group experience, to whatever extent fits in with the family's need and life style and the child's adjustment. Parents and children both get a chance to lead separate lives for some time each week, and return to each other enriched. It can indeed be limiting for young children and their parents to be together all of the time. If a husband and wife spent every day together all year long, they'd probably get on each other's nerves too! People need variety. It's the quality of the time we spend with our children, and not the number of hours, that makes good parenting.

Undoubtedly, some preschool programs are better than others. In this, as in so many areas, parents do well to take a close look and be informed consumers. The things I feel it's most important to look for are warm, loving, and attentive teachers who are understanding of children's developmental abilities, plenty of appropriate play materials, and a manageable number of children. In such an environment, children often have a more interesting life than they would by just being at home all of the time. The experiences themselves are positive for many young children, and more and more parents seem interested in these opportunities.

Susan was finding it difficult all of a sudden to get Sam, at two and a half, to take his usual afternoon nap. For several days she battled with him, getting upset, yelling, finally having him nap for only a few minutes, as it took what was most of his usual naptime to get him into bed. After a week or two, she realized that Sam was ready to give up his nap. Instead of fighting with him for an hour to get him to sleep (fidget) for five minutes, she decided to use the naptime to do something constructive with him.

When Susan told me about this, I recalled a similar chain of events I had had both with Joshua and Jesse at that age. Living with children means constant adjustments. Just as parents are getting used to a certain routine, the child changes. It usually takes a bit of time to recognize that this is what is happening and that the child is branching out into another stage. Then when we do realize it, we need to readjust. Susan had been used to having Sam's afternoon naptimes as time for herself. It can be annoying to lose this needed time and have to readjust the daily schedule to fit in quiet time at a different hour. Parenting involves guiding ourselves as well as our children through the stages of their lives.

A two-and-a-half-year-old had begun to get up at 5:30 A.M., wide awake and ready for the day. The parents were not as eager to start the day at that hour and wanted to know what they could do about this situation.

Unfortunately, many toddlers do go through an early-rising phase. Sometimes a parent can convince them to go back to sleep, but quite often they really are up for the day; they just cannot fall back to sleep. Besides going to bed earlier themselves, parents don't have too many options.

At two, a child cannot be left on his own, as much as the parents would love to remain in their own bed and sleep. So many kinds of accidents could occur, like falling off a chair while attempting to reach the cookies. This isn't because the child is bad; a two-year-old simply doesn't have the self-control to supervise himself properly.

An alternative to getting up all the way is to go into the child's room and lie down on his bed (or, if he is still in a crib, to sit on a chair in his room) while he plays, and close your eyes trying to get a few more minutes rest. Parents can feel consoled to know that most children keep this up for only a few weeks—a few months at most— and then go back to waking at a more reasonable hour. Also, as a child reaches three, parents will find that he can be trusted to remain alone for a time if he wakes up early. Many three-year-olds can find an appropriate activity on their own and play quietly in their rooms, looking at books or playing with cars or blocks until their parents get up.

A couple were having a conflict over how much responsibility Beth, their two-and-a-half-year-old, could handle. The mother allowed Beth to play alone outside of their house, and she had taught her to cross their quiet street to the other side. The father was horrified. He realized that his daughter was extremely verbal and so she appeared to be older than she was, but in reality she was only two. He felt that his wife had very high expectations for a young child. Beth's mother defended her actions; she felt that she had an unusually mature child who was thriving under her expectations. She saw no reason to hold Beth back from whatever

responsibilities she seemed able to handle. This had become a very heated issue between the two parents, and they appealed to me for advice.

I agree with Beth's father that a two-year-old does not have reliable self-control. Some children this age do show astonishing verbal ability, but their emotional maturity is another matter. Though Beth may have looked both ways to cross the street on some occasions, there is too strong a chance that she will forget to look, should something distract her. Two-year-olds get very absorbed in their activity of the moment and often neglect to pay attention to what is going on around them. A child can get so absorbed in wanting to see the big kid across the street, she simply forgets there is a street that cars traverse separating her from him. Also, at this age a child's spatial perception is not reliable; she can easily misjudge distances. She may not realize an oncoming car is as close to her as it really is.

I feel it is important to emphasize this point: A two-year-old cannot be depended on to extend the proper precaution! She needs an adult (or a responsible older child) to supervise her outdoor play at all times.

It is good to keep in mind that three-, four-, and five-year-olds need supervision too. They are also young children. Around four to five most children begin to play outside on their own, near their houses, and around five or six they are getting ready to learn to cross quiet streets alone. Until then, adults need to provide the supervision that young children cannot provide for themselves.

A three-year-old was "slow as molasses" about everything: eating, getting dressed, brushing his teeth, picking up toys. His mother was having a hard time accepting his rhythm.

In fact, this three-year-old was just acting like a three-year-old! It can be hard for adults to adjust themselves to a child's level. Children are not as physically capable as adults are, and they get very absorbed in what they're doing. They are not in a hurry to get to something else; they take time and they pay close attention to details.

Talking about our own feelings can be very helpful. I suggested to this mother that she just keep on reminding herself that her child was only a child with a line like "My son is acting normally for his age; it's okay" or "He's just a young child." This kind of reminder can help her be more aware that her son's capabilities are different from her own, and more tolerant of the discrepancy.

A father was concerned because his daughter, almost four, was a messy eater. She enjoyed playing with her food and didn't always hold her utensils properly or eat with her plate directly in front of

her. He understood that preschoolers, like toddlers, can be interested in handling food, and he did let her eat in her own way. He also would show her how to hold her fork properly and would remind her to keep her plate in front of her. He wanted to know if it would be wise to pressure her to eat more like an adult, or if it was all right to keep on in the way he had been handling the situation.

I believe this father was striking a good balance. He was allowing for some normal exploration and also gently reminding his daughter of correct eating habits. I suggested that he might notice when she did remember to hold her utensils properly and acknowledge this by saying he is proud of how well she can handle her fork, or that he likes it for the family to be eating together in this grown-up way. Appreciation like this can encourage the child to keep up her efforts.

The changing moods of her four-year-old were giving one mother a hard time. One moment her child was rational and easy to deal with, and the next minute she was hysterical and demanding. The mother wanted to know how often she should give in to the childish qualities and when she should take a stand.

Four-year-olds are rebellious, as are two-and-a-half-year-olds and the one-and-a-half-year-olds. Ilg and Ames' description for many aspects of four-year-old behavior is "out of bounds." Fortunately, much of the four's uneven behavior retreats by age five, though it will crop up again for a while around six. Knowing that this uneven behavior will come and go can help us to ride it out more calmly each time it reappears. Certainly we can't give in to everything, but we can be aware that four-year-olds do get in ruts where they demand things in certain ways. We can let up a bit on limits that aren't essential, while sticking firmly to those that are. This kind of compromise can make life easier with four-year-olds. Growing involves struggle! It is hard on parents, but we do want our children to grow, so we must face the struggles and uneasy times this involves.

I felt it would help for this mother to spend time appreciating her child's strong points. Jesse, too, was difficult at four. To help me through the year, I kept a written list of our better moments together, which included things like a serious discussion we had about God, his rubbing my head when I had a headache and sharing his special blanket when I was sad, and many instances of his entertaining Dick and me with dancing and imaginative play-acting.

Toby was having a particularly intense four-year-old stage. His mother found herself repeatedly setting limits on his disruptive behavior. She began to think that so much of their relationship

was centering on her limit setting that too little easygoing time together remained. Toby was acting up quite a lot and, she believed, did need her to set limits. How could she spend time with him that was also positive?

Special time can be the biggest help at times like these. I suggested that the mother take Toby to some places alone and tell him that this is special time for them together. They might go for a short walk or visit the park or spend time in their home, but alone together, without the other siblings. While spending time with him, the mother could comment, "It's so nice to be looking at this book together with you on my lap," or "I'm enjoying being with you at the park, talking to you while I watch you climb."

It's very important that these special times with Toby be pleasant; they should not be occasions for conflict or fault finding. The mother should not bring up the fact that fifteen minutes before, the son had been acting uncooperatively or that she was still upset because yesterday he had been rude. The focus of these special times should be on mother and son enjoying each other's company.

If Toby and his mother can enjoy this type of nice, relaxed time together, it will probably make it easier for him to accept her limit setting when it's necessary. Toby will not be getting attention from his mother only for his disruptive behavior, but they will be having good times together as well. Parents do need to set limits, but I encourage them not to make discipline the core of their relationship with their children. Let the heart of the parent-child relationship be the positive feelings and times that are shared together, even during the more difficult stages of a child's life.

It would also be helpful for the mother to make a point of noticing her son's better behavior and comment, for example, "I'm so pleased to see you putting your toys away now," or "Thank you for helping to set the table," or "It's so nice being with you when you are pleasant like this." This kind of positive reinforcement, acknowledging how good his cooperative behavior makes her feel, will help her to see more and more of it.

A father thought his four-year-old daughter was particularly aggressive. I asked him what he meant by this, how aggression was revealed in her behavior. He said that whenever she got angry because of a limit he set, she would say things like, "You idiot! If I can't do it, I'll kick the wall," or "I'll spit if you won't let me."

Young children, from two to about six, even seven, do come out with these kinds of remarks to express their frustration or anger. This is normal. Anyone who's spent time with a four-year-old could probably give lots of examples of these angry comments.

This "talking back" is difficult for a parent to endure, but it is wise to ignore as much of it as possible, as children need some leeway to express themselves—four-year-old style. This is part of their struggle to achieve more independence and show us that they are growing up. It is not a sign of an aggressive personality.

I often hear children called fresh for this type of comment. This is not helpful. In fact, it is doing the same thing the child has just done—calling names and hurting feelings. If parents respond by coming down hard and saying things like "How dare you talk back to me" or "Stop being fresh," they are setting up a power struggle between themselves and the child, and this struggle may then last for many years. Of course, a parent doesn't have to approve or always allow disagreeable behavior that is characteristic of an age. I wouldn't expect this father to say, "Hooray, I'm so thrilled my four-year-old is now rebellious and talks back," but parents can be understanding of each stage and try to set the necessary limits firmly, yet kindly.

If a four-year-old's talking back has gone too far, the parent might say, "I don't enjoy being spoken to like that. I won't be able to listen unless you find a better way to tell me," or "What you said hurt my feelings. I don't call you names when I'm angry. You can be mad, but there are better ways to tell me about it," or simply say that it is unpleasant to hear talk like that. In these ways we accept that the child is angry and help her to learn appropriate ways to express her feelings.

A father and mother were very worried because their five-year-old was still wetting the bed at night. Is this normal?

Yes. Bed-wetting is very common. Many children do not stay dry at night until eight or nine years old, some even older. Knowing this can make it easier for parents to accept this fact as part of many childhoods.

It is sometimes helpful to have the child cut down on liquid intake as bedtime approaches. Some parents like to wake a child to urinate, hoping to avoid changing wet sheets the next day. It is essential that the parents do not ridicule the child in any way or make him feel bad or babyish for wetting, and they should never punish. Nighttime control takes time.

It's wise to let children who are wetting know that many other children are in the same position. Anxious pressuring won't help, but keeping relaxed will.

It is a good idea to check with your pediatrician to be certain the wetting is not caused by an emotional or physical problem, but usually the child just needs time. Almost all children do stop bed-wetting on their own when they are ready. Sometimes a child feels ready to stop wetting but is unable to and wants help. In that case (and only in that case), one of the battery-operated alarm systems on the market may be of use. When one of these is attached to a child's bed, a bell rings as soon as he starts to wet, alerting him to get up and finish urinating in the bathroom. After weeks (or months) of this, he develops the habit of waking without the alarm.

Parents of school-age children wonder what kinds of behavior patterns can be expected in later childhood.

Like younger children, school-age children go through definite stages, and certain behavior patterns are typical of each age.

At age six we see a child entering his school years with an eagerness to explore and learn new skills. This is an exuberant time in which he goes forward to embrace the world and the experiences it has to offer. While this is delightful to watch, for parents there are hard moments too. The six-year-old is still quite self-centered. He likes to be in charge and have as much of his own way as possible, and will respond with anger when thwarted.

Seven-year-olds usually have a quieter disposition than six-year-olds. At six they were collecting data from the world, and now they are synthesizing and integrating their experience. The seven-year-old is introspective. This year we may find him observing from the sidelines, while the year before he was probably at the center of the action. The seven-year-old is not as defiant and bold as the six-year-old, who demands that his point of view be carried out, but he is often moody and complaining.

The eight-year-old is outgoing. He is feeling pretty good about himself and his world. He has collected a lot of information, pieced it together, and is skillful in many areas. He shows increasing self-confidence, cooperative efforts, consideration for others, and a renewed enthusiasm for learning what the world has to offer. He is pleasant to live with and is making strides in the art of relating well to others.

Nine continues much like eight with still more self-confidence, increased independence, and ability to be a pleasant companion to friends and family. In the nine-year-old we see many self-initiated projects and involvement with friends.

Age ten is the climax of childhood. The child is feeling very good about himself and his world. He especially enjoys good family relationships and takes much pride in his family. The ten-year-old likes where he is—no longer a small child and not yet a teenager with complicated demands. The ten-year-old, for many parents, is a sheer delight and brings memories of how he was at age five, another high point of harmony.

When Joshua was seven years old, it suddenly seemed, that whatever I would say or do was wrong. The slightest remark I made received a moody, grumpy response from him. The simplest things were becoming difficult. If I said, "I'm making alphabet soup" (his favorite), Joshua might retort, "You know I hate alphabet soup." We had just begun to celebrate the end of the stormy sixes, and here we were already in the throes of the moody sevens. I wasn't sure I could take it! I was even beginning to wonder if I still liked Joshua at all.

Then the revelation! I remembered my own advice and was able to switch my focus from the negative stage characteristics to Joshua's good qualities at ages six and seven.

At six, he *was* quick to react, but that was hardly the whole picture. Much more of the time, I was gaining great pleasure from seeing him learn new skills and reveal maturity and independence as he went from kindergarten to first grade.

At seven, Joshua was showing a great deal of initiative and creativity. He was an avid collector of trading cards, and spent hours cataloging and sorting his collections. It seemed whenever I walked into his room, he'd be in the middle of an interesting project. One night he was making a telephone book, stapling together pieces of paper and writing down his friends' phone numbers. He was interested in whales, sharks, rocks, and fossils and enjoyed reading and discussing these subjects. Also, he played really well with his friends and with Jesse, and was actually very considerate of his brother.

Once all of this sank in, I changed. I started to lay low on some of the unpleasant times, ignoring many of them. When I was really upset, I stuck with the specific behavior, refraining from any general remarks about his personality. I made a point to set aside more special times with Joshua. We had many bedtime talks accompanied by back rubs and hand holding. I'd let him know how much I enjoyed this time together and did not use these occasions to comment on anything unpleasant he had done. I took more time to point out to Joshua the things I liked about him. Dick also joined the campaign, and it worked.

I had found that when I looked for the good things, the negative things fell more into place. They were there, but I wasn't making such a fuss over them. The less attention they got, the more everyone, including Joshua, could concentrate on better things. The negative aspects had a place, but not such a big one anymore. With relief, Dick and I realized that we had a wonderful son after all and had almost gotten taken in by a temporary negative stage characteristic.

A mother was dismayed to see her cooperative ten-year-old daughter becoming a rather difficult eleven-year-old. Was this a turning point, she wondered, and could she expect all of adolescence to follow along like this? She stressed that for several years just before age ten, life had been delightfully smooth; the sudden shift at eleven seemed so jarring.

This woman's daughter was indeed going through a normal transition period, but that doesn't mean it is the beginning of uninterrupted hard times. Adolescence, like childhood, has its ups and downs. It is a time of intense physical, emotional, psychological, and social changes. I gave this mother an overview of the adolescent years, to help her and her daughter through its stages.

Eleven is sometimes called preadolescence, indicating its transition role between childhood and adolescence. The stress and turmoil come as the child envisions the teenage years just ahead, along with some of the changes this will entail. She is still a child, but she experiences new thoughts and feelings that prepare her for the years ahead.

The twelve-year-old is better adjusted to entering a new phase and takes pleasure in being considered an adolescent. She is peaceful, friendly, and quite easygoing. Leaving elementary school is a source of pride to her.

At thirteen, a child is likely to become more introspective and touchy. Thirteen-year-olds tend to seek privacy to think things through, and they are quite sensitive to criticism.

Age fourteen is another period of balance and equilibrium. A sense of contentment may characterize this age, contributing to better relationships all around.

The fifteen-year-old has started to get a closer view of the adult world, and suddenly realizes that at a time now not too far off, she will be a part of it. This is a provoking thought, and many fifteen-year-olds feel the pang that soon they will be on their own, away from the support of their family and familiar nest. They begin to prepare for this by struggling now for freedoms and new independence. They choose to do much more on their own and with friends. They are trying very hard to be independent and are no longer as interested in communicating with their parents. Getting along with a fifteen-year-old is not so easy, but at sixteen, parents reap the rewards of bearing with it.

The adolescent at sixteen reaches a high point of self-understanding and appreciation. She has accepted that the adult world is just around the corner and in fact she is becoming eager to enter it. She is feeling on a more equal par with adults, without such a need to fight for her freedoms as at fifteen; by now a great deal of independence has actually been gained.

From this summary, it is clear that early adolescence is a time of alternating moods, with the even years generally pleasant and the odd years more difficult. The difficult years are necessary times of new thinking and growth. A more negative phase will always have promising aspects too, such as the eleven-year-old's ability to maintain good relationships with friends or a thirteen-year-old's renewed interest in reading. Each adolescent also still has her or his own endearing personal qualities. We need to continue to tell our teenagers what we like about them and focus on the positive aspects of each stage.

The overall picture is one of annual alternations, but in any one year we can also expect our adolescent's mood to swing up and down considerably. She will feel moments of joy as she contemplates her adulthood, the ability to form her own family, pursue her own career, and make her own decisions. At times, however, this prospect will seem terrifying, and she will cling to the benefits of childhood: freedom from serious responsibilities and an ability to enjoy the present enthusiastically, without an adult's concern for the future. The rapidity with which adolescents go back and forth between mature and childlike behavior is often confusing to the adults around them.

Parents and children both feel mixed emotions about the increasing independence of teenagers. It is often difficult for parents to watch their once-little girl or boy blossoming physically and emotionally and socially, yet they also feel delight in witnessing this maturing. Sometimes parents feel jealous looking at their youthful, attractive sons and daughters facing a full life ahead. It is common for parents to feel sad that they will no longer be so influential, as their child makes more and more decisions independently. They see this as relinquishing a role that has given them a sense of importance. At the same time, they will probably welcome the new freedom this will bring them.

Adolescence is confusing as parents try to capture the right balance of guiding and letting go. If a child is early to mature physically, parents can tend to have unrealistically high expectations, forgetting that her emotional development may be lagging behind. With other teenagers, emotional maturity may come well before physical development. Parents need to observe each child closely so they can help her grow and take on increased responsibilities and privileges as she is ready for them.

Parents of young children say that they look forward to the time when their children get older and won't need them as much as before. Parents of older children and teenagers say that they are, in fact, needed quite often.

Some parents say that they feel close when they do things with their teenagers, like riding bikes together, going to films, playing games at home, and cooking together. During these relaxed and enjoyable times, teenagers will often bring up the important issues on their minds, sometimes even more than when the parent and teenager sit down with the expressed intention of having a serious talk.

Parents need to make themselves available, even though teenagers are spending so much of their time with peers. Parents need time alone too, and should plan for it, but they should remember to leave room for their older children and teenagers.

A father said that he was having a hard time with his teenagers. He was trying to convince them of his value system, and communication between them wasn't going as well as he wished it would.

Teenagers are sorting out and piecing together many things and creating their own value systems. It is not realistic or even desirable for parents to expect agreement on all issues. Parents need to provide the soil from which their children can grow and become true individuals, each fulfilling his own unique potential. This is going to involve his departure from some of his parents' ways.

Certainly, this process is stressful in most families, for it entails the teenager's placing the parents' values and beliefs under close scrutiny. At times nothing the parents say, believe in, or do will be quite right to the teenager. If we can recognize that the questioning and disagreement are essential parts of adolescence, it will be easier to keep our integrity intact. Instead of insisting on conformity to his point of view, a parent can simply say, "You feel one way, I feel another. We are two different people and we do not always need to agree."

When parents put down their children for believing or feeling a certain way, the children may stop sharing their thoughts with them altogether, turning to friends for support. Strong opposition also makes a child even more determined to stick to his own views. When parents can disagree and yet accept the other's view, children do not feel threatened and they'll be more amenable to considering their parents' side of the issue. We want to keep the lines of communication open by establishing an atmosphere that says, "Let's share our differing beliefs and learn from one another. Let's discuss life together and help each other to grow and change." This way parents and children will have a lot to give and a lot to get from one another.

Often, as teenagers grow older, they do come around to accepting quite a few of their parents' values, while taking on some new ones of their own. As they move into young adulthood, their beliefs become more secure, and generally they are once again able to love and appreciate their parents for being the good people they are.

CHAPTER 4

Sibling Issues

Helping Children in the Same Family Get Along Well

The birth of a sibling is a cataclysmic event to a child. While she will feel love for the baby, she will feel jealousy as well. Positive approaches help, and I offer here suggestions on helping the older child deal successfully with feelings about the new family member. Once the baby is older, the children can be expected to play well together much of the time, but not always. All children need a balance between playing alone, with siblings, with agemates, and alone with each of their parents. When the siblings are together, they will quarrel at times. In this chapter, I examine some of the reasons for this and suggest how a parent can help resolve the conflicts, as well as teach the children skills to solve many issues on their own. I also discuss rivalry and the dangers of comparing children. The chapter closes with some general suggestions for minimizing competition and encouraging affection between brothers and sisters.

A pregnant mother asked for suggestions on how to help her two sons, ages three and ten, adjust to the new baby's arrival.

Siblings will feel jealous of a new baby. This is most evident with toddlers and preschoolers, who are still very dependent on their parents, but even school-age children and teenagers feel jealous when a baby arrives. They worry that they will be left out or loved less. They do feel love for the new baby too, and this mixture of strong emotions is hard to handle. Young children often show their mixed feelings by first kissing and then biting or poking the baby quite hard.

Parents can help in various ways. They can let their children know that it is all right to feel jealous. It is helpful to say things like "Sometimes you'll like the baby and other times you'll wish we'd take him right back to the hospital!" or "It's hard getting used to the baby. You might feel angry at us for spending time feeding and diapering her."

They can even tell the children that they find the baby annoying at times too, blurting out, "All this baby ever does is cry, cry, cry!" Every parent does feel this way at times, and it is a great release of tension for a child to hear it expressed.

The first few weeks of the baby's life are often hardest on the other children. Parents can play down some of the inappropriate behavior they see, realizing that much of it is an expression of jealousy, perhaps saying, "It is hard getting used to the baby." This can go a long way to reassure the child that there is enough love to go around after all. Soon parents do need to reestablish limits on disruptive behavior, but they can keep in mind the child's plight.

Attempts to hurt the baby in any way must be stopped and the hostility redirected. The parent can be sympathetic to the feelings, but unequivocal about not tolerating aggression. "I know you feel like hitting the baby. It is okay to want to pinch or hit her, but your sister is not for hurting." The parent may add, "Come and hit this pillow instead," and even join in hitting a pillow so the child can see that it really is okay. His feelings of anger and jealousy are accepted, and he is helped to find an appropriate release.

Another outlet for his hostile feelings can be a doll. A doll can safely be punched, hit, or thrown across the room, and it can also be a recipient of tender and nurturing feelings. Some parents object to giving dolls to boys, but this is unfair. Many boys will be fathers someday, feeding and diapering and loving their own babies. Young boys can act out their healthy fathering feelings by caring for dolls.

Parents also need to reassure each of their children directly of their love. They need to tell each child (teenagers included) that he or she is loved, valued, and enjoyed in a very special way, and that the baby will not take his place in their hearts. He needs to know that he will still have lots of their time and attention. A parent can say, "You might feel left out when I take care of the baby, but you won't be. I love you and we'll still have lots of special times together doing things that you like to do." Then it is essential that the parent does spend time with each child, away from the baby, during which he or she dotes on that child alone. The child needs to hear that he is still loved and see that he will continue to get focused time and attention from his parents, as before.

At infant feeding time, a child may feel most abandoned. Reading to him or holding him close at these times helps make him feel loved. If he's happy alone just then, this wouldn't be necessary, but often at feeding time the child just happens to act up because he is feeling left out of the intimate scene.

It also often happens that a child finds himself waiting around for a drink or a story while the baby is getting needed attention. It is wise on occasion to make the baby wait and even to say, "Oh, Baby, you will just have to wait. I need to get your big brother a drink first." This way the older child doesn't always feel that he is playing second fiddle.

Each sibling also needs chances to help out with the baby. Giving the child a role can minimize feelings that he is being left out while the baby's needs are being abundantly met. This doesn't mean that the older child should be constantly catering to the baby, but the three-year-old can occasionally get the pacifier, bring a diaper, or help to hold the bottle. The ten-year-old can even prepare the formula or rock the baby at times. He can also feel grown-up by helping out with the three-year-old while the parent is with the baby. Both children will feel important if the parent points out how the baby appreciates their efforts, saying, "Look how she calmed right down when you rocked her," or "She certainly loves those noises you are making. Every time you do it, she laughs." Too much child-care responsibility will make an older child resentful and rob him of his own childhood time for fun and play, but a moderate amount of helping out will lay the groundwork for a satisfying relationship between each of the boys and the baby.

The three-year-old can be reassured that once the baby gets older she will be a better playmate. Children are often disappointed by how little a baby can do. Parents can sometimes address the infant in a tone of pity, saying, for example, "You can't ride a bike yet like your older brother." This can help the child feel proud of his accomplishments.

Children love to hear stories about themselves as babies. You can tell each child about how you rocked him, diapered him, and fed and bathed him, and how much you enjoyed him as a baby. You can do this sometimes as you both look at his baby pictures. He will love to hear you tell all about his first step, his first words, and any other details you remember about his past. You might add, "And now that you're three, I do other things for you. I read you stories at night, I set up fingerpaints for you in the kitchen, I take you to the movies." This reminds him that the new baby isn't the only one who receives special care. He got that kind of care when he was a baby, and you're still there for him now to provide the kind of attention he needs as he grows.

Parents need not act guilty about a new baby, but should show that they are glad to welcome a new family member. They may want to point out how lucky the baby is to join such a wonderful family. Two excellent books to read with young children are *That New Baby* by Sara Bonnett Stein (Walker & Co.) and the old favorite, *A Baby Sister for Frances* by Russell Hoban (Harper & Row).

Keep in mind that using positive approaches will not make jealousy go away. Parents can minimize it and help a child to deal with his feelings in healthy and realistic ways, but his feelings will not go away in a few days. The child will need lots of time to work through these strong emotions. Expect to take a few months to help children adjust to a new baby and air their strong, initial feelings of jealousy.

A father mentioned that his four-year-old son had begun to show jealousy toward his sister, Melissa, as she was nearing her first birthday. Before this he hadn't noticed any jealousy at all. Does jealousy just pop up like this?

Usually the jealousy is there in the preschooler from the time the baby is born. Most parents recognize jealousy when they see it expressed as aggression, but it may have taken a different form in this case. Jealousy can show up as regression in eating, toileting, or sleeping routines, or it can manifest itself as bad dreams, whining, moping, unexplained temper tantrums, or exaggerated concern for the baby. Sometimes a child seems unrealistically kind to the baby. The child really has jealous feelings but is afraid to show them for fear that his parents will not love him if he has these kinds of feelings.

It is helpful if parents simply accept the fact that an older child will be feeling some jealousy. The parents are wise to encourage the child's jealous feelings to come out in the open and find appropriate expression from the very beginning. When hurt feelings are out in the open, they lose their intensity and make more room for positive feelings to grow. Many parents think that they shouldn't mention to their child that he may feel jealous, for fear that they will be putting ideas into his mind. Don't worry; the jealousy as well as the good feelings for the baby exist already. When parents accept this reality, children see that their feelings do not shock their parents. They see that their parents love them even though they have jealous and angry thoughts. It's so much better to share feelings than to have to hide them.

What the father was noticing as Melissa neared one was therefore probably not the beginning of jealousy. Things do change between siblings at about a year, however. A one-year-old is an active creature, quite different from the helpless baby who first came home. One-year-olds like to mess things up and knock things down. When the four-year-old is building with blocks, his fast-moving sister may be there to topple his structure. This is annoying to an older child, to say the least.

Parents can help out by making sure the older child gets some chances to play away from the baby's path of destruction. At other times the parents could show the four-year-old some things to do with Melissa that could be fun for both of them, like rolling a ball back and forth. This helps the older boy be more accepting of his sister's age and abilities and see that there are ways to enjoy her company.

A three-year-old girl had recently become an older sister. She now felt like being a baby at times too, so her mother would put her into the baby's stroller and wheel her around a bit. The mother wanted to know if it was wise to give in to the girl's desires to pretend to be a baby again.

Many preschoolers get the urge to regress when a new baby joins the family. The older child sees the baby getting lots of attention and feels that maybe she will get attention too by acting like a baby.

If the parents allow the child to regress now and then, the urges don't build up. The child comes to see that the attention she gets for being her own age is even more satisfying and the activities appropriate to her age are more fulfilling to her. It is important, therefore, to let her act out her babyish fantasies, while also letting her know that she is deeply appreciated for being herself.

Jason was four years old. He was expected to dress himself each morning, but he was resisting now, even though he used to do it cheerfully. A new baby had recently joined the family. His parents knew that Jason was experiencing jealousy, but they were afraid that if they helped to dress him now he would continue to be dependent when he was twenty.

It is important for the parents to see that their son's growth to independence isn't straight, but circular. Helping him get dressed now will not make him dependent when he is twenty. A four-year-old child seems so huge and grown compared to a helpless infant, but he still has lots of need to be dependent. Helping him now when he needs it will help him be able to give up this assistance when he no longer has use for it. If children are satisfied in their dependent needs they grow out of them at their own pace.

Jason doesn't, of course, really need physical help in dressing, but is asking for this assistance as a way to receive extra time and attention from his parents as a result of the baby's arrival. He needs this extra attention during normal routines, in addition to the special time his parents give him setting up projects and being alone together.

A father and mother were concerned about their daughters, ages six and three. They said that the girls never seemed to enjoy being together at all. I asked the parents if they ever took time to get their daughters started up at playing together, and they answered

no. They thought it was just a natural thing that sisters would play together, and that's why they were distressed.

Parents are in a position to encourage their children to play together, help each other, and be warm and caring toward each other. Just expecting children to do these things on their own is usually not enough. Parents need to show how it is done.

Parents can make helpful suggestions—for example, that the six-year-old read her younger sister a story or help tie her shoes, or the three-year-old get her sister an apple or help put her toys away. Parents can provide ideas for activities both girls can do together, like playing games or digging for worms or riding their bikes. It sometimes helps for the parents to join in the playing. One parent could sit with the girls while the six-year-old reads a story, or a parent might build a block house with the children or play a card game with them. Once the girls are playing well, the parent can say that he or she expects them now to continue playing on their own. The parent can check in periodically to see how the girls are doing, perhaps to suggest another game, or even stay for a few minutes more and watch the children at their play. It helps to make statements appreciating their cooperation. Comments like "It's really nice to see you enjoying each other" or "You both are thinking of such interesting things to build with the blocks" reinforce their playing together. This can help the sisters realize that they can enjoy being together, and they will then be able to do so more and more as time goes on.

Both parents can also encourage the girls to be warm and affectionate toward each other, suggesting that they give one another a hug and kiss or a back rub. Even if they say, "Ugh! What, me kiss my sister!" their parents do well to convey that they consider this fine and reasonable behavior.

One morning a five-year-old girl, Heather, told her mother that she wanted to stay home from school that day. In discussing this, the mother discovered that what her daughter really wanted was a chance to play alone, without her three-year-old brother, Steven, hanging around. Usually when this girl played, whether alone or with friends, her brother was with her. Her mother wanted to know if it would be fair to Steven to insist that he stay apart at times.

It is certainly good to encourage siblings to play together, but they also need to play alone or with peers. Eventually Steven will want this too, and it will actually be good for him to learn now to play on his own. His mother can talk with him about how sisters and brothers need to be alone at times.

At first, Steven's mother could help him set up interesting things to do while Heather is elsewhere. Eventually he will be skillful at keeping busy without her help. These might also be good occasions for the mother and son to have some special time together, or for Steven to play with another child his own age. When siblings get these opportunities to be away from each other, they return refreshed and more eager to play together again, and even to include each other when playing with their friends.

Whenever he heard shouts or name calling coming from the upstairs playroom, a father said that he'd go berserk and race up to reprimand his children for their yelling and fighting. He began to realize that his approach wasn't successful, that in fact he was merely contributing one more shrieking person to the scene—himself!

I believe this situation holds a key to understanding how parents can help their children get along well. Let's stop and think about the time the two children had been playing together, before the fighting began. What about the hour, half-hour, two hours, they'd been playing on their own, peacefully and creatively, going from one game to another, keeping busy and happy? The father needs to focus on this time. He even needs to point it out to his children when they are playing well, and let them know how good he feels to see them getting along so nicely.

I understand what it can do to a parent's nervous system suddenly to hear his children yelling and hitting. It's so tempting to approach the children angrily. It is more helpful, however, to stress how well they'd been cooperating before.

One way to do this is to go to the children and say something like "You've been playing very nicely together until now. I don't know exactly what happened; perhaps you hit her first, perhaps she hit you first. You know what? I'm not interested in the details. I just want you to go ahead and begin playing nicely again." Very often this approach, making light of the few minutes of quarreling, will clear the air. If, according to the parent's or children's judgment, there is really an issue that needs intervention, the parent can still first comment on how nicely the children had played together until now and then help them solve the problem.

Another approach at these times is to ignore the quarrel altogether and grit one's teeth well away from the scene. It may well die down on its own pretty quickly. Many times I have heard my children screaming, "I hate you," only to see them two minutes later, arm in arm, the best of pals.

Sometimes children call each other names back and forth ("You're a dummy." "No, *you're* a dummy," etc.) or give each other a quick whack, and it's more in the nature of letting off some steam than real hostility. When the children are pretty equally matched, emotionally or physically, parents are wise to ignore what's going on and see if it blows over. When any child is being hurt, of course the parent needs to be protective.

Sometimes quarrels begin because the children need help making a transition from one game to another. They're starting to tire of what they're doing, can't think of what to do next, and could use the parent's temporary presence to get them absorbed in something else. Perhaps they've been alone together for too long and need a parent to join in and play for a time to change the pace. If they've been playing inside, maybe they need to get out, or the other way around. Maybe they need a short break from each other and would do better in separate rooms for a while.

Whatever the solution, the key is to stress to the children how well they were playing before the quarrel began. We need not dwell on the fighting, and we can use positive skills to redirect the children's energies back toward cooperation.

One mother was extremely uncomfortable about minor quarrels between her children. She winced, hearing them say to each other, "I hate you." She didn't like it when her son would come to her to say that he couldn't stand his sister, or when her daughter felt this way toward her brother. She believed that brothers and sisters should like each other all of the time.

It is unrealistic to expect children in the same family to enjoy each other all of the time. There are going to be moments when they are angry, feeling jealous, or just getting on each other's nerves. It is helpful when parents can accept this.

Many parents do not like to recognize that children in the same family will not always get along. Then they get unduly upset and feel frustrated when their children quarrel. The children are certain to fight at times. This is normal and healthy. Parents help by being realistic and having reasonable expectations.

It would be good if this mother could openly say something like "A lot of the time you and your sister get along well and have fun together, and sometimes it seems that you just can't stand each other. That's the way it is with all brothers and sisters." Sometimes she could make this kind of comment to each of her children individually, while at other times she could say it in front of the whole family. I consider it crucial for all parents to say this kind of thing to their children at times; it relieves everyone's feelings to "tell it like it is."

Children feel more comfortable with their varied feelings when their parents can accept them as a normal part of life in a family. When the grumpy feelings are accepted, then the fond feelings actually have a better chance to emerge and children aren't left feeling guilty for hating their siblings at times. It's important for a child to know that he or she is as normal as any other child in this regard.

With my own two sons, I also find it helpful to let them know that when I was younger I used to fight with my brother and that their father used to fight with his sister and that both of us hit and teased our siblings at times. Then my or Dick's mother or father would come in to us and say, "No hurting" or "No name calling." I feel this is comforting for young children. They find they are not the only ones teasing or hitting; their own parents did this when they were kids too. It also gives them hope for the future. I go on to explain that now Daddy and I no longer fight this way with our brothers and sisters, and someday they won't fight this way anymore either. All children love to hear stories about when their parents were children.

Each afternoon eight-year-old Naomi would come home from school and, according to her mother, start right in fighting with her younger brother, Zack. The mother noticed she was approaching this in a negative way, repeatedly making angry statements such as "How come you're always fighting with Zack?" or "You never get along with your brother!"

These kinds of statements can make Naomi feel that her mother actually expects her to fight with Zack each day, and also cause her to dwell on the more negative aspects of their relationship.

Expressing ourselves positively helps children live up to our positive expectations. The mother would be more helpful if she said, "I expect you to come home and find something you like to do," or "I know you can come in without getting into hassles with your brother." This can make Naomi more confident of her ability to stop this pattern of fighting.

The mother should also be aware that at times Naomi may be retaliating against an attack that was initiated by Zack. She should not just assume that the older child began the quarrel but should hold the younger child accountable for his part in these daily battles too. I know that I sometimes jump to protect Jesse from his older brother, Joshua, but I have realized that this is not always fair. We get used to thinking of the younger child as the baby, but a six-year-old is quite as able to give out trouble as to take it.

It is also important for the mother to say to Naomi that it is okay for her not to like her brother all of the time, and that she knows there will be times she will like him and other times when she will feel that he is a pain and wish he'd disappear. If the mother can encourage the daughter to share these feelings with her, it may help to lessen the fights. Siblings need opportunities to express the negative feelings they've got toward each other with a parent's understanding ear. The parent should not take sides, but just listen. These and other positive approaches are more helpful than attacking a child without offering any way out of the situation or alternatives to change it.

A mother saw one of her daughters pinch her other daughter quite hard for no reason at all. The mother was furious and felt like smacking the offender. She was trying to apply positive methods, however, so instead of hitting, she took her daughter by the arms, held her firmly, and said, "When I see you do that, it makes me feel like slapping you. Your sister isn't for pinching!"

I was happy to hear that this mother had resisted her urge to hit. She could have gone on to make clear for her daughter the example she was setting by saying, "I was so mad I felt like hitting, but I didn't. I expect the same from you. It's okay to feel like pinching your sister, but it's not all right to do it. When you're mad at her, *tell* her that you're mad and why."

We need to be aware that there are times when a child pinches or hits a sister or brother out of generalized jealous feelings, and the child is not able to verbalize any specific reason why she feels like hitting. Deep down, the older sister is harboring remains of the strong jealousy she felt when her sister was born. Every now and then these generalized jealous feelings make an appearance, and we see them in kicks and pokes that come, so it seems, for no reason. Younger siblings also experience generalized jealousy toward their sisters and brothers who go to bed later, go to the movies on their own, ride their bikes longer distances, and the like. The pinch the three-year-old gives her six-year-old sister, seemingly for nothing, often comes from these feelings.

It's helpful for parents to try to get their children to talk about these feelings directly. If the older child is going off on a bike ride a few blocks away and the younger child can't go along, the parent could try to have the younger child air her feelings about this. If the child can't verbalize them, the parent could do it for her, saying, "You're looking mad. You'd like to be able to ride far away, too. It's hard to wait, but you'll be able to do it when you're older."

In my own family, when one of my children has hurt the other, I say, "When I'm angry with you, I don't hit you; I tell you. I expect you to do the same thing with each other. If you're mad for a reason, tell each other why. If you don't have a reason, then just say that you're feeling mad. I didn't bring you into this world to hurt each other's bodies, and I get very upset inside when I see it happening." Then I try to redirect everyone's energy to better things.

A mother felt that the fighting and squabbling that took place between her two children every morning was so annoying that it interfered with her ability to get the housework done before leaving for work. She needed to do her chores in the morning in order to free her afternoons to spend time with her children, ages five and seven.

There are several appropriate ways to handle this. The mother mentioned that she'd wake up at the same time as the children and felt immediately plunged into hassles. I suggested that waking up a few minutes before they do might help her to gain a clearer perspective on the morning.

The mother had never confronted her children with her real feelings about the morning fighting ritual. She could tell them how unpleasant it was for her to have to listen to it and waste time breaking things up instead of getting her household work done. She could let her children know that when they cooperate with her, it makes her feel like cooperating with them. She could point out that they like her to do things with them after school, and she likes to be able to do these things also. But she will need that afternoon time to get her household jobs done if she can't do them in the morning.

After expressing her feelings, the mother could take some positive steps. She might say that she expects her children to be able to give up their squabbling and find things to do alone, or together, in comparative peace. She could let them know she has faith in them to establish a new morning routine. She could even be understanding of her children's feelings by saying that she realizes it can be hard to get along so early in the morning. She could ask her children for their ideas of what they could do in the mornings that would be pleasant and constructive. By making her needs explicit, she teaches her children that family living requires a balance of needs. The more parents are willing to face their children as people (not just as kids), the more children will be willing to regard their parents as people with legitimate needs and feelings also.

Both working and nonworking parents might consider occasionally setting aside special time for children early in the morning, before everyone's active day begins. A parent can take a few minutes to read a story, play a short game, or chat. This can start everyone's day off with warm feelings. Taking even a few minutes to do something with her children might make it easier for them to continue to play together while their mother takes care of her chores.

A mother was worried that her seven-year-old daughter was becoming a terrible tattletale. She seemed to thrive on catching her older brother and sister in trouble.

The best defense against tattling is to avoid blaming. The parent should be searching for a positive solution, not a culprit. Blaming fosters a competitive spirit among siblings. If the children expect someone to get the blame, then they are forever involved in power plays, tattling and trying to win the parent to their side. This intensifies the natural rivalry they feel. It is much more helpful to maintain an attitude of cooperative problem solving.

One afternoon I was in the kitchen doing the dishes when Jesse, then five, stomped in. He huffed, "I hate Joshua. He pinched me and scratched me." I listened to him with interest, answering only with "Hmm" or "Oh." Jesse seemed satisfied and was about to walk away when I lightheartedly added, "And what did you do to Joshua?" Jesse exclaimed (with a hint of pride), "I had only kicked him!"

Jesse had come in to express his feelings to me. He wasn't interested in having me get involved in figuring out what had gone on between the boys; no more detail was necessary. One minute later, as soon as he reached the spot where they had been playing before, I heard the sounds of both boys playing happily together again.

A father had begun to use positive methods when conflicts came up in the family. He'd especially been working on expressing his anger in constructive ways. He was noticing that his two sons were beginning to follow suit, and shared an impressive example with the group.

Often, when the six-year-old became annoyed at his younger brother, he would threaten to take away everything he had ever given him, and actually begin to collect the toys. His brother would, of course, become hysterical, and the father would have to intervene. One afternoon, the father overheard his older son exclaim, "This makes me so mad I feel like taking away everything I've ever given you," but he did not go to gather up the things. The younger brother stopped his annoying behavior, and the two boys went on to play cheerfully once again. The father became more aware of the ways children learn the behaviors we model.

A mother was very upset that her ten-year-old son kept calling his twelve-year-old sister "Chubby." The girl was just beginning a diet and was very sensitive to the name calling. The mother would blow up at her son and wanted to be more effective.

First, the mother could take her son aside and explain to him his sister's situation, that it isn't easy to lose weight and she needs everyone's help. The mother could add that she doesn't want any of her children hurting another's feelings and that she'd give him the same protection if he needed it. The son may need a few reminders.

If the boy persists in his name calling, then the mother should curtail it by asking him to go to another room until he can be cooperative. Whenever two or more children are calling each other names or hitting one another, and someone is being hurt either emotionally or physically, and the children don't seem able to come to a peaceful settlement on their own, then separating them for a few minutes (sometimes even for a few seconds) can help to restore order.

Another approach is for the parent to let the children know how their behavior is affecting her. For example, she might say, "When I hear my children calling each other names, I get so upset it ruins my day. I expect my children to get along. There is to be no name calling in our house to hurt feelings!"

An eight-year-old girl had come home from her grandmother's with several dolls. She told her four-year-old brother that he could keep a certain doll, and then several minutes later changed her mind. This caused a struggle, with both the brother and sister crying over this doll. The mother got so disgusted that she threw the doll away.

Some situations occur at bad moments, when parents just can't handle them in positive ways. Parents are human and can't think rationally all of the time. We're entitled to our bad moments, too.

When things are more peaceful again, the mother might wish to tell her children, "There would have been a better way for me to have handled this, but I wasn't up to it then. All the crying was getting to me." And then it would have been helpful to speak with the daughter about her ambivalent feelings toward the doll. Part of the daughter did want to give her brother this doll, yet part of her was having trouble giving it up. The mother might say that she realized it was a hard decision for the daughter to make and that sometimes we do feel two ways in a situation. Having her feelings understood might make it easier for the daughter to share or give something up at another time. The mother could have spoken to her son as well, and let him know that it was a hard decision for his sister to make.

One father, trying to be considerate of his children's individual preferences, brought gum home for one child and candy for the other. The children were four and five years old. It turned out that

they didn't appreciate their father's efforts and were unhappy about not receiving the same thing.

Young children sometimes just want the same thing a sibling or friend has. Older children would be more likely to appreciate this father's consideration and able to sustain their own preferences, but younger children often find this difficult. We do want to foster each child's individuality, but two young children very close in age are going to be competitive at times. I advised this father not to feel hurt that his plan had backfired, and to try again when his children are somewhat older.

A four-year-old boy would complain because his eight-year-old sister was allowed to go to bed later than he was. Their mother would have the sister pretend to go to sleep when the brother did, and as soon as her brother was asleep, she would come out to play. Is this a helpful tactic?

It is best to be truthful with children. The four-year-old should know that his sister stays up later because she is older. Children need to see that privileges and responsibilities increase with age. The mother can accept the son's feelings by saying, "I know you don't like it that your sister goes to sleep later than you. When you're her age, you'll get to go to sleep later too." This way, the mother allows the son his displeasure, but helps him to look forward to increased privileges as he gets older. The mother needs to help her son accept and face reality. Having his sister pretend to go to sleep earlier doesn't help the son adjust to the real situation and isn't fair to the sister.

Two brothers, ages seven and nine, kept each other awake every night. They were in their own room, but their mother couldn't relax hearing a lot of horseplay coming from their direction. She'd go in to tell them to sleep, but this didn't work. She also tried punishments like forbidding TV the next night, but that didn't work either. What could she do?

I suggested that this mother tell the children how she feels about the situation and then try problem solving. She told them that she couldn't enjoy her evening and that without a good evening it is hard for her to be a pleasant mother the next day. Then the mother asked her sons how they would handle this problem. They said that as soon as she hears them begin to play around, she should come in and tell them it is time to go to sleep. The mother reported mainly peaceful evenings thereafter.

When children are included in decisions that concern them, they are more apt to cooperate, as they are then following guidelines that they helped to form. This kind of problem solving can work sometimes with very young children and is one of the most often used positive tools for children over preschool age.

A father often compared his children with one another. For example, he would say to his six-year-old son, "Why can't you be more easygoing like Kathy?" To his ten-year-old son he might say, "Your older brother likes baseball. What's the matter with you?" The father wanted to know if this was all right, or if it would make the children unduly competitive.

Parents are not helpful when they negatively compare children with each other, implying that one child should be more like another. This does make children resent each other. Children don't want to be like their brothers and sisters; they'd rather feel free to be themselves.

Parents are helpful when they appreciate each child for his or her own specific qualities and strengths. When children see they are being valued for their own qualities, they feel secure, and they are more likely to be able to appreciate their brothers' and sisters' varying interests and strengths. They can feel positive about these because their parents aren't trying to get them to be like their siblings. Parents can sometimes comment to the children, when they are together, on their different qualities; for example: "Jeffrey, I appreciate your interest in the pet fish. You take such good care of them and always read up on their varieties. Julie, I like your stamp collection. You're working so hard at finding unusual stamps. You're two different people, and it's nice to see each of you pursuing your own interests."

When two or more siblings do enjoy a similar interest, that's fine, and it's good for parents to comment on this as well. "How nice to see that you both enjoy baseball and can play catch and sort cards together," a parent might say. The parent is appreciating a special bond the children share. This type of comment unites instead of divides the siblings.

A mother had a harder time with her thirteen-year-old daughter, Joan, than with her seven-year-old son. She was thinking, "What a lemon I got the first time around. What did I do to deserve a kid like this?" She was particularly troubled by Joan's relationship to her brother.

Many parents find one child easier to get along with than another. Each child has a different temperament, and sometimes a parent's own style fits more easily with one child than with another.

It is essential to see that the child who is more difficult is not bad, nor is the parent inadequate for finding her difficult. It is just a matter of personal rhythm, mood, and temperament.

Instead of feeling cheated, this mother can learn to see this situation as a challenge. By concentrating on the strengths in herself, in Joan, and in their relationship, she can learn to develop the strengths and build upon them. This relationship with her daughter will very likely require extra thought, energy, and creativity on her part. However, the positive results she'll get will be a satisfying reward for her efforts.

I suggested that the mother try to improve her own relationship to her daughter before expecting Joan to get along better with her brother. I asked if she ever spent special times alone with her daughter, enjoying her, showing interest in her life, and not criticizing her in any way. The mother answered, "No, not really." I encouraged her to do so, and to show physical affection as well. Perhaps inviting her daughter to go to the corner store with her for a soda or taking a walk together could be a good beginning, especially if she makes a point to let Joan know that this would be time just for the two of them to enjoy each other.

Two months later at a follow-up session, this woman was eager to share her experiences. She told the group that her problem with her daughter had been resolved and the thing that had done it was "personalizing" her relationship to Joan, spending special times together and telling her daughter how good it was to be with her like this.

Their better relationship carried over into other aspects of their life as well. Joan began to make her bed and help with household chores on her own initiative. Best of all, the troubling sibling relationship changed into a close bond. Joan began paying attention to her younger brother and acting courteously toward him most of the time. The mother then suggested to Joan that she spend some special time playing with her brother just as the two of them had been spending together, and the girl readily agreed. She was now able to follow her mother's example of a nurturing and meaningful relationship.

One father expressed his feelings of guilt for spending more time with his six-year-old son than with his four-year-old son. This father did love his four-year-old very much too, but found himself enjoying the new skills and companionship age six had to offer.

Many parents enjoy certain ages and stages more than others. This father need not feel guilty for appreciating his six-year-old's new ability to swing a bat and the pleasure he gets from being with him. Yet the father felt that he was not spending as much time as he could with his younger son, whom he also loved and enjoyed. A better balance would be achieved if the father also scheduled time to do things with his younger son that they both enjoy. The father reported that there are many things he enjoys doing with his younger son. He loves and enjoys both boys, and certainly does have the right to especially enjoy the skills and companionship of a six-year-old.

It was bedtime, and Dick had just played a board game with the boys. Then I went to lie down with Jesse, and Dick went to snuggle with Joshua. After a few minutes, Dick left Joshua's room, but Jesse was still asking for one more story. I became impatient. I told him that I wanted him to cooperate now so that I could do some work, and this way we'd have more time to do things together next week during school vacation. My voice was edgy.

At this point Joshua came in. He looked at Jesse and said, "What can I do to make you feel better?" Jesse answered, "Read me a story and play the Emperor Concerto or Superman" (his two favorite records). Joshua said, "Not the record; Daddy's working in the basement and the noise could bother him. I'll read a story to you." As Jesse got the book, Joshua said to me, "I'm the best help with Jesse. You were just talking fast and getting excited!" Joshua read the story, I stayed to hear it, and then they both went right to sleep.

I hadn't had the patience to read another story right then. On the other hand, the same five minutes I was using to tell Jesse to cooperate was the same time it would have taken me to read the story. *But* (the big *but*) Jesse would probably have asked me for one more thing after that. He was in that kind of mood, and my edginess was aggravating it. Joshua really did help out. He did well, and he felt good about helping to solve the problem, and Jesse appreciated his efforts.

This incident made me realize that if one child is feeling unhappy about something, the parent doesn't always need to be the one to help out. We can ask another child if he can think of a way to make his brother feel better. This teaches children to help each other, and gives them a good chance to work on their problem-solving skills.

Parents often feel torn when each child clamors to be the most special. "I got more than she did," "I'm the best," and "He's a copycat," are typical of statements that parents hear. How can we reduce this kind of sibling rivalry?

The underlying issue in sibling rivalry is usually the desire to obtain the lion's share of a parent's love and attention. That's why parents need to show their children that they love each one of them uniquely. It is not wise to compare children with each other, favoring one child's looks, capabilities, achievements, or qualities over another's. It is best to show our children that we appreciate them because of their individuality and differences, and truly love each of them for being the special person she is. This frees children to be themselves, without striving to be like a brother or sister in order to gain the parent's love.

To reinforce her individuality, each child needs to have some belongings and a space that is all her own, and special time alone with her parents. Then it is easier for her to share them at other times. It is also meaningful for parents to spend special time with several of their children together, doing things as a group that are interesting or relaxing for everyone. Younger children enjoy storytelling; older ones might enjoy listening to a record or playing a game together. These activities can help children in the same family to value each other and enjoy each other's company. This sets the stage for children to do things together at other times when the parent is not around.

Sibling rivalry will not disappear, but these measures help. When children feel secure in their uniqueness and confident that they are valued for being themselves, they don't feel as deep a need to fight for a place in their parents' hearts. They know that a special place already exists for them, and then they can even appreciate their sisters and brothers for being the special people they are.

I want to stress how important it is to let our children know that we understand they will have both good and bad feelings toward each other. Parents can encourage siblings to tell each other when they are mad. Brothers and sisters need to know that it's okay to express angry feelings and whenever possible to try to work out these feelings and their cause with each other. Parents can also help out by just being there to listen to a child's anger.

At those more peaceful times when brothers and sisters *are* feeling good about each other, it is helpful occasionally for parents to comment that it is nice to have a brother or sister, and even ask each child to say something he or she really likes or appreciates about the others. It is nice for parents to listen to and encourage the warm feelings their children have for each other. One mother asked her two daughters, ages five and three, to do this. The three-year-old said she liked it when her sister came to the bathroom with her, as she didn't like to be in the bathroom alone. The five-year-old said she liked to draw with the three-year-old. Another mother asked her children the same questions. One of her sons, age seven, said that he liked his nine-year-old brother because he never tattled on him. The mothers had the children tell each other these things. If children have trouble verbalizing these feelings, parents can help out. A parent may say, "One thing you seem to enjoy about your sister is that she plays chasing games with you," or "You seem to enjoy your sister's funny jokes," or "Both of you really enjoy playing Batman together," or "One of the things you seem to like about your brother is that he helps you think of interesting projects to do."

We can also let our children know what we like about the way they're relating to each other. For example, on Saturday mornings Joshua and Jesse often get up and whisper their dreams to each other. They strike up other conversations, laugh, help each other get dressed, bicker a bit sometimes too, and then get each other breakfast. All this time Dick and I are still resting. I like to let them know how good we feel about their getting along so well, enjoying each other, and helping us.

We need to put the emphasis on the warm feelings and good times siblings share with each other, and at the same time to respect jealousy and grievances, accepting them as natural and handling them in constructive ways. We also need to provide children with skills they can use to resolve some of the conflicts that come between them.

CHAPTER 5

Children's Feelings

Adults Accepting Children's Feelings and Children Learning to Express Them with Sensitivity to Others

> *Children need freedom to express their feelings, both positive and negative. Sharing positive feelings—joy, pleasure, contentment—enriches the quality of family life. Learning to express the negative emotions—anger, hatred, jealousy—in appropriate ways is just as important. These feelings seem so strong that people often like to push them aside, in themselves or their children. But feelings are real, and part of being human. Getting them out in the open furthers the individual's mental health and the family's ability to communicate well. In this chapter, I discuss how to help children be in touch with the full range of their feelings and express them in ways that respect the feelings of others.*

The human potential movements of the 1970s have brought many adults a better understanding of their feelings, but this knowledge has been gained painfully and with great effort. How, parents wonder, can they help their children to know themselves better now, to be more in touch with their feelings from the beginning?

The new interest in children's feelings is a very healthy development. All people are entitled to a full variety of feelings. Many people have grown up having their feelings invalidated. Remarks like "What do you know, you're just a kid" or "You've no reason to feel like that" hurt children by separating them from their feelings. Our goal as parents should be to help children know how they feel and to teach them appropriate ways to express feelings.

We benefit from this too. Feelings that can be expressed clearly are less likely to pop up unexpectedly in the form of tantrums, nail biting, or nightmares. When parents can accept the feelings, they can help the child to express them in a way that will not hurt himself or others. Also, by helping the child to be aware of his feelings, parents help him to state his needs. As parents we need to be clear with our children, letting them know what we expect and want of them, and it is good for our children to do the same. This way we avoid much guessing and misinterpretation, and increase the chances for mutual understanding.

Positive feelings like happiness, contentment, joy, and serenity are good places to begin. Parents can help make children more aware of feeling good with comments like "You really enjoy playing with clay," or "Hearing that story really helped you to relax."

Often, children feel two ways about the same thing. Instead of saying, "What's the matter with you? Do you like your friend or hate him?" parents can respect the ambivalence. "Sometimes you like Pat and sometimes you don't. Sometimes you like him and hate him at the same time!" Ambivalence is normal; adults often feel it too.

Some feelings of children are hard to bear, like anger, hatred, jealousy, and fear, but they, too, need opportunity for expression. When these feelings are bottled up inside, they can fester and grow, to the detriment of a person's body and mind. Feelings that are allowed out in the open lose their sharp edge. Expressing feelings is not a luxury; it is essential to mental and physical health.

Adults can model the expression of feelings with statements like "I'm so relieved you got home safely, but I was furious you didn't call to say you'd be late," or "I enjoyed myself at the ballgame today," or "I'm not in the mood for doing laundry right now." Doing this shows that it is appropriate to express feelings and demonstrates how to do so. Adults also help children by striking up conversations about feelings—the adult's or the child's—often. It is good to discuss feelings both when they are fresh and later, when the experience and the emotions can be reviewed and absorbed. For example: "You really had a terrible fight with your sister this morning about the lunchboxes. Are you feeling better about it now?" or "It was nice to see you and Daddy going off fishing together last weekend. That was a very special time for you, wasn't it?"

For a long time, the right to feel pain and sadness seemed to be reserved for females only in our society. Girls and women felt more comfortable having certain feelings and expressing them. Boys and men knew that many expressions of feeling were taboo for them and kept their emotions inside and did not reveal them. Similarly, anger was reserved for boys and men to feel.

Today, times are changing and people are realizing that a wide range of feelings is an essential part of being human. Nonetheless, many adults still feel uncomfortable seeing a boy cry or are shocked to see an older girl get angry. It feels good to express positive and pleasurable feelings, and also to express anger, disappointment, or sadness, when this is done in appropriate ways. It feels good to get feelings out in the open. We need to be able to do this within our own families and with our friends. All of us, men and women, boys and girls, can find our feelings, give them form and expression, and learn to listen to the feelings of others.

A mother was discussing her four-year-old daughter's fussiness. Laurie would get upset over many things. For example, if her mother said it was time to go into the house for lunch or that the family was having hamburgers for dinner, Laurie would scream because she didn't want to come in yet for lunch or because she wanted chicken for dinner. If they were having chicken for dinner, she'd cry for hamburger. The mother usually told Laurie to stop crying and leave her alone, but then Laurie would only scream louder.

All parents need to be left alone at times, but when children fuss like this it can help if we also at times respond sympathetically. Laurie's mother might say, "I see you are upset and need to cry about this," or "You'd like to stay outdoors, but it's time to come in." This way, Laurie is allowed to feel out of sorts.

Parents, of course, have feelings too, and in this case the mother just couldn't tolerate listening to her daughter anymore. While still granting Laurie the right to fuss, she could say, "I see you feel bad and need to cry. That's okay, but I need to go in the house and prepare lunch now. I'll be thinking about how upset you are as I do." Then she could go into the kitchen alone, while Laurie finished fussing somewhere else.

A mother described a situation where her own embarrassment made it hard for her to allow her son, Tom, to express his feelings. The family was visiting Tom's aunt and uncle and cousins, and the parents had promised to take all of the children to a puppet show. The day's routine got confused, however, and when they went to the station, they had missed the train. There was no other way to get to the show. Tom was very disappointed and cried and carried on quite a bit. The mother didn't know if it was right to let him fuss like this, although somehow she felt it was. Her sister-in-law

was a more authoritarian disciplinarian, and Tom's mother felt that her sister-in-law would never have let her own children cry like this. The mother was feeling confused.

It's difficult at times to follow our own instincts if we feel someone is judging us; but the mother's natural feelings were right. Her three-year-old son was very disappointed about missing the chance to go to the puppet show and he had every right to be. When adults are disappointed, they often spend a good deal of time complaining, talking, and even crying about their letdowns. Three-year-olds do it their own way. It is reasonable for Tom to cry and fuss to express his disappointment.

Tom's mother could have helped him to put his feelings into words, saying that she knew he was looking forward to the show very much and she understood that he was disappointed. She could have also helped him to cry, saying, "You need to cry it out, it was a horrible disappointment for you. Go ahead and cry, it's all right." She could hug him as he did. If he didn't want to be hugged but preferred to stomp around, she could still be supportive, standing by him, letting him know it's okay to be that upset. This approach would actually help him to recover sooner. A child feels better when his feelings have been heard.

A father said that when his three-year-old son was mad, he often reached out to hit. Many children hit when they are angry, and parents want to know positive ways to handle this unpleasant occurrence.

Children, like adults, need to learn to express anger in positive ways. For many children, hitting is a spontaneous reaction to anger. The parent needs to remember that this outburst was not premeditated. He can stop the hitting and also teach better ways to express the anger.

Often, a simple statement will stop a child from hitting; for example: "I don't like that" or "Stop that now" or "You can be mad, but I'm not for hitting!" Then the father can help the child put his anger into words by saying, "You are mad and I'd like to hear about it. *Tell* me that you're mad and why you are." If the child is too upset to speak at the moment, or is not really talking yet, and the parent knows why the child is mad, the parent can verbalize it for him. "You're mad about ———. You have a right to be mad." Even if the parent doesn't know why the child is mad, he can still recognize the anger. "You're mad now. That's okay, but you can't hit me. People aren't for hitting."

If it appears that the child needs an outlet for further hitting, the parent can offer a pillow, saying, "You're mad. You need to hit.

Pillows can be hit, not people." In a few seconds the child will feel better. If he continues to try to hit people, the parent can hold him, firmly but gently, to show that he won't be allowed to do this, while still repeating that it is okay to be angry, and trying again to have him verbalize his feelings when he is calmer.

One mother explained that when her nine-year-old boy didn't like a rule she'd set, he'd throw a full-scale tantrum—crying, stomping his feet, jumping up and down. She'd tell him he was acting like a baby, but he would keep it up for as long as half an hour. She wanted to know how to handle this behavior.

Parents need to help their children learn to act more reasonably. It would be important for this mother to let her son know that at nine years old she expects him to talk things out with her when he is upset, instead of thrashing around. If he starts to have a tantrum, she could intervene, saying, "Let's talk about this instead. You're older now and we need to be able to discuss issues more reasonably." Or she might say, "Crying and acting like this isn't helping to solve the problem. I'd like you to use your energy instead to start thinking of ways to work this out between us."

When this mother began using these approaches, she found that her son's tantrums were not occurring as often, and when they did, they only lasted for a couple of minutes. He was learning to express his feelings verbally in many situations. Like all children, however, he still needed to fuss at times. When he did, he was encouraged to do so, but out of his mother's earshot. He was no longer called a baby for this, and he appreciated his mother's acceptance of his need to let go at times.

A mother felt she usually got along well with her son but was worried that deep down he really did not like her, because whenever he was mad, he'd shout, "I hate you" or "You're a mean, horrible mother."

Actually, it is a strength of their relationship that this boy could express anger so clearly to his mother. These are his momentary feelings, and she need not worry that they represent his truest, most constant emotions. She can say to him, "You're feeling that way because you're very angry with me right now. In a while you'll feel better about me again."

The mother could also let her son know that she, too, feels this way at times: "When you don't cooperate with me, sometimes I get so mad that I don't like you very much, and sometimes when your father does something I don't like, I feel that way toward him, but

then after a few minutes I'm feeling good about each of you again."
Parents can stress that most of the time we feel good feelings toward
each other, but when we're angry we all get those hateful feelings,
and then they go away again.

The mother can help her son to rephrase his anger in a way that is
not so threatening to her. "You'll need to find a better way to tell me
that you are angry. When you say it like that, it hurts my feelings and I
just cannot listen. Tell me in a better way so I can try to work out the
issue with you." She may need to suggest the better way. "Here's
how I'd like to hear you tell me you're angry: 'Mom, I'm very angry
that you said I couldn't go out again tonight because it's too dark. I
wanted to go out!' That would be a good way to let me know your
feelings."

Responses like "It's not nice to hate your mother" or "How dare
you talk to me that way!" aren't helpful. They deny the child's feelings, and feelings that are denied get shoved inside and usually last
much longer. A sarcastic response like "I hate you, too!" is not helpful either. This kind of reply will aggravate, not minimize, the son's
angry feelings. The boy needs to be able to tell his mother when he is
very angry, and he can learn to do so in nonhurtful ways.

**Linda, age four, was very angry at her mother and shouted that
she was going to kill her. The mother asked her daughter how she
was going to do it.**

Linda was expressing feelings, not intentions, and the mother
would have done better to help her distinguish between the two.
When a child expresses such strong feelings, it is best for the parent
to help the child keep the feelings in the domain of feelings, with no
hint of giving them actuality. Linda's mother could have said something like "Sometimes people get so mad at someone they feel like
killing her, but they don't really do it, and you're not going to kill
me." This way Linda sees that her feelings are accepted, but that her
mother will protect her by making sure that they remain controlled.
The initial response had offered Linda a chance to believe she might
actually kill her mother—a frightening thought for the child.

Linda's mother can help her to express her anger better by saying,
"I can see you are very angry with me right now. Instead of making
threats, you can say that you are furious, and why, and then I'll be
able to hear you out." It is possible that Linda had heard an adult say
to a child, "I'll kill you if you don't stop that now!" Her mother can
let her know that this is a very unpleasant way for people to express
their anger and that both grownups and children can find better
words to use when they are angry.

Since Linda was four years old, she probably was experiencing Oedipal feelings, having fantasies of replacing her mother as her father's wife. These feelings are strong in four-year-olds. Yet children deeply love the parent they are secretly competing with. Especially during this time, children need reassurance that their strong wishes will not come true.

Parents report that sometimes their children get angry and threaten to leave home. Some parents react in a sarcastic manner and say, "Who cares, leave!" Others encourage the children by saying, "Where are you going to go, and when will you be leaving?" Still other parents feel rejected and think their children don't love them. What is a helpful response?

When children become angry or upset about a rule, they sometimes get the feeling they'd like to leave home. They don't really want to leave; the threat is an expression of the anger. It is hard to be the target of these strong feelings and, understandably, adults are often flustered by the attack. None of the above approaches are helpful, however.

Sarcasm cuts a child down and threatens his feeling of being loved and his sense of security. When adults say, "Leave! Who cares!" they're not being truthful. Adults do care, and children should know that they do.

When parents ask the child to detail his plans, they are playing into his fantasy. They need to help the child acknowledge what is real— his feelings—and help him to work through them, instead of encouraging fantasies of escape.

Parents shouldn't feel rejected either, and it's not good to ask children, "Don't you love us anymore?" Of course children love their parents, and want and need them. Treating children like this gives them great power over their parents. We should assume we are loved and help our children to believe that it is all right to feel angry at someone they love.

A parent can say, "You feel like leaving home. You're mad now. But you really won't be leaving. This is your home and we are your family. Sometimes you get that angry and dissatisfied with the way we do things here." When children are feeling better, it's nice to add, "Most of the time you really like living here. But sometimes you're dissatisfied with a rule or get mad at me. Mainly we do try to work things out to satisfy all of us, but sometimes we need to set a rule you don't like. That's the way it is in all families." This helps children to see things realistically.

The *Runaway Bunny* by Margaret Wise Brown (Harper & Row) is a good book to read to young children if this theme is common in your family.

A four-year-old had previously had difficulty expressing anger. One morning, she was so angry at her father for finishing her candy the night before that she lashed out at him, "I'm very angry at you. And you are a pig!"

The father was glad to hear his daughter displaying anger, but he still didn't like being called a pig. He said to her, "You're mad at me and I'm really happy you're telling me about it. I liked the way you said, 'I'm very angry at you.' But I don't like being called a pig; that hurts my feelings. When you're angry, let me know the first way, by saying that you are mad. That sounds good."

The father went on to apologize to his daughter. He told her that the candy was so good he couldn't stop eating it, and he would get her some more. He also said, "You never care if I take a few, and that's nice. But you sure do have a right to be mad when I go ahead and eat the whole bag!"

It's at least as important to praise children when they show improvement as it is to correct mistakes. This father did both, in a constructive and courteous manner.

A mother described a situation in which hearing out her son's feelings brought them closer together. Her nine-year-old was having a conflict with a classmate, who would pretty regularly kick him in the leg. The teacher would tell the boy not to do this, but her intervention was unsuccessful. Finally, this boy began to hit the other child a few times. The teacher went over to stop him, and he swore at her as he continued to hit the other boy. The teacher contacted the mother to tell her that her son had hit another child and had used swear words.

In the past, the mother said she would have smacked her son for what he had done, but as a result of her group experience she had made a commitment to stop hitting. This time, she did not even approach him until the next day when she was less upset. Then she asked him to describe the incident. He told her that he had reached his limit of being bothered by the other child and had to hit him back. He said he wasn't even aware he had sworn at his teacher. The mother listened and accepted her son's view, and admitted that as a result she felt a closeness to him, and he to her, that wouldn't have been present had she plunged in to hit him for what he had done.

Certainly, this situation might have been avoided if the teacher had thought of ways to deal with the anger and aggression of the boy who had done the initial kicking. Perhaps he was upset for a reason and needed help to verbalize his feelings instead of kicking. The mother was considering a meeting with the teacher to discuss constructive outlets for anger.

Meanwhile, the next morning, on his own initiative, her son brought a piece of cake to his teacher—his way of apologizing for swearing.

A mother said that the other morning she was angry about something and took it out on her eight-year-old daughter. As the morning wore on and she finally composed herself, she took a few minutes off from work and called the daughter at school to apologize to her. She was very glad that her mother called and said with understanding, "We all make mistakes, Mom." This mother said that recently she had become more and more aware that her daughter is a person who deserves to be treated with respect and consideration. In the past, she would not have been concerned that the child might be upset in school because of the morning quarrel, nor would she have apologized easily. She was so pleased with her new perspective.

This mother's apology was a very good response. The more parents accord their children the consideration that is their due, the more they see their children following suit. The daughter took her mother's feelings into consideration and made her feel loved and accepted, even though she had made a mistake. She took it in her stride that her mother, like all other people, is entitled to make mistakes on occasion; no one is perfect. Her warm feelings, however, would not have surfaced, I am sure, if the mother had not first acknowledged her mistake and made a conciliatory gesture.

Justin sometimes expressed sadness about being an only child. His mother asked how she could help him deal with these feelings.

It would be constructive for the mother to acknowledge her son's feelings when he mentions them. She might say, "Sometimes you do feel you'd like to have a brother or sister" or "Sometimes you feel gypped." She could encourage him to talk out his feelings and listen to him respectfully.

The mother could also talk with her son about the fact that every child grows up in different living circumstances, each with advantages and disadvantages. She can help him appreciate the good things about being an only child, such as getting a lot of his parents' time and having his own room, as well as talking about the drawbacks. This treats the situation realistically. It is not helpful to feel sorry for her son. He needs to deal with his life situation as it is, as every child must, regardless of the circumstances.

Ben, seven years old, felt rejected by Jim, a friend. While spending the afternoon with Jim, Ben discovered that he had not been invited to Jim's birthday party. Later, when his friend went home, Ben tearfully reported this to his father: "Imagine that, one of my best friends not asking me to his birthday party. He probably doesn't even want to be friends with me anymore!" Ben looked hurt and very sad. The father dealt with his son's strong feelings and the situation beautifully.

Ben's father helped him continue to express his feelings: "That makes you feel very unhappy, doesn't it?" Ben said, "Yes, it was hard to believe." The father sat with a gentle hand around Ben's shoulder. After listening for quite a while, he offered an explanation: Since the boys live in different towns and didn't visit each other often, perhaps Jim invited only children from nearby who went to his school. He said that since both boys really liked each other very much, this was no reason to stop being friends. Ben agreed and commented that they had had a great time together that afternoon. Again the father acknowledged how sad this news had made his son feel.

In this intimate sharing, the father helped Ben express his feelings, which seemed to take the sharp edge off them and also gave him the strength to keep up a good friendship. In any friendship things will happen that we don't like. Sometimes it is wise to hash them out with the friend; at other times it is best to handle the feelings in other ways. By hearing out his son's hurt, this father brought himself and his son closer while helping Ben learn more about friendship.

The mother of a nineteen-year-old girl shared an experience. The daughter had recently moved to a new city, and while her mother was visiting she confided that she was lonely and it was hard for her to get used to her new environment. The mother agonized over this, saying, "Oh, my poor baby, this is so hard for you, so terrible." The daughter faced her mother and said, "Mom, I want to share things with you, but when you react like that, you're not helping me out. I need your support and encouragement, not for you to get caught up in it like I am."

Parents need to see that their children are separate people and that all children, younger and older ones, will experience times of disappointment, unhappiness, and frustration. Parents are not responsible every time their children feel bad, and they don't need to alleviate the situation either. A helpful approach is to stand by, respecting their feelings, offering encouraging support and a good listening ear. By doing this, we help children to develop their own strengths.

Though the mother may not be the one to alter the child's situation, she may be in a position to do something special to make her child feel better. For example, she might have given her daughter a boost by taking her out to a show or getting a lamp to perk up her new apartment. For a younger child, a new coloring book or a surprise pack of baseball cards might be a welcome morale-booster. The child will still need to face the situation herself, but a gesture like this will show that she is loved, and will be appreciated.

A mother was quite shaken because when she asked her daughter what she liked about herself, the girl had said, "Nothing. I hate myself." The mother felt she had done a terrible job if her daughter could say a thing like this, and was almost desperate to repair the girl's self-esteem.

This mother had not done a terrible job, but she needs to see that her daughter is entitled to all of her feelings, even self-hatred. This is probably a momentary feeling that will pass, and it is all right for her to experience it. If she felt this way all of the time, the mother would indeed have cause for concern, but in fact this girl was almost always quite cheerful and self-possessed. As parents, we can give our children the tools to deal with their feelings, but it is not our role to protect them from having them.

A mother and father found their twelve-year-old daughter crying in the closet, for no apparent reason. They asked many questions to try to find out what was the matter and how they could help, but they got no answer.

Sometimes adults and children feel a certain way and don't know why. We can be helpful at these times by simply accepting the feelings and not probing for a cause. Our focus can be on getting the feelings out.

Crying is healing; it is a way to express the feeling and restore equanimity. If a child is crying because of any kind of hurt, whether physical or emotional, it is often wise to allow her to cry and say something like, "Go ahead. It's okay to cry. It will help make you feel better. Then we can talk about it." Often the child can talk after crying, whereas she could not before. Even when a child knows the cause of her sadness, we still want her to be as comfortable expressing feelings directly as discussing the reason. We can hold the child's hand or hug her while she is crying. This contact often makes it easier for the tears to roll.

I also feel it's healthy for parents to cry at times in front of their children. We need healing mechanisms too. Children can learn that being older doesn't mean not crying; even adults get hurt feelings and cry to help heal them. We should never call a child a baby for crying. Crying is appropriate for people of all ages and of both sexes. Talking through feelings has its place too, of course, but this should not replace more emotional expressions.

Many parents, familiar with the writings of Haim Ginott, have tried his technique of reflecting back feelings. For example, if a child appears disappointed, the parent says, "You seem really disappointed about what happened." Some of these parents have reported instances in which the child lashes back, "I'm not!" It's as if the child doesn't want his feelings clarified or understood like this. Some parents have said that even when the child comes to them saying himself, "I'm so angry about this," and the parent tries to mirror the child's feeling by saying, "Oh, you're really angry," the child seems put off. They have questioned the usefulness of this approach.

Children are different, and need a variety of adult responses. Sometimes a child wants to keep his feelings to himself and doesn't appreciate a parent's interest. At other times, when children share feelings, they might prefer a more simple response, like "I see" or "I'm glad you told me," rather than have the parent dwell on the feeling.

There are also times when reflecting feelings will be helpful. It can help to get the feeling expressed better and show the child that his feelings have been accepted by his parent. Having his feelings understood and clarified may help him look more clearly at the situation and be able to think more creatively about it. If a parent says, "You seem disappointed that the party was canceled," it may be just the opener the child needs to say more about his feelings, and after getting them off his chest, he can think more constructively about what to do that evening instead. Without his parent's understanding assistance, he might have spent the whole day moping, stuck with the bad feelings, and unable to find a good alternative entertainment.

As parents we need to take our cues from our children. No one method is helpful all of the time.

A mother was concerned because her children were not talking to her as much as she would have liked. She was especially worried about her ten-year-old son, who didn't seem able to share his feelings at all. When I asked if she stated her own feelings and thoughts to her children, the mother said no.

Young children often express their feelings quite spontaneously, but as they get older, they become more reserved. Parents can help to maintain good communication by sharing their own feelings and ideas with their children. This shows them we trust and respect them, and they are more likely to return our trust.

When a child does talk to you, it is very important to listen well, without making fun of his feelings or ideas. Then he will see that he is respected, and he will be encouraged to open up further.

It also helps for the parent to tell the child she is interested in his thoughts and feelings. Statements like "I'm interested in knowing your thoughts on _____" or "How do you feel about _____?" are good openers. Then, of course, the parent needs to stick around and hear the child's response. When parents want to invite further conversation, they can ask questions like "What were some of the things you did today at your friend's house?" instead of questions that lead to a blunt yes or no answer, such as "Did you have a good time at your friend's house?"

One father was interested in hearing more from his children and set up structured family rap sessions every few days. All the members of the family sat down together and talked about anything on their minds. It was a good time to share feelings. Each person had a chance to relate things that had gone well or poorly for her or him recently. They discussed issues that concerned the family and also events that took place outside of it. Family members listened to each other and also helped out by offering suggestions. This was a supportive, intimate sharing time. Everyone's needs were considered. The meetings emphasized the community spirit of the family, a unit in which individuals live together as independent people with strong interdependent bonds. Whether at structured meetings or informally throughout the day, it is wonderful when family members take time to listen well to one another. The emotional support they give to one another helps each of them to move on in positive directions in the family and in the wider world.

CHAPTER 6

Building a Positive Self-Image

Appreciating Children So They Will Like Themselves

At home and in school, attention often centers on what a child has done wrong, on what she needs to improve, on what her parents and teachers don't like about her personality or perform-ance. The good side—what she is doing well, her strengths and positive qualities—is too often taken for granted. This is unfortu-nate. In this chapter I discuss ways that parents and teachers can correct this imbalance and focus on the positive, using tech-niques like physical affection, verbal appreciation, focused indi-vidual special time, and constructive criticism. When parents let their child know they see her as capable of being loving, respon-sible, competent, cooperative, and enjoyable, she will demon-strate these qualities more and more. When parents and teachers hold up a positive mirror to children, they will reflect back a positive self-image.

Many parents are in the habit of relying almost exclusively on words, rather than touch, to communicate good feelings to their children. Group members have remarked on a need in our society for families to open up more to the benefits of physical affection.

I also believe that both verbal and nonverbal communication are necessary and that more can be done to emphasize physical closeness between parents and children. Hugs and kisses express love. Holding a child's hand, caressing her hair or forehead, leaning over to put a hand gently on her shoulder are gestures that create strong bonds and often speak louder than words. Sitting together for a moment with your arm around your child's shoulder adds warmth and closeness, and feels good.

Parents can add even more to the benefits of touching by telling their children how much they appreciate the physical affection shared between them. A father can say to his son, "Thanks for that wonderful hug. It made me feel so good." Or a mother might say, "I appreciate your good-bye kiss; it helps to start my day. I love you."

Children of all ages, both boys and girls, need plenty of physical affection. Many parents still believe that it is for girls only to be affectionate and that boys over five or so no longer need to give or receive too many hugs and kisses. In this way we direct boys away from their natural tender feelings. i encourage both fathers and mothers to be as affectionate with their sons as with their daughters, throughout their childhood. It is wonderful, too, when parents and their grown children are able to express closeness by touching. People of all ages need physical affection; it is an essential part of being human.

Some parents ask what to do when they attempt to hug or kiss a child and the child is not in the mood. Other parents have said that sometimes the reverse occurs—the children want to hug and kiss them and the parents don't feel like it. One mother said that her daughter would try to kiss her so many times in a row that the mother would say to her, sometimes quite nastily, "Cut that out already!"

If a child doesn't seem to be in the mood for physical affection at a certain moment, I would not force it on her. I would stop my attempts gently and without sarcasm. I would definitely continue to offer the child physical affection at other moments when she may be more receptive. I would also let her know how important it is to me to be able to touch her, that it helps me to feel good and to feel close to her.

We can keep in mind that there are many ways to show physical affection. Joshua went through a long period when he couldn't stand to be kissed, so I often made a point to rub his back or affectionately touch his shoulder. There are many ways to keep in touch.

If a child is kissing a parent so many times that the parent has had enough, it is important to avoid a snappish response, as that could make her feel bad and perhaps reluctant to be physically affectionate at other times. A sarcastic remark invalidates the child's tenderness for the parent. Instead, the parent can try to appreciate the child's affection by saying "Thanks for the kisses," or "Give me one more good hug now, and then I'll need to go and do my work," or simply, "I'm not in the mood for kisses now; come and snuggle me later." This way the child's affection is appreciated even though it is cut off for the moment.

I always begin Parent Awareness groups by asking parents to think about, and then share, what they like about themselves as parents, and also what they especially appreciate about each of their children.

It sometimes seems easier to think about what we don't like about ourselves or our children than what we do like. Often, when I ask parents what they like and appreciate about themselves and their children, they automatically start to discuss what they don't like. They've never taken the time to think specifically about what they do like about each of their children, and there is a social taboo on liking ourselves.

I also work with parents on what they'd like to improve in themselves as parents and on what they find difficult about each child. A child may be going through a certain stage (like the tantrums of toddlerhood), and once a parent can accept the child's ways as normal and learn better ways to handle them, the going gets easier. Sometimes parents need to learn to accept a certain trait in a child, as when a particular child has difficulty facing new situations. At other times parents can help a child to change—for instance, by helping her to give up whining. Exploring what we don't like is an important first step in making changes.

I like to *begin* each group with appreciation, however, and then have parents take the concept of appreciation home with them and make it part of their daily lives. So much emphasis in our society is on criticism. People who look for fault will usually find it, both in themselves and others. When parents can look for the good in themselves (until they find it), then they are more likely to look for and find the good in others, including their children. And when parents find the good in their children, it makes it easier for children to recognize and discover it in themselves. All people flourish when the atmosphere is appreciative.

Therefore, I encourage parents to think, now and then during the day, about what they like about themselves as parents and to observe what they really value about each of their children. I then ask parents to share their feelings and observations. This means taking time to let each child know that your are glad you are a parent, and specifically his or her parent, and what gives you your greatest joys and happiness from parenting.

These appreciations can range from general qualities to very specific observations. For instance, a parent may say to his children, "I like the way I take time to take you places." To his five-year-old son, a father may say, "It's really nice for me to see you listening so carefully to your records. You know all the words and you can tell just when a certain melody is going to begin," and to his thirteen-year-old daughter, "I love the energy you give to your schoolwork and hobbies, and the devotion you show to your friends." A mother may say, "I'm very glad that I'm a mother; I love watching you change and grow," or "One of my greatest moments as a mother was witnessing the drama of your first tooth falling out," or "I'm so lucky to have you as my child, and I'm proud to be your mother." When parents let their children know what they like about them, they feel good. When parents share with their children their joys and pleasures as parents, they show their children that parenting is a worthwhile experience.

Sometimes parents have a particularly difficult time thinking of appreciations for one of their children. I ask them to think about the child's earlier years and remember good things from then. All parents should do this occasionally. Children love to hear about their past. They can't remember the good things about themselves, and it builds their self-image to hear them. A parent may say, "When you were two, you ran so fast," or "When you were five, you used to help answer the phone," or "One day when you were seven, you played so quietly when I was sick." This will help the child build a sense of historical perspective about herself and also help make her feel good about herself in the present.

Parents can encourage their children to learn appreciation skills by asking them what they like about themselves and their parent, sibling, grandparent, or friend. In response to this question a child may say something like "I like about myself the way I run so fast," or "Dad, I like the way you cook," or "I like it when you read to me, Mom." Sam Falkoff once said to his mother, Susan, "I like you because you have curly hair like me." Parents and children can talk about the things they enjoy doing on their own and with each other. A parent may say, "I love reading and baking," or "I like it when we cook together, and I like riding our bikes alongside of each other."

We all keep on changing, too. It is good to consciously notice the changes and verbalize our approval. When we appreciate growth and improvement, children feel rewarded for their progress. The more we think about the positive parts of our life, the richer our lives can be.

During a group discussion of our childhood experiences, a mother commented that her parents had always favored her brothers. This had been very painful to her and damaging to her feelings of self-worth. She explored her relationship with her own children and found that she had been favoring her daughter over her son. She realized that each day after school, she was quick to hurry him out to play. She knew her own confidence and self-appreciation was lowered during her childhood because of not receiving the love and

attention she needed from her parents, and she didn't want to do this to her son. She wanted him to feel as loved as his sister. How could she begin to do this?

First of all, the fact that the mother became aware that she'd been favoring her daughter and putting her son in the position she had been in as a child was a great beginning. The mother then started to look closely at her son. She saw how much he needed her, and also how important he really was to her.

I suggested that she concentrate on her son's capabilities rather than on his weaknesses, as she had been doing. Letting him know that she appreciates him, his accomplishments, and strengths would begin to help build up his positive self-image. Since children see themselves reflected in their parents' eyes, this would help the son to see himself as a fine human being who matters to the people around him.

I also urged this mother to give both her daughter and son special time alone with her, either by going out somewhere like the park or the library or by staying alone together at home. This way, her son and daughter would both receive conscious positive attention from their mother. I cautioned her to be especially careful at these times to focus her attention on the child she was with, and avoid talking about the other child. I also recommended that the mother set aside a family time when she and both of the children would have milk and cookies and a sharing time together. It is very important that she take great care to listen well to each of them at these times.

This mother followed these suggestions, and reported that they helped enormously to create the feeling of a strong family unit.

Four-year-old Matthew was fortunate to have several close friends on his block. He would often come home from nursery school and go right out to play again. When given a choice between spending time with his family or a friend, he would always choose the friend. Yet his mother noticed that if he hadn't seen much of her for a few days, he would seem very angry at her. Should she force him to stay home sometimes?

Here, too, special time is the answer. Increasingly as Matthew grows older, he will have his own life away from home. While peers are very important to a four-year-old and his friendships should certainly be encouraged, his parents need to continue their efforts to give him focused time alone. All children and adolescents need this special time. It is essential for their positive self-image.

Matthew's time with his parents need not cut too drastically into his time with friends. The quality of special time is more important than the quantity of time. Spending even five or ten minutes a day with each child and letting him know that "This is our special time together" helps to cement a good bond between parent and child. Matthew will appreciate it if his parents make efforts to include his friends in their life—taking them on family outings at times, inviting them to dinner, welcoming them in their house. These gestures should not, however, replace Matthew's individual time with his mother and father.

I suggest that parents always comment to their children about their nice times together, either while they are happening or later. Children need to hear it emphasized that the times they spend with their parents are enjoyable and meaningful to them. Matthew's mother might say, "I'm enjoying playing dominoes with you right now," or "Last night it was pleasant having our special time listening to records together." If a child learns that the people he admires value his company, he will conclude that he is a pretty fine person. Soon parents will hear their children saying these things back to them. It's good to hear a comment like "I'm enjoying having breakfast with you, Mom," or "It's great playing cards with you, Dad."

Christopher, a three-and-a-half-year-old, was adjusting well to nursery school and was very skillful with small toys like Legos. Nonetheless, his mother considered him quite babyish. Christopher was not totally toilet-trained and he was not very comfortable in many social situations. Rather than say hello to people, he would sometimes make a woofing sound instead. His mother told him these were babyish traits and was trying to get him to act more his age, but it seemed to her that the more she did, the harder he clung to his babyish ways.

All children grow at different rates. Like most children, Christopher was advanced in some areas and slower in others. Apparently, the pressure his mother was putting on him to stay dry at night and be socially graceful was only slowing his development in these other areas.

We need to accept children as they are. We can encourage their growth by being calm and friendly, not by being anxious and pressuring. The mother was starting to feel that maybe she had a problem child, and that really came through in the way she talked about her son. Even her mother-in-law had said, "He is a baby. He'll be like this for a few more years, I bet. You're going to have quite a time with him."

It is important for the mother to change her way of seeing her child. She needs to see him as the person he is, who has, like all of us, certain strengths and certain limitations. He is not a "baby." If the mother can accept her son for who he is and adopt an attitude of confidence that he will grow and change, then the child will relax, accept himself, and grow comfortably at his own pace.

110

During the course of her group, this mother did relax about her son, and as her attitude changed, she noticed that his did too. He went on to be fully toilet-trained and to greet people with less shyness in quite a short period of time.

I noticed that a certain mother would always refer to her younger daughter as "the whiner." It seemed as though she was using that label instead of taking any positive steps to make the whining go away.

When a child is given a label like "whiner," she will often live up to the parent's expectations and continue to whine. Even if the child has not been directly called a whiner, but the whining itself is labeled by remarks such as "Stop whining or I won't get it for you," the child becomes focused on whining. It is better to avoid mentioning the words "whining" or "whiner" and give up making negative statements. If this mother can stay detached, even lighthearted about it, and make positive comments like "I prefer it when you use your big girl's voice," it will be more helpful to her child. She may need to demonstrate what a "big girl's voice" sounds like. When the child sees that her mother has confidence that she does have and can use a pleasant voice, then she will believe this of herself too.

In my own family we have a humorous jingle that sometimes works when the children whine. Once I was watching cartoons on TV with them and a skit came on with a catchy melody about the kids who "whimper and whine." So at times when my children are screechy, I sing to them, "We are the kids who whimper and whine," and they jokingly mimic their own whining. We all have a good time with this, and they get the message.

Often parents label a child as "shy" when she won't respond to a conversation. The parent announces, "Oh, she is shy."

Identifying a child as shy may keep her on the fringes for longer. Parents can help a child better by saying things such as "She'll talk with you as soon as she's ready." This way, parents demonstrate confidence that she is able to join in, without pushing her to do so.

By labeling a child as shy, the parent is acting as if she were like that in *all* situations. Children, like grownups, demonstrate different sides of themselves at different times. We are creatures of many qualities. The same child who is taking more time to ease into a certain situation may feel confident and assertive at another time. We'd be wrong to claim the child as "shy" or "assertive"; we are best off dealing with a child's behavior in each specific instance.

A mother saw her seven-year-old, Alex, as clumsy. He often spilled things and tripped over objects. She asked what could be done about his clumsiness and whether it would be okay to call him clumsy every so often.

Criticizing Alex will make him need his energies for defense. If his mother says, "You're so clumsy," he might answer, "I am not clumsy!" (though deep down he's beginning to think more and more that he is), or he might say his sister made him spill. Children should not have to use their energy to defend themselves; they need it for learning and creativity. Calling Alex clumsy, even every so often, will do nothing to improve his coordination and will be damaging to his self-esteem. It is best to eliminate negative labeling completely.

Alex's mother can help him focus on solutions. If he trips or bumps into things, she can give positive advice like "Walk around that," or "Squeeze through that way," so the emphasis is on pointing out what needs to be done. Or the mother could ignore his actions, indicating that she feels he'll do just fine. If he spills juice, she can calmly ask him to wipe it up, or they might clean the floor together. In addition, providing opportunities for Alex to exercise his body through sports and gymnastics would be valuable in helping him to develop a good feeling about his body and increase his physical skills.

Some parents say that they are constantly reminding their children to stand up straight, yet they still hunch over.

When children feel good about themselves, it shows in their entire attitude. Instead of telling children to stand up straight and focusing on their posture in this negative way, it is better to help children feel good by concentrating on their strengths and capabilities. When children feel good about themselves, they are eager to face the world and walk beautifully through it.

A mother shared her memories of feeling victimized by negative labeling. As a child, she was called "stupid" so often that to this day she needs to combat the voices (now internal) saying she is stupid and unworthy. She now likes herself and enjoys her life, but she stressed that it had been difficult to throw off a negative view of herself, and she is still struggling against it. She urged her group members to consciously work at building self-confidence and self-love in their children.

This woman had come a long way on her own to break out of a negative self-image. I suggested that she repeat something like "I am really fine, loving, intelligent" to herself whenever she felt the old feelings surface. Because of her keen awareness of the effect of negative labeling on her growth, her warning to group members was particularly poignant.

Some parents say that they do not label their children in a serious way, but merely "joke around" calling them "stupid" or "clumsy" in jest. One woman said that she would say, "Hi, brats," to her niece and nephew, meaning it lovingly. These parents feel that it is good to take a humorous view of childhood.

Any kind of labeling of a child is unwise. Children learn what words mean, and "brat" has a negative meaning. The parent may think that certain labeling is done in fun, but to the child it's a different picture. Children take name calling and labeling seriously, and it wounds their self-esteem. When a child is called stupid in jest, she may still feel deep down that she is considered stupid by her parent and she thinks, "If my own mother and father call me stupid, then probably I am." The joke is not worth this risk; we need to eliminate name calling and labeling of any kind.

One mother shared with the group a dramatic instance of this danger. As a child, an uncle would "kid" her with the following refrain: "You can have her, I don't want her, she's too fat for me." He thought this was quite amusing, but she hated her uncle for this. When he died, she remembered feeling glad. Labeling, even in jest, is painful to a child. It's best to show our affection with words that denote affection.

One mother said that her husband often teased the children excessively. He'd say, "Let's go to the park," and then, after the children had become excited about going, say, "I was only kidding."

Parents will fool around with their children at times, and gentle teasing has its place. Heavier kidding, like this, makes children feel foolish and helpless. It weakens their self-esteem, and needs to be avoided.

By accident, a girl had banged a door on her mother's finger. The mother experienced such pain that she began to swear and call her daughter names. Later, she felt terrible about this episode.

When the mother calmed down from the pain, she had apologized. She assured her daughter that she hadn't meant what she said, but had been in such pain that she just didn't know what she was saying.

The mother was able to answer her own concerns about the incident. She knew it was okay to lose her cool and that this was normal under the circumstances. She felt comfortable about apologizing afterward. Yet she also felt that the next time she really lost control, she would try harder to use strong words in isolation, without connecting them to anyone's character. Instead of saying to her daughter, "You're a moron," she could say, "Oh, damn!"

A three-year-old boy was trying to draw a circle. His father glanced down and said, "That's not a circle; it's not round!" The boy began to cry, and his father felt stumped. "I shouldn't lie and say it's a circle if it's not, should I?" he wondered.

Criticism that puts down a child's efforts without indicating any way to improve is not helpful. When grownups emphasize a child's failure or lack of success, they aren't helping. Criticism is constructive when it indicates how to do better or helps the child himself to think of ways to proceed. For example, the father might have said, "What do you know that's round? Let's look at some round objects. Put one in front of you to get a better idea of how to draw it, or trace one." Also, criticism is positive when it builds upon the child's existing strengths. The father might have said, "This part of your circle looks round. Make the rest more like that."

Parents comment that many teachers focus on what children can't do or aren't doing correctly and that they often do not point out to children how they can improve. A teacher may write negative comments on a child's assignment: "Wrong" or "Too short" or "Not detailed enough."

It is best to phrase comments in positive terms, pointing out to children how they can make changes that need to be made or encouraging them to find a better way on their own. It's helpful for children when teachers (and parents) indicate what they have done well so they can build up from there.

In school as in the family, attention often centers on what a child has done wrong, on what needs to be improved, or on where teachers are having problems with a child. Time and energy is spent on pointing these things out in a negative way. The good side of the child, what the child is already doing well, her strengths and positive qualities are too often taken for granted. Children learn about themselves from the perspective of teachers as well as parents. A child's home and school setting both need to be encouraging. The important adults in her life should be campaigning for, not against, her positive self-image and developmental skills.

A group of parents and teachers were discussing the connection between a parent's attitude toward homework and a child's self-esteem.

The consensus of the group was that children need to assume the major responsibility for their homework, but a parent's attention could be helpful in various ways. Parents can show sincere interest in the content of the work, asking questions and taking time to discuss the subject matter with the child. The group agreed that parents too often put their main energy into seeing to it that the child does the work, forgetting how important it is to show interest in the work itself.

When parents take the time to be interested in their child's schoolwork, they show that she is important and that the work she is doing is of value. Occasionally a parent doing his own work alongside of the child doing homework can be a positive sign for the child, showing that both she and her parent are each busy at their own special work, together. Initially, children may need help from their parents in learning how to set aside time for homework. Parents may offer their child a choice of the afternoon or evening, for example, but soon children can begin structuring their own time for this.

Teachers do play a major part in helping to motivate a child's interest in learning, thought, and skill development. It seems, however, that a good balance of parent and teacher interest in a child's work can go a long way toward building and maintaining a child's enthusiasm for learning. When a child sees that her work is of interest to the significant people in her life (parents and teachers), then her work assumes greater value in her own eyes as well.

Parents sometimes don't like the way a teacher is handling their child or a given situation. Perhaps a teacher calls a certain child bad or lazy, or picks on her and in this way contributes to a negative self-image. Parents are wary, however, about interfering, and wonder if it's wise to speak to the teacher under these circumstances.

Parents have a right to see that their children are receiving meaningful school experiences. Many parents have been successful talking things over with their child's teacher. The best way to do this is to refrain from attacking the teacher in any way, but explain your belief in positive approaches and discuss how positive approaches contribute to a child's good self-image.

All teachers need to learn to look for the positive in children and to show all children that they are regarded as fine human beings capable of achieving. Then more children in school will live up to their teachers' positive expectations for them and succeed. If a child is having trouble with a teacher who really doesn't see her as a unique person capable of fulfillment and success, then the parent can try to find a teacher for the child who does. It is so important that children be with teachers who will supplement the positive feelings about themselves that they receive at home. Many teachers are using positive methods already. I encourage all teachers to follow their lead.

A father asked if there is such a thing as giving too much praise.
There is no such thing as too much of the right kind of praise. Children benefit from unlimited amounts of *descriptive* praise. Parents can praise a child's efforts, accomplishments, or creativity in a descriptive way so the child sees that the parent has taken the time to appreciate her efforts. A parent might say about a child's drawing, "I like the colors you used; they make me feel good inside," or about the yard the child cleaned up, "The yard looks beautiful now; the leaves are cleared, the chairs are arranged. That was a hard job. I appreciate the help." When parents take the time to describe the child's efforts and thoughtfulness, and also add how they feel about those efforts and accomplishments, children feel loved.

The danger is in praising a child's character directly, as in saying, "You're Daddy's good boy" or "You're such a sweet girl and always so helpful" or "You're a perfect child." These comments can indicate that the parent expects the child to exhibit only good behavior, and any lapses will result in a loss of love. No one is perfect all the time. It isn't fair to children to indicate to them in words or through more subtle means that we always expect this of them. The child herself knows that she can't always be counted on to demonstrate appropriate behavior and she is certainly possessed of many hostile and jealous feelings. Just three minutes ago, she may have been wishing her baby brother a few nasty things, or maybe last night she pinched him quite hard, not to mention that nobody had found out yet about the candy she'd taken from the pantry that morning! So instead of making her feel good, judgmental praise can make her feel bad, guilty, and ashamed for not living up to the label.

I do believe that it is possible to appreciate a child's total being in an affectionate, accepting manner. If a parent says, "You're just so wonderful" or "You're such a good person" or "You're great" in a loving way that tells the child, "I love you completely as a person, I accept you, misbehavior and all, and in my eyes you are wonderful," this can help a child feel totally loved and accepted.

Sometimes parents ask how to apply descriptive praise to general good behavior. If a child behaved nicely throughout a certain day, parents can still thank him best by being as specific as possible. "You've been a good boy today," is judgmental, but saying, "It was fun to be with you today. I loved building castles with you at the beach, and later you sat very still in the restaurant and ate all your food," is descriptive and very appropriate. A comment like "It was kind of you to help your sister put her toys away this afternoon" fares better than "You're such a helpful brother." In these ways, parents can appreciate their child's efforts and personal qualities, without being judgmental of his or her total character.

A father insisted that my techniques of appreciation and positive reinforcement would work well with most children, but that his five-year-old daughter Gloria really is bad, it's not just his impression of her!

Gloria is *not* bad. It is so important for parents to realize that every child is a good person. Here, both in conscious and in more subtle, unconscious ways, the father was giving his daughter the message that he expects her to be a bad person. This five-year-old girl will not develop confidence in herself or a good self-image if her father regards her like this; she will pick up his opinion of her and live up to it. Children are tuned in well to their parents. Even if a parent doesn't openly label a child, but deep down believes a certain child is rotten to the core, the child may get the hidden message and act accordingly.

This father needs to begin to look for the good that exists in Gloria. The more he looks for it, the more he will find. Then he needs to point out to his daughter the good that he finds, and he will see her begin to blossom. The child will not see herself as a good individual unless the important grownups in her life see her that way. All children can build upon their positive natures and show their best self more to the world and to themselves, when the people around them nurture their goodness.

Even when Gloria misbehaves, her father must take care to distinguish between the person and the behavior. Comments like "I don't like what you are doing" should replace comments like "You're a bad girl" or "You're being naughty right now." His criticism must go toward correcting the child's behavior, while leaving her personal integrity intact. Adults can understand this. If an adult did something that wasn't so terrific and a friend or spouse remarked, "What a bad person you are," he certainly would feel insulted and less worthy. If, instead, his friend or spouse said, "I don't think what you did was such a good idea," he could consider things better. His integrity is intact, and he is simply being asked to reconsider his behavior.

Every child is a good person and needs to be seen as such. Children are still good even when they're doing something we cannot approve. They themselves are not bad, rotten, no-good, or naughty, and it is harmful for them to see themselves in these ways. We need to aim disapproval at the child's behavior, not at her as a person. This deserves emphasis.

A father and mother asked me to sum up the ways they can help their children become self-confident.

Parents build confidence when they make encouraging comments that bolster their child's esteem. They need to refrain from all comments that are disparaging: "You never do anything right," "You can't do anything right," "Didn't I tell you that would happen?" "You're driving me nuts," "You're giving me an ulcer," "I've explained that to you a hundred times," "Let me do it for you already," "You'll never grow up."

Parents can start the day with comments like "It's so good to see you" or "I'm enjoying having breakfast with you." They can continue on during the day with "You're doing such a good job putting the toys away," "I like the way you're trying hard at your schoolwork," "You did great! Congratulations for doing so well on the test" (even if it wasn't 100%), "It's okay to make mistakes; that's how we learn," "I like listening to your wonderful ideas," "Learning to swim is hard work, but knowing how will be well worth the effort." At bedtime, a snuggle and a statement like "You had a good bike ride today," "I love you," "We've had a wonderful day together," or "It's so good being with you" make a happy end to the day.

Some parents say, "Why do we need to verbalize our feelings like this? Our children know when we're enjoying being with them or are having fun doing something together." Actually, very often children don't know our thoughts or feelings on these occasions. Saying these things (or occasionally writing them in notes and letters) lets them know very directly our positive feelings about being with them. When parents hold up a positive mirror to children, they will reflect back a positive self-image.

Another thing that builds confidence is for parents to be aware of each child's developmental level and help each one to grow and branch out at her own pace. Pushing children when they are not ready does not create confidence but sets them ahead on shaky ground. It is better to let each advance be made confidently, when the child is truly ready. Nor does it help to hold a child back when she is ready for a new effort.

Children need to feel competent. They need chances to do things on their own and think for themselves. They even need to make their own mistakes, and they will learn from them. Sometimes children want help, and that's fine, but parents shouldn't push help when it is not being appreciated.

Parents should not deprive their children of learning experiences by taking away hope and enthusiasm. One girl had told her father that she was planning to enter her grade's art contest. His reply was, "Don't bother. You'll never win." He would have given a boost to his daughter's growing self-esteem had he instead replied, "That's a nice idea. If you win, it will be fun. If you don't, it doesn't matter. Preparing your artwork and entering will be a fine reward in itself and you'll enjoy it."

When parents take an active interest in their child's world, children of all ages feel important and appreciated. This can mean playing with toys with a young child, or playing cards or going biking with older children and teenagers. It is important to take the time to talk with children about their interests, activities, and hobbies and at times to participate, as by attending a sports event or concert.

Children also benefit from learning more about the adult world. Children can take part in many ways. A young child can use a dull knife to help her parent cut up vegetables for a salad; an older child can help to shovel snow or fix a leaky sink. Children can take part in household activities and also in some leisure time interests of parents, like fishing or jogging. Parents can occasionally take their children to see their workplace, and they can talk about the kind of work they do. Children can learn from an early age about the many fields of work available and that work can be a fulfilling part of life. They can also see that using free time well is equally important. When parents share their lives with their children, including them in various ways, the children feel valued and important.

Parents sometimes acknowledge that inwardly they want to hold back time and keep their children babies. It's healthy to admit these feelings, for then it is easier to leave them behind and go ahead toward the future, growing and changing along with our children. It is also helpful when parents can focus on some of the things they now enjoy with their child that they couldn't have enjoyed with her when she was younger. Each stage has its own beauty. By finding what we can enjoy about our children at each stage and letting them know these things, we contribute toward their feeling good about themselves as they continue to grow and change.

CHAPTER 7

Fears

Role-Playing Fears and Talking Them Through

> *Childhood fears are a common and normal phenomenon. At times parents help by providing clarifying information, in other instances by simply accepting the fear without ridicule, while being reassuring and encouraging. This can be done with words or touch, or acted out in play. In this chapter, I explore these ways to handle some of the concerns and fears that are common to many children, such as school anxiety; fear of strangers, dogs, water, and doctors; feelings about handicapped people and hospitalizations; and nightmares. I also deal with a parent's responsibility to acknowledge real fear of legitimate dangers.*

A father was concerned because his four-year-old son seemed afraid of being left alone whenever he and his wife left for an evening out together, though the boy knew and liked his baby-sitter well. The son also became upset when his mother went out alone to an evening meeting. The parents were beginning to wonder whether they should go out, since it bothered their child so much.

Parents certainly need to go out, and they also need to help make their children comfortable with this. With many childhood fears, a combination of the following methods is helpful: having a reassuring attitude; accepting the fear; talking about the feared object or event with the child; using play materials to familiarize the child with the situation.

If parents show their child that they are anxious and they are having doubts about leaving him, then the child may think that there really is reason to fear being left with a sitter. Parents help children best by being calm, confident, reassuring, and sympathetic. The father could say to his son, "I know you don't want us to leave, but we need to go out now. You might fuss for a while; that's okay. I know you'll stop soon and will enjoy your time with the sitter.

Tomorrow we'll play together again. You visit your friends, and we need time for this too." The father could then give his son a nice reassuring hug. When parents are confident, children will adjust sooner. Most children will not cry for long.

Play is one of the most useful tools for facing fears. This boy's parents could act out the evening routine with him during the day, to help him practice the parents' leavetaking. Together, the boy and a parent could set up props to establish the scene that will be enacted. Parent and child can be the players (playing themselves, each other, or the baby-sitter), or dolls can be used to represent them. The father or mother could create a dialogue like this one:

> The son doll: I don't want you to go out!
> The parent dolls: We need to enjoy ourselves by going out together sometimes. You don't want us to go, but we know you'll have fun with your sitter.
> The sitter doll: Come on and play with me.
> The son doll: (crying still and fussing) Don't go!
> The parent dolls: (kissing their son good-bye) We'll be back later.

This boy's mother chose to act out the situation without toys. One afternoon she said to him, "Let's pretend that you're me and you need to go to a meeting, and I'll pretend to be you." Her son liked the idea and took his mother's pocketbook and started to go. The mother, playing the son, said, "Have a good time, Mommy." Here her son stopped and said, "Don't say that. Fuss and cry like I do!" So the mother pretended to cry and fuss. The little boy said emphatically, "I'm going to my meeting." He added, in a more soothing tone, "You'll have a nice time at home and tomorrow morning we'll play together." Then they laughed and hugged.

This kind of role-play can accomplish a great deal. The little boy, in his role as Mommy, gets to identify with an adult who needs to go to meetings even if her child fusses when she leaves. The next time his mother needs to go to a meeting, he may still make a scene, but somewhere in his mind he might recall playing the mother and understand her position better. It also will help him see his mother play a fussing boy and get an idea what this behavior looks like from the outside. When the son himself is able to comfort the fussy child, perhaps he can better appreciate the sincerity of these assurances.

The parent might also at some point suggest (but not insist) that the scene be acted out differently. She might say, "It would be so nice if when Papa and I left next time, you could say, 'Good-bye, have a nice time,' instead of fussing. Let's pretend we're going out to dinner now and you wave and say, 'Have a nice time.'" He may not wish to, and even if he does it won't guarantee he will adopt this new way to say good-bye the next time they really do go out, but it gives him the chance to try a more cheerful approach and maybe he will find it's easier than he'd thought.

Role-play like this works so well because children are more relaxed away from the crisis. Acting out the situation before it occurs can help them prepare for what will happen and better handle the real event. Acting it out afterward can help them to absorb the emotions they felt and be better prepared for a similar event in the future. Don't be surprised if a child wants to go through it several times. Children benefit from repetition, and gradually their concerns can be minimized.

A father and mother were planning to go away for a week without their children. The children were going to remain in their own home with professional baby-sitters (a mother, father, and child). The father had the children meet the woman several days before he and his wife were going to leave for vacation, so that they would know in advance who was to be caring for them. He wanted to know if there was anything else he could do to make the situation comfortable for his children and minimize any apprehension they might be feeling.

As this couple recognized, when parents will be away, it is helpful to let their children know ahead of time just where their parents are going and for how long they'll be gone. The children should also know what their own routine and schedule will be for the week. (For example, will they still be having their music lessons on Tuesday?) They should always meet beforehand the person who will be caring for them.

In this case, since the sitters weren't people the children knew well, it would be helpful for the parents to notify some of their close friends or relatives and ask them to call or visit the children a few times during the week so the children can have some contact with familiar people. It can be helpful for the children if the parents, too, call from their vacation. This mother, however, felt strongly that she'd enjoy her vacation more if she didn't speak to her children on the phone. That makes it especially important for relatives or friends to call instead. It is also good for parents to leave pictures of themselves and perhaps a note or message saying something like, "We love you very much. Have a good week. See you soon." If children can't read yet, the baby-sitter could read this to the children at the moments they seem to be missing their parents the most. If the family has a tape recorder, cassette messages could even be left so the children can hear their parents' real voices and feel their presence.

Careful preparation ahead of time can minimize apprehension and create a more secure and pleasant attitude in any new situation.

A mother described her child's separation problem when she started nursery school. Martha would cry and cling to her mother's leg, not wanting her to leave. This made the mother feel guilty. Other parents expressed the same concern about kindergarten, day-care, or nursery programs.

Many teachers today suggest that parents help their young child adjust to a new school environment by staying in school with her for a few days, or for some time each day for several days. This way the parent gets the opportunity to ease her own child into the school experience. The mother can play with her child, or sit nearby as her child plays with other children.

If a child continues to cry when her parent leaves, but the parent and teacher both feel that the child really is capable of adjusting and having a nice time, it is helpful to be firm, reassuring, and not anxious. The parent can say something like "I know it's hard to say good-bye, but you'll have a good day and I'll be back for you when school is over" or "It's okay to cry, but soon you'll be ready to play." It helps when a teacher stands by to be with the child as the parent leaves and for the parent to leave without dragging out her good-bye.

Sometimes a special toy from home or even a picture of her parents can help to make the adjustment from home to school easier. At home, if the parent shows an interest in the child's school and asks about the interesting projects, the teachers, and the other children, this can help the child to realize that her school is really a special place. If the child seems to like one of the children particularly well, the parent could arrange for that child to visit at home. Playing with a school friend at home can build a special bond that helps adjustment dramatically.

It can also be helpful if parents and children act out difficult parting scenes at home using dolls or role-play. They can also go beyond good-bye scenes to playing school together. Then the parent and child can re-create the fun things that happen at school, like drawing and singing.

Parents should not be dismayed if it takes the child time to like school. Some children will take several weeks or even longer to get comfortable with this new experience. With their parents' and teachers' understanding help, and at their own pace, children gradually ease into the new environment and will become stronger for it. Through school experiences, meeting new people, and learning more about life, children grow in independence and self-esteem.

An eleven-year-old boy was crying and acting very fearful about moving to a new school in a different city. His parents felt he was too old to be showing such concern and tried to get him out of his babyish ways by saying, "What are you so nervous about? You'll make friends fast enough!"

Fear is a normal human emotion. Parents should not ignore, put down, or try to force their children (of any age) out of their fears or concerns.

This boy's fear is real, and his parents' response was not understanding. The child's fear does not go away because they tell it to, and he is not given any comfort. Instead, the parent can be accepting. "It's hard to be moving and to have to make new friends. It'll take some time, but soon this place will be home and you'll have friends here too."

Sometimes older children have fears about more routine events, like a shot at the doctor's office or taking a final exam. Remember, the fears may seem silly to you, but to your child they are very serious and deserve the same respectful attention as your younger children's fears.

Parents say that their young children often act silly or unsociable when company arrives. They may call the parents' friends silly names, hide, run away, or even tell the company to go home.

Many adults feel uncomfortable around new people. We can expect this from children also. Usually the parent can let the company know that it takes the child a little while to adjust to new people, but once they get to know each other everything will be fine. If the child's annoying behavior is going on for too long, the parent can talk with the child along the following lines: "When your friends come over, I do my best to make them feel at home. I talk with them, give them snacks, and even play with them. When my friends come over, I expect you to help make them feel at home also. Calling my friends silly names and telling them to go home makes them feel bad. I know it can be hard to get used to new people, but you'll like them soon. What can you do to help them feel welcome? How about showing them your toys?"

Sometimes a child's behavior is a reaction to feeling ignored by both his parents and the company. You won't want him to monopolize the visit, but it helps to create an atmosphere where the friends are visiting the entire family. If the child is given special time to talk to the guests, then he may accept it more easily if the parents ask for special grown-up time with them later.

Jesse did not like to get his hair washed when he was two years old. He just hated to put his head back to get rinsed. Sometimes he would scream ferociously, as if in terror.

Sometimes parents get mad at children for being afraid. When a child is afraid and fussing, he is not helped by an angry or hysterical parent. Comments like "You've nothing to be afraid of" or "I want you to stop your ridiculous fussing" only make things worse. Sometimes if a parent says, "Don't be afraid," in a soft, comforting way, it will calm the child down.

When possible, it is helpful to allow a child to confront his fear gradually, but on certain occasions, this is not realistic. A child does need to have his hair washed from time to time, and you cannot wash it halfway. Parents are most helpful in this situation by being firm and confident, while accepting the child's fear and offering reassurance and encouragement. As I washed Jesse's hair, I would tell him that it was okay to be scared and scream (accepting his fear), but that it had to be done (being firm and confident) and that I knew he would get through it okay (offering reassurance and encouragement). Once the shampoo was over, I'd say something like "It was scary" or "You hated it, but you made it through very well." This can help to give a child a sense of achievement. Though afraid, he did see the experience through. This can give him more courage for the next time.

Since play can be used to help children work through fears, I would sometimes let Jesse have some shampoo and a rubber doll and suggest that he wash his doll's hair and tell her to put her head back to be rinsed. Sometimes I would even wash Jesse's hair as he washed the doll's hair. This was an effective distraction, and gave Jesse more control. Once, we acted out a situation in which I pretended to be Jesse and he pretended to be me. Then Jesse-as-Mommy washed my hair as I pretended to be him (screaming and fussing). There is always more than one way to approach a situation, and combining a variety of approaches is often effective.

A father would take his three-year-old daughter to the beach and could not get her to go in the water. He realized that the vastness of the ocean and the waves could be upsetting to her and didn't want to force her in, but he was eager for her to overcome her reluctance. Here's what he did.

The father used blocks and other toy props to create a beach scene in his daughter's room. Then he and his daughter pretended to go into the imaginary water together. Sometimes, instead of doing the acting themselves, the father used small dolls to represent himself and his daughter. The father would provide the dialogue. He would have the doll representing himself say to the doll representing his daughter, "Let's go into the water now. First we'll get our toes wet, then our feet, now up to the knees." The daughter doll would say, "This is fun, Dad. I'm enjoying getting wet." He encouraged his daughter to provide similar dialogue, and sometimes they did it together, each taking a different role. The father would always be sympathetic to his daughter's fear. He would say to the daughter doll, "I know this is scary for you. But soon you'll get used to it." Father and daughter played this way at home quite often over a period of weeks, and gradually the daughter got used to going into the water at the real beach. In the safe atmosphere of home, with familiar play equipment, she was able to overcome her fear.

The father did something else that was quite inventive. He wrote and illustrated a short story about a little girl who was afraid to try out the water at the beach. In his story, the girl got braver at each beach visit, from the day she put her toe in until the day she went in all the way. At the end of the book, the narrative said: "It was scary at first; now it's fun." His daughter loved this book about herself.

When Jonas was four, he spent most of the summer resisting going into the lake at camp. Instead, he'd play at the water's edge. His counselors were understanding of his fear while trying gradually to help him get into the water.

On a very hot day, the hottest of the year, everyone in the camp was being required to go into the water to cool off, for health and safety reasons. Jonas's counselor couldn't stand watching him at the edge of the lake in this excruciating heat. She went over to him and said, "Jonas, I know you've preferred to play at the water's edge, but today it's just too hot. Everyone needs to go into the water to cool off. I'm going to help you go in." Jonas's strange reply was "Do it fast!" From that day on, Jonas went happily into the lake and enjoyed learning to swim.

When a child is ready to give up his fears, he will.

A father reported that his three-year-old daughter, who was afraid of dogs barking, would sometimes go around the house pretending to be a barking dog. What was going on here?

Children, on their own, turn to play to work through their fears. By becoming a barking dog and making those loud sounds herself, this child was becoming more familiar with the thing she feared. She could turn the barking sounds on and off at will, which gave her a control over them she wished she could have in reality. When we set up play situations to deal with fears, we are only doing in a more structured way what children do all the time by themselves.

A mother reported that her seven-year-old son had noticed a man with one arm and had expressed concern that this might happen to him some day. The mother felt at a loss for words, and was surprised to find it so difficult to face this issue with her son.
Often adults do get overwhelmed when confronted with such things and find it hard to share feelings and information. This mother realized, however, that it is helpful to children when we give them information and reassurance so they don't remain confused and worried. This boy needed to know that this kind of thing happens rarely, usually as a result of a serious accident, although a person is occasionally born that way. The mother could point out to her son that most likely this would never happen to him, as it is very unusual.

After giving this reassurance, the mother could go on to explore her son's feelings about what he saw. Most likely he will have questions about what life is like for such a man. She could explain that when these things occur, people can learn to live with their handicap and go on functioning and living full lives; they are as fully human and rich with resources as anyone else.

It is possible she would find her son acting out this handicap, playing games about one-armed men. He would need to be told that it is fine to play like this at home, but not to ever imitate anyone like this in front of him, as that could hurt the person's feelings. She may also find her son pretending to be lifting weights and performing other feats of strength to show just how intact and strong his own two arms really are. It is so scary for the child to think of losing an arm that he may need to remind himself in vivid ways that it is not true. This is one way he becomes comfortable with what seems scary, strange, or new.

Parents can read to children who express such fears the book *About Handicaps: An Open Family Book for Parents and Children Together* by Sara Bonnett Stein (Walker & Co.). This book acknowledges that it is hard for most children to understand, at first, another's handicap, and it shows how children can learn to deal with their fear and realize that although a person is different on the outside, he is a complete person nonetheless. Another beautiful book to share with children is *Like Me* by Alan Brightman (Little, Brown & Co.). This book deals with retardation and depicts retarded children learning, loving, and growing. The message is that all children are more alike than they are different. Every child has some things he can do well and other things he does with more difficulty.

Many of us were brought up believing that differences are to be feared and shunned and that people who are different are somehow not quite human. Of course, this is untrue, and it hurts the people we avoid. It is important to teach our children that each individual is a complete person and that each human being shares the desire and capacity to live life to his own fullest potential.

A four-year-old boy hated to go to the doctor. His mother said that he became frightened before each visit, and she was embarrassed about having to drag a scared child to the doctor. Was there any way she could help him?

This mother had never prepared her son for his doctor visits. Some visits were for checkups, others for shots, and others because of illness. It's necessary for adults to talk with children about what will happen at the doctor's office and to be truthful about it. This way children know what to expect and can resolve some of their fears. If the child knows what to expect, he can even look forward to some parts of the exam, like being weighed or having his heartbeat checked. Parents can help the child to see the doctor as a friend who helps him stay healthy.

It might help to act out the doctor's visit at home before it happens. The mother could set up props such as a toy needle and stethoscope, and talk with her son about these instruments and their function. This way they won't appear so strange to him at his actual visit. The mother and son could take turns being the doctor and patient, or they could use dolls to act out what will happen. This is fun to do and adds a playful element to a scary experience.

There are some informative and comforting books to read to children about doctor and dental visits, and these are another excellent way to prepare them for the experience. *My Doctor* by Harlow Rockwell (Macmillan) is suitable for very young children, as is *My Dentist* by the same author (Greenwillow Books). *My Friend the Doctor* and *My Friend the Dentist* are both done in cooperation with the Menninger Foundation by Watson, Switzer, and Hirschberg (Golden Press).

It is especially important to prepare the child for any part of the exam that may be unpleasant. If he will be getting a shot, the parent should be honest and let him know that shots can hurt and that it's okay to cry or feel scared. Sometimes parents don't want their child to cry or be afraid because they are embarrassed for the doctor to see this behavior. Don't worry about a show of bravery for the doctor. Expressing feelings is a sign of strength, not weakness. A parent's job is to be the child's ally, and the doctor will be able to handle any expressions of pain or fear that he makes. Reassurance is necessary too. The child should know the shot will hurt, and it's fine to express the pain, but he also needs to know that the pain won't last long and that he's having the shot to make sure he will stay healthy. At the office, touching can be the most helpful form of reassurance. Depending on the situation, a parent could cuddle a child, rock him, or hold his hand to be supportive and comforting. This can make him feel much safer.

After the examination, his mother could help him a lot by going over what actually took place. She might say, "That shot really hurt you. You cried and that was just fine. You took it and you were brave," or "I liked the way you breathed so well for the doctor." This can help the child to develop a new sense of strength. Though it was hard, he did it.

One mother reported what a horrible experience it was when her six-year-old daughter had her tonsils removed. Several other parents had similar horror stories about this operation.

Fortunately, tonsillectomies are done much less often now than in the past. Many parents believe that this procedure is minor, yet these mothers felt it was a major operation and hard for both parent and child. They both need to be prepared for what will happen. In all fearful situations, a child's fear is lessened sooner when knowledge and helpful information replace what is unknown or mysterious, even if the knowledge includes unpleasant parts. If the mother has any questions at all about the operation or hospital procedure, she should not hesitate to ask the doctor about what is on her mind. Then she can pass on to the child as accurate a picture as possible of what to expect.

Parents should talk with their children about feelings of fear. It can be scary going to the hospital, seeing strange-looking instruments, other sick people, a whole different world, and needing to have one's tonsils out. One mother had a doctor friend who brought home hospital masks, a gown, and other hospital gear for her daughter to see before she went. This helped to familiarize the girl with the hospital environment.

The mothers all said that their children were very angry at them after the operation was over. They felt it would be wise to talk beforehand with a child about the fact that she might feel mad at her parents for sending her to the hospital. They urged parents to let the child know it was okay to feel mad even though they can explain that they also wish the operation wouldn't have to happen.

In the hospital itself, the mothers recommend that if it is at all possible, a parent sleep in the hospital room with the child overnight. The children who had a parent with them felt much more secure.

Going into and coming out of anesthesia can be a difficult time. One mother said that the laughing gas didn't cause her daughter to fall right to sleep, so she was still awake when she was being wheeled into the operating room and cried very hard for her mommy. It was very trying for the mother to stand by. Had she been prepared for this possibility, the mother felt she could have handled it better, and even insisted on accompanying her daughter. In the recovery room, while still asleep from the operation, this daughter cried again. The mother could have gone into the recovery room, but didn't know a child could cry under anesthesia and felt so upset to hear her daughter cry in this unconscious state that she chose to stay out of the room. Again, had she been made aware of this possibility, she might have felt better prepared and waited in the recovery room for the girl to awaken.

Another mother mentioned that when she saw her son right after his operation, there was blood on his nose and he didn't look so good. She wasn't expecting this and was shocked. Knowing what to expect would have been much better. Don't be afraid to ask!

The child should be told how she will feel after the operation. She will very likely have a bad sore throat. She needs to be told that the operation will make her better, but it will take a few days before she feels good.

It is also good to know the general hospital routine ahead of time. It helps to know what kinds of food the child will be permitted to eat, what time she will need to sleep, what clothes and belongings she may bring from home. Children feel more secure when their parents know what will happen and share this information with them. Learning these things all at once upon entering the hospital can make them feel overwhelmed, rushed, and confused.

Often a child will need to wear hospital pajamas. It would be helpful if she could keep her own slippers or some other item that will help her to feel more at home. Favorite toys and books help too.

Once home again, the mothers found that their children had nightmares for several weeks, and they recommend that parents be aware of this possibility. The children continued to be really angry at their parents, saying things like "Get away from me." One perceptive nurse said the anger was a sign of recovery, for the child was herself again and dealing with her feelings about the situation. These parents found it helpful to talk out the whole experience again at home, to listen to the pain, the scared feelings, the mad feelings, and accept their validity.

Some children act babyish upon returning home. The hospital was strange and things were not like home. They need extra attention and reassurance. Other children may have more tantrums and be bossy and demanding. In the hospital they lost a lot of what was their usual familiar environment and at home they need to be able to exercise control over their life. Parents need to be supportive and understanding so that children can work through their experience and move forward.

An excellent book to share with a child is *A Hospital Story* by Sara Bonnett Stein (Walker & Co.). Illustrated with photographs, this true story of a girl's tonsillectomy is easy for a child to understand. There is also an excellent side text for parents. *Curious George Goes to the Hospital* by Margaret and H. A. Rey (Scholastic Books) is a favorite classic for parents and children to read together.

A father wondered if it's okay to use a night light in a child's room if the child is afraid of the dark, or if it would be better to force him to sleep in the dark to show there is nothing to fear.

If a child is already afraid of the dark (or shadows or monsters), then, for him, there *is* something to fear. Saying "There's nothing to fear" is not true and is not recognizing the child's experience and feelings. Parents do much better to accept their child's fear as real (which it is) and provide him with opportunities to gain more control over it. In this case, the night light can gradually adjust the child to the dark. In the dark he would imagine scary shapes and animals in his room, but with a small light on he can see that the chair is really only a chair.

When Jesse was four, he was afraid of the dark and imagined scary monsters appearing out of the shadows. Instead of a light, he used something else to help him. He had found an old discarded crib bumper and decided to take this to sleep with him so that, should monsters appear, he could "bop 'em" with the bumper. He felt protected and slept well. Whatever will help the child feel more in control of the situation (within reason, of course) can be used. Other children feel protected by certain toys or a special stuffed animal. These safety figures are fine, and when the children feel ready to do without them, they will let us know.

When Joshua was about three and a half, he went through a monster-superhero phase. During the day he fearlessly played an assortment of intriguing roles, but at night these same monsters and heroes would cause bad dreams and disturb his sleep. We were aware of the dreams but hadn't been much help to Joshua

until he himself found a way to use role-play to deal with his fear-ful dreams.

One afternoon, Joshua and Dick were playing together in Joshua's room. Dick was lying down on Joshua's bed, trying to sneak in a nap. Seeing his father asleep on his own bed seemed to remind Joshua of his bad dreams. He began flapping his arms up and down, saying, "You sleep, Joshua; I'll be a dream," indicating to Dick that he should take on the role of Joshua. He continued to flap his arms and hands and began to chant to Dick-as-Joshua, "I am the dream. The dream is bothering you, Joshua." The flapping idea was quite effective in getting across the notion of being bothered, and while doing and saying these things, Joshua was also laughing and really enjoying himself. Dick shouted, "Go away dream! Don't bother me! Go away!"

At this point, Joshua himself felt ready to confront the bad dreams. He said he was going to be Joshua and that Dick should be the dream. So Dick went over to the corner of the room and flapped his hands up and down while chanting, "The dream is bothering you—I am the dream." Joshua said, "Go away dream! Go back to your own house! Don't bother me! Go back to your own house!"

That night Joshua wasn't as troubled by his fears of bad dreams as he had been on previous evenings, and went to sleep quite easily, shouting once or twice before falling asleep, "Go away dreams! Go back to your own house!"

Joshua repeated this scene several times over the next month. The troubling dreams did not stop altogether for quite a while, but they decreased dramatically. We were impressed at how creatively Joshua had found his own solution to this problem.

A nine-year-old was having recurring bad dreams as a result of an accident he'd had while getting out of a car. He had opened the door without looking, and a truck that was too close to stop had knocked him unconscious. Fortunately, the boy was left with only a few minor bruises from which he recovered after a few days' rest. The incident was very scary for him, however, and his night-mares continued long after the physical injuries had healed. He often woke up in the middle of the night and he also found it hard to fall asleep in the evening.

When a child awakens from a bad dream, he is helped by physical reassurance and comfort. The parent can go in and sit with him for a while, rub his back, or hug him to make him feel better and relieve him from the scary dream. While doing this the parent can say, "I know the dream was scary, but it's okay now. I'm here. I love you. You can fall back to sleep now." If the child is awake and wants to describe the dream, that is a good way for him to be rid of it. No one enjoys being up at night with a child, but this is a time when he really needs special help.

It is a good idea to talk with children during the day about the bad dreams they have, and to ask if they remember what the dreams were about. We should not force them to talk about the dreams, but we can offer an attentive ear if they wish to do so. It will help them sometimes. It is also beneficial to talk with children about the good dreams they have and let them know that all dreams are not scary.

This particular boy talked quite freely during the day about the many concerns he had about his accident. His mother would listen to his worries and let him express his fears and feelings. He expressed anger that it happened to him, relief that he wasn't really hurt, and worries about what might have happened, that he might have lost a leg or been killed. His mother responded by saying that she knew it was so scary for him, and for her too. "It was horrible to think that you might have been seriously hurt or even killed, but everything is okay now and I am so glad that you really were not badly hurt." They also talked about how important it is to make sure to look all around before getting out of a car. Gradually, these methods worked and the dreams subsided.

If the boy had not been so open about his concerns but nonetheless was revealing anxiety through dreams, his mother or father could have helped by asking him how he was feeling about the accident or giving him the chance to act out the accident with toy cars and trucks. Some parents think that talking to a child about his fears like this will put more fears into his mind. They feel that if a child says, "I was so afraid I was going to die," the parent should try to hurry past the comment or say, "Well, don't worry, it didn't happen." Brushing aside a child's fear will not make it go away. It only leaves the child alone with it and won't help him to work through his feelings and resolve them.

Children need to develop a healthy understanding of what is truly dangerous. One day my husband was very slowly starting to drive our car out of the driveway. Joshua, who was four years old, leaned forward to open the moving car's door. I was shocked that he did not exercise the proper degree of caution.

Although we had talked before with Joshua about moving cars, in this instance he acted on impulse, forgetting to stop and think about safety. Fortunately, I was standing by and instantly leaned over to catch him. I told him that this is a very dangerous thing he must never do because he could be badly hurt that way.

Later on, we talked again about safety and the real dangers involved in these kinds of situations and had these talks on several occasions thereafter. Parents need to help their children resolve their unrealistic fears, but parents also need to teach children about real dangers so they will develop a healthy sense of self-protection.

One afternoon a mother noticed a stranger in a parked car near her house. After a while, she heard a conversation beginning between him and her very outgoing son. She went outside and questioned the stranger enough to ascertain that he was in the neighborhood for a legitimate reason, but the incident made her realize that it was time to talk with her son about "not taking candy from strangers."

Such talks are an unfortunate necessity of bringing up children. It is natural for parents to wish they lived in a world that was totally safe for their children, but it is not, and children need to learn wariness. This mother explained to her son that there are people who do terrible things like try to steal children, that they may try to tempt them with candy and other presents, that he must never, never get into a car or go away with a person he does not know. Her son asked many questions and was quite upset about this; he even had some nightmares. In the long run, however, his mother felt it was better for him to have this fear than not. I agree.

CHAPTER 8

Sex Identity and Education

Respecting Our Bodies and Shedding Old Roles

We are fortunate to live in a society that tolerates open discussion of sexual matters, where body functions are not treated with shame and secrecy, and a child's natural curiosity can be adequately satisfied. Parents are in a key position to help children develop a healthy, positive attitude toward their bodies and their sexuality. In this chapter, I discuss helpful ways to present children with the information they need about the human body and its functions. Children's body image will be influenced tremendously by their parent's attitude toward such things as household nudity, sex play, and masturbation. I offer positive suggestions for handling occurrences such as these. I also discuss sex role stereotyping, appropriate responses to the preschooler's romantic feelings for the opposite-sex parent, and giving adolescents the information and emotional support they need as their bodies change.

A father noticed that in the nursery school his child attended, boys and girls shared the same johns and were permitted to observe each other toileting. The children were two to five years old. The father wondered if this was a good idea, as he didn't think that children needed to learn so young about sex differences.

Young children benefit from seeing boys and girls their age naked. They can learn from observation that boys and girls are built differently. It is reassuring to a three-year-old girl to see that other girls have a vagina; a three-year-old boy is glad to know that other boys his age have a penis too. Observing one another nude in a casual way helps young children be comfortable with the sex they are, and also understand better the differences that exist between the sexes. Children will also compare the appearance of boys and girls at school with that of older siblings and parents, and they will note the physical changes that come with maturity. By this kind of observing, children become at ease with the human body and how it grows and changes.

Young children are not, however, getting all the information they need just by observing. They need to be given facts as well, or fantasies may take over. Young girls may wonder if they once had a penis or if they will ever get one. Boys may wonder if they will lose their penis and get a vagina. One four-year-old girl said to her mother, "I know, when I grow up I'll get a penis." Adults need to provide young children with accurate and reassuring information. The following are some important facts for children to be given.

Boys are born with a penis and testicles, and they will always have them. Boys become men. As they grow up, their entire bodies grow. Growing is a gradual process that occurs slowly, and when a boy is older, his penis and testicles will increase in size. At a certain time (puberty to adolescence), hair will grow—in his genital area, under his arms, and on his face, and his voice will deepen.

Girls are born with a vagina and clitoris, they always will have them, and girls grow into women. They have never had a penis. When a girl is older, she will have hair in her genital area and under her arms and she will have breasts.

Although young children observe other children and adults, they are not certain how they themselves will grow and change. Getting correct information is necessary and reassuring. Boys and girls both need information about both sexes and they should learn the correct language for discussing these matters. It's best for the grownup to refer to a penis as a penis and a vagina as a vagina. If children go on to use words such as "wee wee" or "dinky," that's okay; it's a child's way of experimenting. Parents, however, should use the correct terms. This treats these important parts of the body with respect.

Parents ask if it's appropriate to walk around nude in front of their children.

Within limits, young children do benefit from seeing the people in their family nude. That's one of the ways they learn about sex differences. If a parent is dressing, toileting, or showering, and the children observe the parent in a casual way, that's fine. When everyone hides from each other, then a child can get the idea that there is something bad about the body. On the other hand, parents should not walk around nude in a showy kind of way. This can be stimulating to children, especially when Oedipal fantasies are present. (See also page 148.)

As children get older, often a parent or child wants privacy. This need should be respected. An older child may say, "I want to get undressed alone, without my younger brother around." A parent may say, "I'd like my privacy showering." In general, most healthy is a relaxed attitude in which children get some chances to observe body differences and the body is neither being hidden shamefully nor flagrantly exposed.

Parents wonder when to tell "the facts of life" and how much the children need to know.

The time to offer this information is as soon as children begin to ask questions. Your answers should always be truthful, simple, and limited to what the child can absorb at the time. A two-and-a-half-year-old may notice her pregnant aunt and ask what is inside her. You can say there is a baby growing in her in a special place. You would not have to go any further right then. You can wait until the child's next question.

If a child has not asked any questions by the age of three, parents can bring the subject up, perhaps by discussing a pregnant acquaintance. Another way to introduce these issues is by reading a good children's book on the subject, such as *Making Babies: An Open Family Book for Parents and Children Together* by Sara Bonnett Stein (Walker & Co.), which includes an excellent side section for parents, or the beautifully written and illustrated *Where Do Babies Come From?* by Margaret Sheffield (Alfred A. Knopf). Two other helpful books are *The Wonderful Story of How You Were Born* by Sidonie Matsner Gruenberg (Doubleday) and *Before You Were a Baby* by Paul Showers and Kay Sperry Showers (Thomas Crowell). These books all offer sex information in a warm, personal style. By introducing the subject in this way, parents show that they are comfortable with this kind of information, and the children feel safe asking further questions.

It is often helpful, before giving answers or information, to ask the child what she thinks, so you can correct any misinformation she has absorbed. Very often, a child's own thinking, though intelligent and creative, is wrong, confusing, or even scary. One boy had mentioned to his mother that he never wanted to start a baby. No wonder! He thought a baby started from a seed that would come out of his penis. He mentally compared the seed to a peanut seed and thought it would hurt a great deal as it came out. When Sam Falkoff was three, he described how he thought his sister Rebecca grew: A seed was planted in their garden and grew to be a plant. The plant was then put into Susan, and then it turned into Rebecca! Parents should listen to their children's ideas with respect and never make fun of them. They have, in fact, probably made creative use of bits of information they have been given. Once we learn where they have drawn incorrect conclusions, we can proceed to tell them what is actually true.

We should give a child roughly the following information: Sometimes a man and a woman get very close to each other and the man puts his penis into her vagina. We can say that this is called making love. Making love feels good, and grownups do it as a way to express love for each other and when they want to have a baby. Babies are started when sperm that is produced inside a man's testicles comes out of his penis and joins with a tiny egg inside the woman. The combined sperm and egg grows inside of the womb, or uterus (but not the stomach—that is where food goes), and becomes a baby. When the baby is ready to be born, it comes out through the vagina, which stretches for the baby and then shrinks back again. Children may ask if childbirth hurts and we can tell them that sometimes it does, but it can also be a very exciting and happy experience. Even though children can't really understand all of this, they begin to register truthful information.

Children ask certain questions again and again, and parents will need to give them the facts many times. The life process is beautiful and deserves to be treated with dignity and respect. Parents should offer the correct information, at a pace that seems comfortable for their particular child, and should answer their child's questions simply and pleasantly.

Six-year-old Angela was revealing her curiosity by giggling over trying to see her father's penis and by acting embarrassed while she was dressing and bathing. Her mother said that Angela had never been told about how babies are born. Should she bring the subject up now?

The daughter's giggling and curiosity is quite normal at this age. All children, whether they know the facts of reproduction or not, are very interested in observing body differences. Both of my own sons at six, upon finding me in the shower, would sometimes take a quick look in and then walk out nonchalantly, while at other times they laughed and chanted something like "You have a vagina" and even added "with hair on it." Joking, laughter, and play are significant ways that children take in, digest, and assimilate information. Though the child's interest in her father might have been embarrassing to him, her curiosity was normal. All children need accurate information about body differences, and observation is one important way to get it.

Angela needs to hear the facts clearly stated, too. I do feel it would be wise for her parents to initiate a conversation about how babies are conceived and born. It is likely that Angela has heard some of this information elsewhere, bits and pieces from friends, maybe in school. It is so important, however, for *parents* to share sex information. They can provide not only the facts, but also a loving, caring, and relaxed narration of them.

Sheila, age seven, asked her father while they were having a snack together, "What does 'fuck' mean?" Then she began to answer her own question. She made a circle with her thumb and index finger and slipped in the index finger of her other hand while saying, "This? A penis in a vagina?" Her father replied, "Yes." "Then how come it's a swear word?" she went on. Her father answered, "Sometimes it's used by some people to mean lovemaking and at other times people use it as a swear word when they're angry, and then it has nothing to do with loving." Some parents in the group were surprised he had not called her fresh for using that word.

The father did not call Sheila fresh or turn her away. He wasn't shocked by her question either. He recognized that children will be thinking and talking about these things, as most of us did when we were children. In fact, as parents we can feel glad when our children come to us with their questions so that we can help to clarify them in ways we'd like. Calling a child fresh hurts her feelings and puts her down. It also turns her away from us, and often for good. Then, Sheila at age sixteen may no longer even consider coming to her father, and he might urgently wish she would talk with him about what is on her mind. When we turn our children away, they often go to their friends who are equally confused or perhaps to a more understanding adult from whom they will get help; but we will have lost the opportunity to share with our own children about these important and intimate matters. By keeping the doors open for our young children, we will be working to keep communication open for our older children too.

A seven-and-a-half-year-old boy said to his mother, "Can a seven-year-old boy start a baby?" His mother answered, "No, seven-year-old boys don't produce sperm yet." He also asked, "What about the penis and vagina part?" (wondering if a seven-year-old can do this). His mother went on, "No, that's not for children, only for grownups."

Children think about these things and need their parents to explain what is and is not appropriate behavior for children.

An eight-year-old boy asked his mother how many times she and his father had made love aside from the times they did it to have their children. He asked, "Do grownups do it about twice a month?"

His mother did an excellent job of giving a direct answer and keeping her response on his level. She said that grownups make love when they are feeling like it, that sometimes it's more often and sometimes less, and that there is no set amount of times. She went on, "When you play Monopoly, sometimes you play it more often and at other times you play it less."

Mothers have asked how to explain menstruation to their preschool children, as it often happens that a preschooler enters the bathroom and notices the mother's menstrual blood.

When a preschool boy or girl has noticed menstrual blood, a mother can explain that she is not hurt and does not have a cut. She can describe the process of menstruation to the child, at a level she can understand. Susan Falkoff described how she explained this to her son Sam: Every month an egg gets ready for a sperm to get to it. If the sperm reaches the egg and joins with it, then fertilization occurs, and a baby starts to grow in her uterus. If a sperm does not join with the egg, then a baby doesn't start to grow and the special lining that was growing in her uterus to get ready for a baby is not needed, and comes out of her body through her vagina, and looks like blood. At this point in the explanation, Sam noticed a neighbor pass by on the street. He turned to Susan and said, "Does Theresa bleed?" We need to appreciate the candor and curiosity of children as they attempt to make sense of the information they receive.

In the children's book *Making Babies* by Sara Bonnett Stein (Walker & Co.), the uterine lining is described as spongy and soft, like a pillow for the growing baby. Blood helps to make this pillow soft, and when a baby does not start to grow inside, the blood isn't needed and comes out through the vagina. These kinds of explanations, stated calmly and matter-of-factly, are simple and truthful. Both boys and girls should know about menstruation, certainly by the age of eight, nine, or ten. It is best for parents to give this information so that children don't pick it up on their own and get an incomplete and confusing set of facts.

An eight-year-old boy had an erection and asked his mother what it was. She said, "What do you think?" to which the child replied, "I guess I have to pee." The mother left it at that.

This mother might have given her son a better explanation. She perhaps could have said that when a penis gets hard like that, it's called an erection, that after a while it gets soft again, and this is a common thing that happens to other boys and also to men. It is important for her son to understand that having an erection is normal so he won't worry that something is wrong with him when it happens.

A father said that his ten-year-old daughter asked what homosexuality meant. She had been watching something on TV and came to him for an answer. He told her that a homosexual is a person who chooses to have sexual relations with someone of the same sex. She then wanted to know what her father thought about this, and he was at a loss for what to say.

Homosexuality is a difficult issue for many people. I encourage parents to foster in their children an attitude of tolerance and respect toward all human beings, regardless of their sexual preference. Parents need not fear that this will affect their child's sexual orientation.

Many parents share feelings of being embarrassed or uncomfortable discussing sex information with their children.

Perhaps it is a comfort to know that many other parents share this difficulty. One way to ease embarrassment is to share your feelings of concern or discomfort with friends. Often they will have similar feelings, and talking together can be a great support.

It is worthwhile to reevaluate your attitudes toward sexual issues in order to provide your children with positive feelings and not have them go through childhood, as many of us did, with confusion, shame, and guilt regarding their bodies and sex. If we look around at all of nature and see our physical selves as one other wondrous and beautiful part of the universe, it can be a helpful perspective.

It is best if you have developed open communication about sexual matters early on by dealing honestly with your preschooler's questions; but if your children are older, it is never too late to begin. You can let them know you are available now to talk about these issues and you can even admit to them that it is hard for you to talk about this, but that you really want to. It is fine to explain that when you grew up, you didn't get the help you really needed and so this is new for you too. Children can be surprisingly understanding. It is not always easy for them to talk about sexual issues either, and they will gain comfort from this kind of sharing.

Both fathers and mothers can be very helpful to children about sex. We should not think that mothers have to be the ones to talk with the girls and fathers with the boys. Fathers do have something special to share with their sons and mothers with their daughters, but the reverse is also true. Hearing both perspectives from someone they love can be so valuable to children. If parents work on losing their own embarrassment, they will find that they can be a very important resource to their children of all ages.

Parents need not think that they have to know the answers to everything their children ask. Parents can let their children know when they are not sure about a certain issue and then together they can go to books for better understanding. This way, children see that their parents are able and willing to help them understand matters that aren't always so simple to comprehend.

As children learn about body processes, it is not always easy for them to incorporate everything they're learning right away. Much sounds strange and hard to believe. One six-year-old told his father that he never wanted to get married. He kept repeating this, and then later on he said, "I never want to get married because I don't want to have to put my penis in a girl's vagina." The father reported that as his son said this, his expression indicated that this notion seemed quite repulsive. Another parent heard her child saying, "Oh, babies come out of vaginas—how yucky."

Though children are beginning to hear the information, unless they are able to accept it emotionally, it will not make total sense to them. The father in the first incident told his son that he could understand his feelings and that when he got older all of this would make more sense to him. He explained that for grownups it makes sense and is a nice thing. The mother in the second incident told her child that our bodies are good and beautiful and work for us in many ways, and that a vagina is a good tunnel to let the baby through.

Just because children can't understand and feel happy right away about everything they learn, this does not mean they don't need accurate explanations. They do. They need correct information and an understanding parent who can take them from where they are and slowly help them to understand life's processes and the goodness of our bodies.

Several parents wondered if explaining to preschool-age children the way babies get started will tempt them to imitate the process.

Parents don't need to worry about this. When parents give their preschoolers this information they can also inform them that these activities are just for grownups. Young children learn that they cannot drive until they become adults. We do not see preschool children having wine with dinner, going to work, or staying out until two A.M.

for a movie. Children can learn distinctions between adult and child activities.

It is true, however, that in their imaginative play children *pretend* to drive, shave, go off to work, drink wine, etc. Two four-year-olds may play house and decide they are going to have a baby. Usually, this involves the girl walking around with a pillow under her shirt and using a doll to be the baby that came out. A parent might occasionally overhear something like "Okay, the sperm and egg will join and now the baby will grow," but most often children won't even get into this aspect in their play.

If a parent ever did find two young children imitating copulation, the activity should be stopped in a nonpunishing and confident manner. The children can be told that these activities are just for grownups. It is very important not ever to punish or humiliate children for their explorations or their questions, as this would leave them with negative feelings about themselves in relation to sex. We want to help children develop positive attitudes toward their sexuality so that sex can be a pleasurable and healthy part of their adult lives.

A mother found her six-year-old son and his friend undressing in front of each other. She wanted to know why they were doing this at age six since when they were two, three, and four years old they had seen lots of children nude in nursery school during toileting. She also wanted to know if it was okay to let them play like this.

According to the Gesell Institute's *Child Behavior from Birth to Ten*, based on studies of hundreds of children, the ages of four and six are particularly noted for sexual exploration. At three, five, seven, and eight, many children are also exploring, but not as often or with as high interest as the four- and six-year-olds. Eight-year-olds show a great deal of interest, but they do less actual exploration. They (like some six- and seven-year-olds) show their interest by giggling, telling dirty jokes, and writing down or saying words related to sex and elimination. Children investigate and observe to gain answers to some of the questions on their minds about the body. And they do obtain helpful information from their investigations. When this is supplemented by accurate information from their parents, they are able gradually to put together a coherent version of the life process.

The way to handle instances of sexual exploration will depend on their scope. Most of children's sex play is of brief duration and can be ignored. If, on the other hand, a parent notices that the exploring/comparing seems to be involving the children for a long time and the parent is feeling uncomfortable about it, she could tell the children to button up and then guide them to other projects, saying, "You were interested in seeing each other's bodies. You're both boys and you each have a penis. Now go and play with the blocks." Or, to a boy and girl, a parent might say, "You wanted to see how you are each different. Boys have a penis and girls have a vagina. We can look at books to get more answers to your questions." This puts an end to the exploration, but not to the child's right to be interested, and suggests other sources for further study and investigation. We should expect some sexual exploration, but it is fine to draw limits when they seem necessary.

In some instances, it is appropriate for parents to set their limits quite quickly. A five-year-old girl was sleeping over at the home of a five-year-old boy. The boy's older brother, who was eight, had joined the two younger children and began giggling, calling his penis a dinky, and pulling down his pajama bottoms. The mother, who saw this, thought this was entirely unacceptable and simply told the older boy to stop it immediately and pull his pajamas back up, which he did. There wasn't a need to say anything about body differences or looking at books, but just to curtail the child's action. Once it was stopped, all the children went about their business very happily.

A father observed his four-year-old son, Steve, playing house with a three-year-old friend, Janie. His son was playing the mother and pretending to be pregnant, and Janie was pretending to be the father. The father wondered if this was to be expected from children of this age or if he should be concerned about homosexual tendencies.

In their imaginative play, young children between two and about six years of age try out many different roles. Girls will often pretend to be the father and boys at times pretend to be the mother. This has nothing to do with future homosexuality; it is one way children learn to understand the world about them.

Young children often wonder what it would be like to be of the opposite sex. One four-year-old boy said, "I want to be a girl and have a vagina." It is common for girls to regard the penis as a playful, powerful thing and feel that they would like to have one. It is natural for boys to see breasts or a pregnant belly and wish that they could also have breasts someday (they seem decorative and nice) or wish that they could grow a baby inside just as girls will be able to do someday. When young children express desires like these, adults should respond with sympathetic understanding, never with ridicule. The adult can say something like "I understand, but we all can't have everything. We are each built one way." Adults can help young children to feel good about the sex they are. We can help boys to feel proud that they have a penis and testicles and someday might choose to help start a baby and take care of it. We can help young girls to feel proud that they have a womb (uterus) where a baby could grow someday, and breasts that will have milk if they have children.

It is normal for children to play out their wishes and fantasies in imaginative play. A girl, while playing, may put a stick between her legs, pretending to have a penis. A boy, like Steve, may pretend to be pregnant, or to have breasts. Adults can sometimes point out to young children that, for example, though Steve is really a boy and will become a man, he is pretending to be a woman, and that though Janie is really a girl and will become a woman, she is pretending to be a man. This can help sort out the real from the pretend. But it is not necessary to do this kind of pointing out often, and it is fine to leave children to their play. Once children reach six or seven, they have the world better figured out and begin to give up most role switching in their play. They begin to identify more exclusively with their own sex.

Many parents feel strongly about wanting "boys to be boys" and "girls to be girls."

I urge parents to steer away from sex-role stereotypes and to allow their children to reach toward their full human potential. Many parents feel that boys should not cry or express gentle emotions because that is "girl's stuff." A lot of parents give more physical affection to girls than to boys, expecting that boys should be tough and aggressive. Too many parents still expect girls to be always quiet and neat and feel uncomfortable when girls assert themselves as people. Some feel that if girls are strong and physically active, they are "tomboys."

Parents need to help free children from these stereotyped expectations. Both boys and girls need to know it is okay to cry, to possess and express tender feelings, to want to hug and be hugged, to be powerful people and have healthy, coordinated bodies. Many parents don't like to see boys playing with dolls or girls playing with cars. This is a repressive attitude. All play materials benefit both sexes. Boys and girls can express tender feelings toward dolls; they can hug and kiss a doll, put a doll to sleep. Both can try out on dolls the future possible role of being a caring parent. Dolls are also excellent targets for aggressive feelings. It's okay to pinch or hit a doll, and harmful to pinch or hit another child.

Parents need to discuss with their children of all ages that both women and men can go out to work and that all jobs and careers are appropriate to both women and men. Both fathers and mothers can be active caretakers of children and both men and women can share the work of a household. Boys and girls should be able to look forward to taking part in society in whatever way they wish.

Parents want to know if masturbation is normal for young children.

It is normal and healthy for young children to explore their bodies. Infants learn about the world with their hands, and their bodies are an important part of their world. If a parent sees an infant or toddler touching her genitals and says, "No," or gives her a toy to distract her, the girl can begin to believe that there is something dangerous or bad about that part of her body, as these limits are not set on touching her nose or arm. Children need to learn to feel comfortable with themselves and to accept all parts of their bodies as good.

An infant's main pleasure zone is the mouth, where comfort is obtained by sucking, but even babies begin to be aware that the genital area is a source of good feelings. As they feel their parents washing them with soft, warm washcloths, or when they themselves touch their genitals, they experience pleasant sensations. The toddler enjoys nice, comfortable feelings from bowel movements.

A preschooler transfers her primary pleasure zone to the genitals. This is a natural step in development. It even is helpful for parents to comment to their young child at this time (at three or four years old) that the genital area is a place that feels good sometimes. This way children won't feel alone or afraid of their physical feelings and discoveries.

Many parents went through childhood believing that masturbation is wrong. This was what their own parents told them. They know they don't want their own children to believe this, yet it seems strange to them to actually mention that touching the genital area feels good. They think it is best to ignore masturbation, saying nothing.

It is a fact that most children do masturbate and discover genital pleasure on their own. If a parent never says that the genitals are a place that feels good when touched, the child may believe that her discovery is a secret one, and perhaps that she is the only one who experiences these pleasurable sensations. This can lead to secret guilt about these explorations. Children need reassurance that their experiences are normal. One mother discovered her four-year-old stroking her genitals. She said to her daughter, "That feels good doesn't it?" Her daughter smiled back at her in agreement. When parents respond like this from time to time, children learn that their feelings and actions are acceptable. If the child is so absorbed in masturbation that it is noticeable to others, the parents can simply tell the child that while it is okay to do this, it should be done in private.

Some parents express concern because their children appear to masturbate often. When these children also have good peer relationships, secure relationships with their parents, and normal interest in play materials, the masturbation is nothing to worry about. In the case of a child who masturbates quite often and seems shut off from other sources of fulfillment and pleasure, the parent can try to encourage the child to play with friends and toys, and in general help her to find satisfaction in other pursuits. It would not be helpful for the parent to focus on the masturbation. It's better to accept it matter-of-factly, while trying to ease the child into other activities.

Masturbation will continue throughout childhood (and after). Parents should expect this and let their children know it's a normal part of growing up.

A mother discovered her four-year-old daughter exploring her body in the bathtub by trying to put a toy up her vagina. The mother told her daughter it was okay to put her finger in her vagina, but that objects may not be used because they could be dangerous and hurtful.

This mother handled this situation well. It is dangerous to put objects into any bodily opening—whether a nose, ear, anus, or vagina—but it is normal and instructive for children to explore their bodies with their fingers.

Kaitlin was an only child. When she was four-years-old, she talked often about marrying her father. Her parents thought this was cute, but they didn't like it so much when she wedged herself between them every time they tried to have a conversation or hug.

Kaitlin was in the Oedipal stage, a stage of child development identified by Freud and named for King Oedipus, a figure from Greek myth who killed his father and married his mother, unaware as he did so of their true identities. Freud believed that the story of Oedipus expresses a universal childhood fantasy. Between the ages of about three and six, children go through a period of wishing to be the romantic partner of their parent of the opposite sex, and viewing the parent of the same sex as their rival. At this time it is common to wish to marry the parent (or parent figure) of the opposite sex. Some children keep this wish more to themselves, while others openly say, "I want to marry you, Mommy," or "When I grow up, I'll marry you, Dad." Parents of only children often report a particularly intense Oedipal period. Since there are no distracting siblings to play or fight with, a lot of the child's energy goes to the parents.

Parents can be helpful during the Oedipal period by giving their child ample attention and affection, and also by setting some limits. When a child makes romantic statements or proposes marriage to a parent, we should not respond with "Oh, how cute" or "Who'll be the bridesmaid?" because it is not wise to allow a child to think that her wish is a possibility. Parents can make it clear in a kind way that they are the child's parents and always will be. Kaitlin's parents can tell her that when she grows up, she will meet someone else to marry.

When Joshua was four years old, he mentioned to me at times, sometimes even vehemently, that he wanted to marry me. I told him that when I was a little girl, I had wanted to marry my father (his Grandpa Sol), and that Daddy had wanted to marry his mommy (Joshua's Grandma Anne), but that when we got older we didn't want to marry our parents anymore and were glad to meet each other. I assured Joshua that I would always be his mother and he would always be my son, and that someday if he had children, I would be their grandmother.

Parents can also deal with interruptions of their time together realistically. Sometimes, when they are hugging, they can include the child in it too, while at other times they can say they are giving each other a hug right now and ask the child to wait for her turn later. The parents can play with the child sometimes and at other times let her know that they expect her to play alone for a time while they have tea and a quiet talk together. In addition, parents can make it clear through their attitude and actions that the relationship between grown-up men and women is a different kind of relationship from the one between parent and child. A romantic relationship is reserved for grownups to share with each other. The roles need to be clearly defined. Certainly at this time, as always, parents do need to give their children lots of love and affection, but this needs to be the kind that suits a parent-child relationship. Adult-type endearments and adult-style hugs and kisses should be saved for the special grownup in their lives.

Expressions of hostility toward a parent of the same sex can be dealt with calmly. Underlying them is the hidden (or not so hidden) romantic intent. Remember that the child still very much wants and needs love and support from the parent she is rejecting in fantasies and dreams. Parents need to be sympathetic to the intensity of these feelings and not get unduly upset about their manifestations.

The long-lasting result of the Oedipal conflict is that children accept that they cannot marry their mother or father (or the significant mother or father figure in their lives) and then make a positive identification with the parent of the same sex. Upon the successful resolution of this stage of her life, Kaitlin will conclude, "I can't marry my father, so I'll be like Mom and marry a man someday." By the age of six or eight, she will begin to lose most of the hostile and competitive feelings she had been harboring toward her mother and will want to spend more time doing things with her and being like her. In cases where the parent of the same sex does not live with the child and is not available at this time, it is important to help her build a good relationship with an adult of the same sex, perhaps an aunt, grandmother, or family friend, to foster her identification with her own sex.

A mother said her four-year-old son was "at that mother-attachment age." He was apparently having Oedipal feelings and was expressing them by kissing and touching her. One day he was sitting on her lap and began playing with her nipples. She felt sexually aroused by this and that made her feel uncomfortable. She simply told him to stop, but wanted to be able to explain to him why he should.

The mother could gently explain to her son that she doesn't like him to touch her that way, and then show him, by holding his hand, hugging, and kissing him (parent-child style) some appropriate ways for them to touch and be close. She might say, "I don't like for you to touch my nipples, but we can hug like this."

One night when Jesse was four, as I put him to bed he looked up at me and said, "When I grow up to be a daddy, I'll be kissing you a lot." I could tell that Jesse was picturing that when he grew up to be the daddy, I would be his wife.

I explained to Jesse that when he grew up to be a daddy, he would have a different wife and he would be kissing her a lot. I explained that I was his mother and always would be and that I was married to his daddy. It is interesting to see the many ways in which young children express their wishes to marry their parents and their confusions about this matter. Parents help by clarifying the issue in a gentle, reassuring way.

Parents ask if the child's Oedipal wishes usually go away entirely by age six or seven or if they ever come back.

Most Oedipal desires do submerge around the ages of six to seven. However, it is common for Oedipal stirrings from earlier times to reemerge during adolescence. The old love feelings felt toward the parent of the opposite sex come to the fore again, as well as the hostility toward the parent of the same sex. This can be a complicated time. Often adolescents are pushing these Oedipal feelings out of the way; they are uncomfortable feelings, and teenagers need their energy to reach out and begin to form friendships with peers of the opposite sex. The Oedipal feelings subside as teenagers branch out more and more in new directions and grow into young adulthood.

A single mother said that she had always spoken with her twin boys about sex up until they were twelve, but then she thought they'd be embarrassed if she talked with them, so she avoided any mention of sex from that point on. Now that they were sixteen, she realized that she had let a lot of confusion persist for an unnecessarily long time, and she was now working hard to clarify their thinking. She wanted to be more helpful to her younger children as they approached their teens and asked me to detail some basic understandings that parents can share with preteens and teenagers about sex.

I suggested to this woman that if her children seem embarrassed, she could say, "This might be embarrassing for you, but I need to give you this information because it's important." Then she could go on and explain the following kinds of things.

Adolescence begins for a boy when he first ejaculates semen, at around the age of thirteen or fourteen. This will usually occur either from masturbation or from a nocturnal emission (also known as a "wet dream"), which happens during sleep. It is important that boys understand that this will happen so they will not be confused by it or frightened that something unhealthy has come out of their body. Instead, they can feel proud that they've entered manhood. Parents may also want to give a detailed explanation of what causes an erection. The interior of the penis is filled with tissues that have spaces. As a result of physical stimulation or sexual fantasy, blood enters these spaces, causing the penis to increase in size and become hard. When the excitement subsides, the penis returns to its flaccid state.

In girls, menstruation can begin as young as nine or ten, or as late as sixteen. Well before it begins, a girl should know why it happens (each month the uterine lining builds up blood cells to provide oxygen and food for a baby; when no baby is growing, the extra lining isn't needed, and it comes out through the vagina as menstrual blood), how often it occurs (once a month for several days), and how to use pads or tampons during the period. When girls are prepared for menstruation ahead of time, they feel secure and can develop pride in and good feelings about their approaching entry into womanhood. When they're not informed beforehand, they may be horrified at seeing menstrual blood for the first time, imagining that something has gone seriously wrong with their bodies.

Menstruation often occurs irregularly during the girl's first year or two. A girl may get her period and then not get it again for a few months, or it may come every two or three weeks. Girls should understand this so they are not surprised that it takes their bodies time to adjust.

All teenagers should have information given to them about both sexes.

Boys and girls often wonder if their bodies are growing as they should. Girls may wonder about breast size and boys about the size of the penis. It is helpful for boys and girls to understand that people develop at different rates. Adult breast and penis sizes vary, as do height and weight. There is no one best proportion or perfect size for all human bodies.

Masturbation becomes more frequent during adolescence for both boys and girls. More sexual feeling is present than before. Masturbation is normal, adults do it too, and teenagers need to know this so they don't harbor guilt about it. During preadolescence and adolescence, masturbation often leads to orgasm, though a preadolescent boy would experience orgasm without ejaculation. Parents do well to describe orgasms to their teenagers—the physical build-up, release of tension, and pleasurable feelings. Teenagers need to understand what is taking place in their bodies. Many teenagers are not prepared for their first orgasm, and it may worry and frighten them.

Adolescents can be informed that one can experience orgasm with a sexual partner, but it is also helpful for parents to tell their teenagers that one's first experience at sexual intercourse may be disappointing. Getting to know another person sexually takes time. When two people care about each other and are considerate of each other in many ways, the sexual aspect of their relationship becomes one more way to communicate and add depth and enjoyment to the relationship.

It is important for both boys and girls to understand that the changes in their bodies mean that now they are producing eggs or sperm, and when a sperm cell unites with an egg cell inside the woman's body, a baby begins to grow. A number of parents express concern because many teenagers who get involved sexually do not understand that pregnancy can result. If the girl becomes pregnant, the teenagers are genuinely surprised. Adults should never assume that teenagers understand the biological process of birth. Each family must take the responsibility for giving its children correct information about reproduction and the various methods of birth control available. Teenagers should also realize that there is a risk of pregnancy even when birth control is used, and they should be aware of the choices open to them in case of pregnancy. None of the alternatives are easy ones, and all involve major decisions and emotional review.

When parents can share this information with their children in a calm, loving, reassuring way, they can help to ease the transition to adulthood. Teenagers also need emotional support and reassurance from their parents to guide them through these times of changes, so they can feel more relaxed, comfortable, and proud about entering a new phase of their lives. Two excellent books written for preadolescents, adolescents, and parents may be helpful too: *Boys and Sex* and *Girls and Sex*, both by Wardell B. Pomeroy, Ph.D. (Delacorte Press). Both books respond to the many questions and concerns that preteenagers, teenagers, and parents have about sex and growing up, and offer the information with warmth and a positive attitude. These books are written not only to help boys and girls better understand their own body changes, but also help them better appreciate each other's development during this important phase of their lives.

Parents wonder how to talk with their teenagers about sexual involvement. Every family has different beliefs and feelings about this, from those who believe that no one should become involved sexually until marriage, to those who feel that reaching out sexually is a natural part of growing up. Others believe it is the maturity of the person that counts. Some parents express the hope that any sexual encounter will take place within a meaningful relationship, while yet others would say it is all right for an older teenager (age eighteen or nineteen) to have sexual relations, but not for a younger teen.

Sexual involvement is a tricky issue, involving values and strong feelings. Parents are wise to listen to their children's feelings, to respect their thinking, and to offer their own views without putting down their teenagers'. Parents should try to keep discussions going and not end them on a sour note. It helps to realize that important issues need to be discussed again and again (once is not enough) and that teenagers need a safe place to air their views and clarify their own thinking. If parents aren't willing to share ideas and only want to dictate views, teenagers will usually turn elsewhere, and then parents lose out on a time of growing intimacy. Sometimes teenagers will speak what's on their mind directly, but other times their concerns come out indirectly, perhaps by referring to a friend's experience or something they've read. Parents need to pick up on cues that indicate their teenager wants to explore a certain issue (the pill, abortion, etc.). Parents, too, can begin conversations that will be meaningful for them and their adolescent. They do not always need to wait for the child to begin. No matter where parents stand on the issue of sexual involvement, I urge them to recognize the fact that many teenagers will become involved sexually and should therefore be aware of the various methods of birth control available. A teenager may or may not be able to handle a sexual relationship, but a great majority of young people are not yet ready to be caring and responsible parents.

Many young teenagers become involved sexually as a result of peer pressure. Parents can urge their children not to feel pressured into sexual relations but wait until they personally are ready. Parents are most helpful when they discuss with their adolescent daughters and sons not only the facts of sex, but also the emotions and responsibilities involved. Teenagers may wish to share with their parents certain aspects of a difficult or a pleasant experience. Parents can help their teenagers in troubled or in better times by being there to share experiences and talk seriously about life and what it has to offer. This will help them as they go forward, slowly and confidently, into the adult world.

CHAPTER 9

Divorce

Dealing with the Intense Emotions of Separation and Adjusting to Single Parenthood

Increasing numbers of children are being affected by divorce. The breakup of the family unit as it has been known is a major life change for the children and adults involved, and one that evokes strong emotions. Each family needs to work out, over time, a way to share children (when they will be shared) that suits its needs, and this may change as the children grow older. In this chapter, I discuss ways to help children deal with their feelings about divorce and adapt to new child-care arrangements. Other questions deal with children's reactions to, and parents' concerns about, remarriage.

The parents of three children were in the process of divorce. Their four-year-old son was expressing his feelings mainly by hitting and screaming over every little thing. Their eight-year-old daughter had said, "You'll need to come to school and tell my teacher about what's happening. I might look sad sometimes, and I want my teacher to know why." Their twelve-year-old daughter had not expressed any of her feelings about the situation at all; she seemed all bottled up. The mother said, "This is a confusing time for all of us and I want to try to do what's best for each of the children."

Children need a lot of adult help while adjusting to a divorce. For one thing, it will be easier for all the children if they are given a clear picture of the situation. Though the truth may be painful, parents can help their children to deal with it. Misinformation leaves children to their own confused thoughts, which are harder to deal with than any reality.

The four-year-old will need to have the situation explained a number of times, as it will take him longer to absorb what is happening. The parents should be sure to discuss only those reasons for the divorce which are appropriate for him to hear, presented at a level he can understand. It may be enough to say, "We are getting divorced because we can no longer live happily together." Parents should use the word "divorce" so that he becomes familiar with it, and also explain what the word actually means—that his parents will be living in different houses from now on. The older children will need more detailed information (as will the four-year-old eventually, when he is somewhat older).

Chances are the parents are quite angry with each other, but it is not appropriate for either parent to make the children listen to vicious condemnations of the other's shortcomings. It is realistic for them to know that their parents dislike certain things about each other, but the children need to continue having love and respect for both their mother and father. It helps for them to see that each parent has good points and some problems, as do all other individuals.

Children should not become a pawn of parents who use them to obtain information about each other or to relay ill will. This confuses their loyalties. They need to remain loyal to both parents.

A divorce brings intense and mixed emotions for everyone involved. Children, too, may be angry at one or both parents. They may also feel relief if the home has been tense, and possibly fearful that the other parent might leave someday too. For everyone, there is a sense of loss at seeing the family unit change; even the adults who haven't been getting along have become used to a certain setup or remember better times. Children may worry that they are the real cause of the breakup, and often they will urge the parents to get back together.

As with any major life change, these feelings will take a long time to work through. The parents, too, will need time to adjust. It is fine for each of them to share her or his frustration and tears. This will make it easier for the children to express their feelings, and sharing strong feelings brings people closer together.

The children's varied feelings need to be respectfully heard. The eight-year-old expressed her feelings of sadness beautifully, and this can be acknowledged, as well as exploring other feelings—perhaps anger or guilt—that she is keeping inside. All three of the children need lots of opportunities to say what's on their mind, and cry and scream about it too. An opener might be: "We're all going through a difficult time right now. You are probably feeling a lot of things. Maybe sometimes you feel sad about what's happening, or very angry, perhaps confused. It would be good to talk together about our feelings. I'd like to hear how you feel about all of this." The twelve-year-old may have been keeping quiet to spare her parents' feelings and she needs to know that the subject is not taboo, that her thoughts and feelings about the family are welcomed.

Besides listening to the children, it helps to answer their anxieties with reassurances that they are well loved and will continue to receive good care, that they are, in fact, a significantly joyous part of each parent's life. When the children express the wish for their parents' reconciliation, it can be acknowledged by saying, "We know that you sometimes wish we could be together again, but it needs to be this way." It is important not to foster false hopes.

The four-year-old, who is in his Oedipal stage, may be especially troubled by guilt. Boys of his age often fantasize about marrying their mothers and doing away with their fathers. When a separation occurs at this time, they may worry that these feelings are the actual cause of the breakup. All children need to be told that a divorce is not their fault, that the reason the parents are separating is that they were not able to get along happily with each other.

This mother realized that the four-year-old's outbursts of anger were related to the divorce. She should be on the lookout for such signs in her older children too. The twelve-year-old may cry and cry over a minor fight with a friend, but it is really her stronger hurt about the separation emerging.

Two excellent books for parents to read with their preschool and elementary-school-age children are *Divorce Is a Grown Up Problem* by Janet Sinberg (Avon Publications) and *Talking About Divorce* by Earl A. Grollman (Beacon Press). Older children will enjoy Dr. Richard A. Gardner's *The Boys and Girls Book About Divorce* (Bantam Books). *The Parents Book About Divorce* by the same author (Doubleday) is a good resource for adults, as is *Explaining Divorce to Children* edited by Earl A. Grollman (Beacon Press). *The Disposable Parent* by Mel Roman and William Haddad (Holt, Rinehart and Winston) presents an impressive argument for joint custody.

A woman explained that she had been divorced for two years and that at the start of the second year, her ex-husband had moved to a distant city. Until this time, he was able to see their two children every week and continue to be active in their care. Now he only sees them during school vacations. Since his move, he had established a routine of phoning the children, who were three and six, once every two weeks. The mother observed that without fail, the children would begin to get very anxious about a week after his call. Right after his next call, they would be content for another week. It was clear to the mother that two weeks in between contacts was just too long.

Both children were adopted, and the mother was also afraid that they might experience an even deeper rejection than children in the same situation with a biological father. They had already needed to deal with their biological parents not being able to care for them and their adoptive parents wanting them so much—and now this! The mother felt that the children's father was not very knowledgeable about the early childhood years and he probably didn't realize how long two weeks can seem to young children. The woman believed that he thought he was being a full-time parent and fulfilling his parental duties by calling consistently every two weeks, yet she also said he was generally open to suggestions concerning the children and did care deeply for them. Should she discuss this matter with him or not? She seemed to want to very much, but needed support and encouragement to go ahead.

This mother received support from the group. Since she would be needing to communicate with this man through the years about their children's growth, development, and well-being, it certainly would be best to set up a pattern now for honest talks with him. The group advised her to call him and explain her feelings about the situation, as well as the children's reaction to the twice-a-month contact. It would be sensible to explain to him that young children need more frequent communication and that a phone call each week, or even several times a week, would be preferable. In addition, letters and drawings sent in the mail would be a fine way to show his interest and help the children continue to feel loved and important.

Several weeks later, this mother reported following up on the group's suggestions and receiving a favorable response. As she suspected, her ex-husband had not been aware that two weeks was too long a time and had thought that his talks with the children were packed with good exchanges that could hold them until the next time. He was glad for the suggestions and said he would not have thought of sending small messages or pictures by mail, other than on birthdays or holidays. He asked that she help the children answer his letters and draw pictures to send to him. As this situation shows, being direct is very often the best way to approach family problems.

A nine-year-old girl's parents were divorced. Johanna lived with her mother and normally saw her father two to three times during the year for several weeks at a time, as he lived a long distance away. Johanna's father was able to arrange a one-day visit for her birthday. He took her to special places and they stayed overnight together at a hotel. They had a wonderful time. Johanna was hard to live with for the next week, however, misbehaving constantly, and finally expressing directly to her mother how angry she felt that the time with her father had to end so soon. The mother asked me how to deal with her daughter's feelings.

The mother could be supportive by helping Johanna deal with her mixed emotions. She could acknowledge how happy Johanna had been to see her father, at the same time letting her know that it was also okay to feel disappointed and angry that it had been so short a time. If Johanna can verbalize these feelings herself, the mother can be a quiet listener; if they seem unexpressed, she could help say them for the child. For example: "You had a special birthday with your father and you were so happy he could come and be with you. I know it's hard to have the time together end so soon. You're used to being with him for longer, and it makes you mad to see him need to go. That makes sense, and it's good that you're still glad he came."

It would have been good for Johanna's father to have helped his daughter with her feelings before they said good-bye. He could have talked with her about the fact that usually they look forward to a good long stay with each other and then they have a better opportunity to make their good-bye more gradual. He might have said, "It's so good being with each other now. I'm going to feel disappointed when I have to leave tomorrow, and I bet you'll be feeling disappointed and angry, the same as me." This way, the father would be letting her know that he, too, has a hard time leaving and that he accepts her feelings about the visit.

Johanna's father may have had a conversation like this with her. Even after talking in this way, Johanna would still very likely feel mad or disappointed for a few days afterward and possibly still misbehave a little as a sign of her inner turmoil. That's okay; it means she's working through her feelings, and with time they will subside.

A mother had been divorced for some time. The children's father lived in another city and made no efforts to see them. She and the children had tried to include him in their lives, but he was unresponsive to their overtures. The mother had built up the children's hopes, assuring them he would change his ways soon. She was feeling drained by this cover-up and began to wonder if it was the best approach.

Initially it was wise to encourage the children to try reaching out to their father; usually even minimal contact with a parent is better than none at all. Once it was clear that their attempts were futile, however, she was correct to curtail them.

Though it can be very painful for children to deal with a parent who is not offering them his love, concern, or interest, we are most supportive when we help them face and deal with reality. Feeding their hopes prevents children from expressing and working through the feelings they have about the situation—feelings of rage, sadness, and confusion. A rejection like this is harmful to their sense of worth. They need to know that their father abandoned them because of his own problems and not because of who they are. The mother can help by telling them that they are lovable people, and point out that there are other people who do care deeply about them—herself and their friends, grandparents, teachers, aunts, and uncles. Her children's energy would be better rewarded by offering love to those who could return it, rather than continually pining for their absent father, as the mother's hopefulness encourages them to do. She is trying to protect them from a painful rejection, but this does not make the rejection disappear; it only prevents them from coming to terms with it and moving on.

Someday the father might contact the children and want to establish a relationship. If that ever happens, the family could reevaluate the situation. To treat this possibility as an imminent reality, however, is wrong. It is only a possibility the future may bring, and it is better to focus the children on the present and the real opportunities for fulfillment it affords.

A recently separated father lived with his two children on the weekends and was upset by how often the boys spoke of missing their mother. How could he help them adjust to their new arrangement?

It is natural for these boys to miss one parent while they are with the other. After all, they are used to having them both together. I am certain that during the week they tell their mother that they are missing their father.

The father can help them best by accepting their feelings. When one of them says something like "I wish I could see Mommy right now," he can answer, "I know you're missing Mommy right now, and you'll be seeing her again tomorrow night. If you'd like, you can phone her." Children love both parents. The father should try not to feel judged or slighted by their interest in their mother.

At other times, this father could talk with his children about how sad it is for them not to be able to have the family all together anymore. Their feelings of loss need to be heard. When they can air their feelings of grief and pain, their ability to heal and adjust will be better.

A father had custody of his two children all week, and their mother had them on the weekends. He said that his typical week

was exhausting; it was a tremendous responsibility to be totally in charge of the children—setting the limits, making all necessary decisions, and seeing to it that the endless details of the daily routine went smoothly. Though he did miss his children on the weekends, he was also glad to have this time to himself to renew his energy, and saw it as an advantage.

A mother in his group had the total responsibility for her three children. Since her divorce a year ago, the father would not see the children, and she found the weight of her task enormous. Between working and caring for the children, there seemed almost no time for herself. She also expressed a recurring fear: Should anything happen to her (a fatal accident, serious illness), what would happen to her children? She was interested in suggestions for coping with this situation.

Caring for children is a very demanding job. Parents from two-parent families also experience child rearing as an enormous responsibility, but without a doubt, parenting is usually easier when there are two to share it.

Other single parents in the group emphasized to this mother the value of building up a support system she could rely on—good baby-sitters she could trust, relatives, friends and neighbors who would be willing to take her children for an occasional weekend. They stressed the importance of having time alone, away from her children and her daily responsibilities, to recharge her mental, emotional, and physical energy.

Some single parents say that although they find single parenting a big job, it is easier than double parenting in certain respects. They enjoy the total freedom of making decisions and caring for the children in the way that seems right to them, without having to undergo the negotiations and make the compromises that parents in two-parent families must make.

Many other parents in the group expressed similar fears about leaving for an evening out and being in a fatal accident. Two-parent families are not immune to this fear, either. Many parents deal with this by making arrangements for the care of their children in the event of their death. They arrange for a close relative or friend to become the legal guardian of their children should the need arise, and also let the children know who would be caring for them under these circumstances. Children, too, often worry about this, and knowing what arrangements have been made brings a degree of relief. Once these arrangements are made, I advise parents to try not to dwell on the matter. It is good to recognize our concerns about this issue, but lingering on the feelings is neither necessary nor helpful to the parents or children.

A mother was divorced, and her children saw their father on weekends. She was having a problem with her six-year-old daughter, Peggy. Whenever the mother and daughter did not see eye to eye, Peggy would say that she was going to live with her father. The mother was beginning to feel that Peggy really preferred her father, and didn't know quite what to do.

A six-year-old child is naturally torn between two parents she loves. Once divorced parents have decided whom the child will live with, they need to help the child accept that decision. They can respect the desire to see the other parent, but be firm about the arrangement: "You wish you could see Daddy right now, but during the week you live with me."

Peggy was trying to manipulate her mother. She was using the divorce to try to get her mother to always give in to her wishes. Her mother could be most helpful by sticking to each real issue, discussing the girl's feelings about the divorce at other times. The mother could say, "You're angry because you would like to stay up later; but it's your bedtime." She needs to show her daughter that she won't let her manipulate her or wound her feelings.

The mother began to do this, and Peggy was actually relieved. She was not comfortable hurting her mother's feelings and needed her to put a stop to this. She also needed to have limits set on her behavior. Both mother and daughter were happier when this was done.

Often children regard the parent they live with on weekends as the "good guy." Weekends seem to be the time for fun, with less responsibility, no rush to get ready for school, no household chores, no lessons to prepare. Parents who are with their children primarily on weekends help if they make their relationship realistic, providing both good times and reasonable responsibilities. A child may be asked to help cook dinner or make the bed. Children need reasonable limits set at all times, and it is essential that parents do this for them on weekends, too. Children need opportunities to talk earnestly with both parents. When weekends become only a time for joking around and going places, the relationship is shallow. Both parents can strive to provide the children with limits, responsibilities, love, understanding, and good times.

A father was living with his nine-year-old daughter, Elena, for the first time in several years. Elena's parents had been divorced when she was one and a half years old, and during all of these years her father had seen her mainly for long vacation intervals. Their times together had always been very pleasant. They got along well, and he had never needed to do more than a minimum of limit setting. He realized that the situation had been quite unrealistic. They were both at their best during vacations—relaxed and easygoing. As Elena got older, he had begun to feel that somehow he was losing out on his opportunity to be a more complete father and that unless he could live with her on a more permanent basis before she reached her teens, something important would be missing in their relationship. As a result, this father arranged to have his daughter live with him for one year and possibly two. His former wife had agreed that this would work out well.

Now Elena and her father were about two months into their first year together. She kept commenting, "How come we don't always get along so easily now? We used to have a lot of good times." Actually, they were getting along very well, but since the father was now in a position of establishing necessary rules and limits, he could not always be the "good guy" anymore. He wondered how to discuss this with Elena.

Elena may be genuinely surprised at the change in her relationship with her father. She may well have fantasized this year as a total vacation, with no rules or responsibilities. She needs help to see that while she and her father are still the same people, different living circumstances will cause people to react in different ways. On a long vacation, one can afford to be more easygoing and permissive, but it is quite another matter when the father now has the responsibility for getting her to school on time each day, seeing that she does her homework, has a good night's sleep, cleans her room, and so on. The father also will have good days and days when he is tired out from work. Elena and her father need to establish a new balance in their relationship.

Elena's father can explain these things to his daughter. He can let her know that the new arrangement will allow them to know each other much better and more realistically. He can reassure her that there will certainly still be good times and remind her that even now most of their days together have been rewarding and enjoyable. He can make it clear that there will also be disagreements and rules, and that living together on a daily basis is different from being together while they are both on vacation. He might also point out that when she visits her mother, their times together will probably be smoother, with less of the organization of day-to-day life. It would be particularly valuable to mention that, for all the complications, he is glad for this change. He can tell her how much he is appreciating this chance to know her better, and that he enjoys the many moods, the learning, and the opportunities for mutual growth that an ongoing, daily parent-child relationship can afford.

A father had been divorced for one year and had joint custody with his ex-wife. The two children, ages four and nine, lived with him three days a week and with their mother the remaining four. They had all adjusted well to this arrangement, yet many friends and relatives criticized the parents for "bouncing the children back and forth like a ball." The father asked, "How can I counter their criticisms with appreciation for our situation?"

Currently more families are considering joint custody than in the past. This kind of shared parenthood can be successful when both parents are fully inclined to participate and arrange their lives accordingly. Many children are quite able to adjust to living in two households when it means a full, continued, caring relationship with both of their parents.

Children in this situation learn that their mother and father do some things differently, and they can accept this. Even in two-parent families, many mothers and fathers think and act differently on important issues. As long as the parents are able to communicate in a reasonable manner regarding the children's welfare, development, and daily issues, joint custody can be a satisfying arrangement.

It is possible that this man's critical friends and relatives were harboring a belief that men are not as well equipped to care for children as women are. Of course, this is untrue. Fortunately, society is starting to alter its views on this subject. More and more individuals are becoming aware that gender does not determine one's potential for parenting (or working), and that both men and women can learn the skills needed to be caring, constructive parents.

This father should not apologize for his choice, but be firm in explaining his position and the specific advantages that joint custody has for his family.

A mother said that when her husband had left her, she and her sixteen-year-old daughter, Tamara, had spent the first two months quarreling. One day, in the midst of a heated argument over a petty issue, the mother and daughter shared the revelation that they didn't want to be fighting with each other. Suddenly, they realized that it was Tamara's father they were angry at, and all this anger at him was coming out indirectly through their fights. They had a meaningful talk about this, and feelings that were too long kept inside were finally shared. After he left, Tamara's father had wanted her to come and see him, but she did not wish to do so. After talking things out with her mother, however, she felt that soon she might feel ready to resume a relationship with her father.

The next day, to her mother's surprise, Tamara came home with a punching bag. She explained that while it had been good to talk with her mother, she had also become aware of the strength of her anger and she just wanted to punch away!

The mother told her group that she, too, had found the punching bag useful and joined in on several occasions. She stressed the importance of recognizing one's own and one's children's feelings more immediately and not pretending that nothing has happened when, in fact, a major transformation of the family has occurred. She also pointed out that while talking is good, even a teenager or adult sometimes needs to turn to a more direct physical outlet for her feelings. The mother said that she and her daughter certainly continued to have the normal number of differences, but once they had openly dealt with the real issue, their usual rapport was re-tored.

It is so important to see that separations bring intense feelings. Ignoring them is not the answer. Parents and children need many direct opportunities to express their feelings, and talking is not always enough, as this sixteen-year-old so perceptively realized. For similar reasons, many teenagers throw themselves into sports. These physical outlets are a good way to get rid of tension due to pent-up feelings.

A mother had been divorced for two years and lived with her four-year-old son, Danny. Danny had always been an extremely verbal child who easily gave the impression of being older than his years. He and his mother had frequent deep and interesting conversations together. Danny's mother realized that sometimes she almost forgot her son was such a young child and began treating him as if he were a peer, expecting more grown-up behavior from him. Then she was surprised by some of his normal four-year-old behavior. To illustrate this, she related the following incident.

One day, Danny's mother noticed him playing with matches. She immediately took the matches away and explained the dangers involved. Several days later, she saw him playing with the matches again. She was honestly taken aback; she had thought that one explanation would be sufficient to curtail Danny's exploring.

It is often easy to fall prey to treating a child as more mature than he is when his verbal skills are high. It is fine to engage in stimulating talks together, but when it comes to other things, it is important to have appropriate expectations for his age.

After a divorce, it can sometimes be particularly tempting to treat a child like an adult to make up for adult companionship that may be lacking. This is true not only with highly verbal children; all single parents should be on the lookout for this occurrence. It's not beneficial to a child's development to make him into an adult companion, and it won't fulfill a parent's need to be in the company of other grownups. I suggest that all single parents make sure to set aside time to be with adult friends. This makes it easier to treat a child appropriately for his age and not place excessive demands on him. A four-year-old needs to be able to be a four-year-old and not feel that he is required to act like a grownup and meet expectations that are too high and, in fact, not emotionally healthy for him to meet.

This mother can take pride in her child's language capabilities and his interests, and still set the limits he needs to grow in a safe atmosphere. Though his self-control and conscience will work effectively for him a good deal of the time and will be improving steadily, at four he cannot yet be trusted to show self-control in a number of situations. He needs a mother's watchful support and guidance.

A father had been divorced when his daughter, Diane, was three, and he remarried when she was ten. Diane had always spent weekends with her father and continued to do so. Diane and her stepmother liked each other, yet the father could clearly see that Diane was very jealous of the new relationship. He wanted suggestions for dealing with her jealousy.

It is a good idea for this father to discuss openly the different kinds of love he feels for the important people in his life. His love for Diane is that of a father for a daughter, while his love for her stepmother is that of a husband for a wife, a grownup relationship. One love does not cancel out or diminish the other; there is plenty of love to go around.

At the same time, Diane's father can respect his daughter's feelings and acknowledge that it may be hard for her at first to get used to this marriage. He can express confidence that she will soon find it very satisfactory. He can also talk with her about the fact that meaningful relationships take time to develop. He can say that he is glad she and his wife get along well and that as time goes on they will probably become even closer. It is best for the father not to try and force a close relationship between them overnight, but to trust that this will steadily grow as his wife and daughter spend more time together and get to know each other in a natural way.

A mother explained that she had married young and that before her children were born, it had never occurred to her and her husband to discuss their views on child-rearing methods. Once their first child had reached toddlerhood, it was already obvious that their approach to discipline was quite different. She was comfortable with the more positive techniques, while her husband was a

yeller and hitter. It turned out that they also disagreed on other important life issues, and subsequently they got a divorce. Once she was on her own with two daughters, the mother became almost instantly aware of a more relaxed tone pervading her home. She attributed this primarily to her way of handling discipline.

Now the mother was dating again, but she had one major worry: She wondered if she would ever be able to find a partner who would fit in with her ways. She also wondered what to do if she met someone she cared about whose views were quite different. Was there anything she could do to influence his thinking and lead him to a more enlightened approach? She realized that one of the biggest mistakes she had made with her former husband was simply not to talk about child rearing, either before the children were born or after they came along, but just to be angry at each other's methods. Still, she felt that her fears were making her wary of all the men she met.

This woman had already alluded to a large part of the solution—talking things out together. Once a parent is involved with someone she feels quite serious about, it is definitely proper to bring up her concerns about child rearing. She can share her views and successes and listen to her friend's ideas. This way, she will discover if this is someone who is willing to open up and share his views or not. If he isn't amenable to this kind of sharing, she might begin to wonder how open he would be for discussions on other important issues. If he is willing to discuss his opinions and listen to hers, that is a good start.

If the two of them don't agree with each other's methods at first, there is still plenty of room for change, as long as the willingness exists to listen to each other and think things through together. It makes a difference if he is someone coming to child rearing totally fresh, with no children of his own and no backlog of child-related experiences, or if he has children and is therefore familiar with their daily life issues. Someone new to children would need time just to get used to being around them, at the same time that he is discovering the constructive methods for dealing with the problems that arise. Someone who has his own children would most likely be more tuned in to the inherent joys and headaches of parenting, but would need time to think through changing his techniques. He would not be able to change overnight, but if he has an open mind, the couple could work at this together. They would also need to work at getting to know each other's children.

This mother need not strive to agree on all issues with the man she dates; this is not realistic. If she and her future partner can come to mutual terms concerning a common philosophy and set of methods, then the situations in which they won't see eye to eye can more easily be tolerated or else be good ground for compromise. I suggested that she also remember that this can be a two-way street. The man she meets may well be doing a number of positive things she isn't. Ideally, they will learn from each other and work together to create a healthy, loving, and positive atmosphere in the new home they create.

CHAPTER 10

#

Helping Children Deal with Death, as a Part of Life

> *All children are naturally curious about death. Their questions deserve thoughtful and honest answers. Children have feelings about death too, and adults can help them to clarify their emotions and concerns. When someone children have known dies, they need the chance to mourn their loss. We cannot protect children from their feelings, but by allowing them to share the experience of grieving, we can help them begin to heal their sorrow and embrace life once again.*

Is it helpful to protect young children from a family's experience with death, in an effort to keep them in the state of "happy childhood" a bit longer, or is it best to include children at these times and share information and feelings with them?

Today there are still many adults who believe that childhood is a carefree time of complete happiness. It is true that young children don't yet have the responsibilities that go with maturity, but childhood nonetheless combines pleasant and stressful times. It is a time of growth, learning, and integrating many kinds of experience. All children fall and scrape their knees, need to separate from their parents to go to school, get rejected by friends. Even unpleasant events help to make a child stronger and more able to cope with the varied experiences of life. A parent's job is not to make a child constantly happy, but to help to build her character.

Death is part of life. Death is sad, and sometimes we fear it, yet parents and children can learn to deal with death honestly together. When adults discuss death with a young child in a calm and accepting way, she can accept death matter-of-factly. When they discuss death with panic or avoid the subject altogether, the child may begin to suspect that it is too difficult to come to terms with death. Anything we hush up for children may be more confusing and scary than what we share with them.

Children often ask questions about death. Sometimes when a close friend or family member is dying or has recently died, they will try to understand what has happened. Parents should not avoid questions about death. They need to give truthful, accurate answers in a reassuring way to children, at a level they can understand.

Children need to know that all people and animals die someday and that death means they won't be seeing that person or animal again. It is realistic and sensible to inform children that sometimes people die young because of a serious illness or accident, but that most people die when they are old and usually parents and children have nice long lives to live together. I feel it is important to instill in children a belief in their longevity, for this will carry them through their daily lives with optimism, looking forward to each new day.

It is helpful to discuss with children, in simple language, the physical symptoms of someone they know and see who is dying. Children notice things, and changes due to illness can be confusing and scary. Talking about these kinds of changes minimizes fearful fantasy. It is important, too, to distinguish between the kind of sickness that gets better, like chicken pox or a cold, and a more serious illness that can lead to death, so young children won't think that being sick means they are going to die. Because children might still worry about becoming seriously ill themselves, it is helpful to reassure them that the chances for that occurring are very small, that the parent isn't even concerned about it, and that the child need not be concerned about it either.

Reading children's stories about death also can help them to integrate any personal experience they're having and to understand more about death in general. *When People Die* by Joanne Bernstein and Stephen Gullo (E. P. Dutton) and *About Dying: An Open Family Book for Parents and Children Together* by Sara Bonnett Stein (Walker & Co.) are two books that explain death in clear and moving prose, illustrated with tasteful photographs. Younger children will also like the storybooks *First Snow* by Helen Coutant (Alfred A. Knopf), *My Grandson Lew* by Charlotte Zolotow (Harper & Row), and *The Tenth Good Thing About Barney* by Judith Viorst (Atheneum).

Children often have many fears, fantasies, and feelings involving death. These are likely to emerge when someone close to the family dies. When my husband's mother, Anne, was dying, Joshua was four. Many of his thoughts about death surprised us, and so did his ability to grieve.

Joshua was attempting to figure out how his grandmother got the terminal disease she had. He shared with me his fantasy that some trees had this disease and others didn't. Grandma, he believed, had climbed a tree that had this disease and she had caught it. I responded that I saw he was trying to figure this out and then went on to discuss how the disease might really have started.

Joshua also expressed fears about death. After returning from a visit to his grandma, he mentioned to one of his teachers that he was so glad to leave Wisconsin before any of us (his mother, father, brother, or himself) caught Grandma's disease. It had not occurred to me to assure Joshua that this illness is not the type that is spread by germs. Fortunately, his teacher shared this incident with us, so we were able to reassure Joshua. During the whole time that Grandma was dying, the adults in our family all expressed our feelings openly. Like us, Joshua loved Grandma Anne dearly. He was able to say, "I'm so sad, I'll miss her so much," or "I'm so angry and upset, I don't want her to die," because he knew it was okay to talk about feelings. He also was introduced to the words and phrases to use for these feelings as he listened to the grownups around him. When parents don't include children at these times, then children not only cannot express their own emotions, but also don't become familiar with the language through which these feelings can be expressed.

Many adults will talk about feelings with their children but think it is weak to cry in front of them. This is not so. Adults are strong when they share strong feelings with their children. Crying helps us to heal. Children should be able to share our grief and express their own. Crying can be warm and intimate, and can bring parents and children closer together during troubled times.

Another reason to allow children to share our experiences with death is that it can create for them memories of intimate times and relationships. Since Joshua knew that his grandmother was dying and that there weren't too many times left to be with her, he made the most of the time there was. Joshua read to Grandma, told her stories, told her he loved her very much and would miss her so much, held her hand, kissed her cheeks, and even talked with her about her sickness and coming death, uttering his hope that the doctors would still be able to figure out how to fix her up. Grandma also talked with him about life and death. These times together were preparing Joshua for the actual death and helping him to integrate intense emotions and a difficult experience. He would always have these intimate, loving talks with his grandma to cherish and remember. These times were also helping Grandma say good-bye to Joshua.

After Grandma Anne actually did die, Joshua continued to express his feelings and confusion. He checked out all of the rooms of her house and looked under all the chairs to make sure she was really not alive. Though a child knows someone has died, it can still be hard to accept the finality. Adults should never ridicule children for these expressions, but help them by showing understanding of how hard it can be to accept that someone we loved has really died. Joshua said that he wished Grandma could be a statue so that he would be able to see her all the time, and again expressed his anger that he could not be with her anymore, and also his feelings of sadness and unhappiness. If Joshua had been excluded from our family's experience with death, he would have had to keep these feelings to himself.

When children are not expressing their feelings, yet we know they are stirred up, it is good for parents to help them by saying, for example, "You miss Grandma so much" or "You used to do so many nice things with Grandma; let's talk about them" or "Sometimes you feel so angry that Grandma died and are very unhappy." Older children as well as younger ones often need help in expressing their feelings. Parents should encourage all of their children to speak about what's on their minds and in their hearts, so that they can gain comfort and clarification from the grownups around them.

Joshua's grief was immediate, but sometimes children have a delayed reaction. Their feelings don't show up right away and we think they are untouched, but then strong emotions surface later. A certain death may not, in fact, involve them as deeply as another, of course, but parents still need to provide their children with helpful information and an open atmosphere in which feelings and questions are welcomed and can be exchanged.

Sometimes parents experience the death of a friend or family member and don't allow their very young children to share in the experience. They briefly tell a child what's happening, but then go on to pretty much ignore him. I did this myself when Joshua was two and a half and a close family friend was dying. Another mother did this when her father was dying and her son was four years old. We felt that our children weren't really aware of what was going on and we might as well not kindle any flames. We were both wrong. About a year later, when I finally realized the importance of sharing these kinds of experiences with children, I found out that my son at three and a half had plenty of questions and concerns about our friend's illness and death. The other mother discovered that her son, too, had many hidden questions and concerns about his grandfather that he finally felt free to bring up when she gave him the green light to do so.

Children sense a parent's openness or lack of it. Both of these children had kept their cares to themselves until their parents revealed to them it was okay to talk about these things. Then came an outpouring of questions, concerns, feelings, and ideas that needed to be clarified and finally could be. Both children remembered very specific things involving the death which adults assumed they had not noticed. My son recalled that our friend's features had changed as a result of his illness and began to ask many questions about these physical changes. For a year he had carried around worries and fears and confusions that had gone unclarified. He even remembered that we had given our friend a record, placing it on his bed, and wanted to know if he had died with the record on his bed.

The other mother also began to talk with her son about his grandfather's death about a year after the event. She wanted to help her son go back and recall the death and integrate it better. She also wanted to help him understand more about death in general. One day she pointed out to him a beautiful sunflower growing in their garden. She told her son (then five years old) that in about two months the flower would die. When this finally occurred, the son took the flower and buried it in the garbage. His mother then talked with him of her own belief of what happens to living beings after death. She said that though people and plants and animals die, they still live on in the memories of those who are living who loved them. "Where would the flower live on?" she asked her son. He pointed to his head and then said, "Papa [his grandfather] is in there too!" This was a beautiful sharing between mother and son.

While Joshua was four and a half during his grandmother's illness, Jesse was two years and four months. Having learned from our experience when Joshua was this age how much death can affect a two-year-old, we made sure that Jesse was free to observe the family crying and expressing grief. It was hard at first to talk with him directly about his grandmother's illness and coming death (showing just how hard it is to do what we know is right), but finally I did begin to talk with him about what he was observing. At first he didn't share any of his feelings or ideas with me, though he was a very verbal two-year-old. I knew, however, that he was absorbing a lot at his own level and probably needed some time to take it all in. Very young children can understand much more than they can usually verbalize, so talking with a two-year-old or with an even younger child can accomplish much more than we realize.

After Grandma Anne's death, the family gathered together at her home. Several times Jesse looked around and said that he wanted to kiss Grandma. My husband and I continued to talk with him about the fact that Grandma had been sick and had died and that we weren't going to be able to see her anymore. We cried and expressed our sadness with him, and also acknowledged how hard it was for him to want to kiss Grandma and not be able to. Once when Jesse noticed me looking sad he said, "Are you sad, Mom?" I said that I was and told him why. For several evenings during this time I would begin to cry as I rocked Jesse to sleep. He would ask me why I was crying and I would explain that it was because Grandma had died. One evening when I wasn't crying as I rocked Jesse to sleep, he looked up at me and said, "You're crying?" I said that I wasn't crying. Jesse continued, "What's the matter?" I said nothing was the matter and that I was okay. Then Jesse said, "Because Grandma died?" So we talked about the fact that I had cried for several evenings as I'd rocked him to sleep because I was so unhappy that Grandma had died and that we wouldn't be able to see her anymore. One afternoon Jesse looked up at me and said, "Grandma Anne died like this," and he put his arms out wide and tilted his head back as he does when he pretends to be dead in his own "bang-bang" dying games. In his own two-year-old way he was showing us that he was beginning to understand what was going on around him.

I hope all this will encourage parents to include their children in the death experiences their families encounter. Children need our protection from unanswered concerns or fears and for the difficult and often new feelings they're facing. We protect them best by sharing feelings and information with them, and by being there to guide them through these times. It is hard for us, too, to face our feelings, but talking and crying together can bring parents and children closer to each other.

One mother found it too difficult to tell her five-year-old daughter that an elderly friend of the family had died. So she told her daughter that Papa, as they called him, had gone on vacation. The mother wanted to know if this was a helpful way of handling the situation.

Children are quick to pick up the messages their parents are trying to hide from them. It is most likely that this child sensed some concern and anxiety, and knew that something was not going along just as usual. In fact, the daughter might even have overheard that this man had died or she might have suspected it on her own. Parents do not help children by keeping this kind of information from them. Instead of getting a chance to absorb the correct information and then be able to deal effectively with fears, fantasies, or feelings that might arise as a result, they remain confused. If a child sees that her parents will not discuss death with her, she may conclude that death must really be a terrible thing if the adults around cannot even bring themselves to talk about it.

Incorrect information can lead to future complications. If this child was aware that the man had died (because she had overheard the hush-ups), yet she was told by her mother that he had gone on vacation, she might well be terrified the next time someone in her family was going on vacation, assuming that going on vacation means a person will die or has died! Children need correct information and the help and guidance of adults close to them to help them absorb, integrate, and deal with the truth.

A father wanted to know if it is appropriate to take children to a wake and to the cemetery.

If the children were not close to the person who died, then I do not believe they need to attend the wake or funeral, but if the person was someone important to them, then I feel it is healthy for them to be included. Death is part of life. Children feel more comfortable being with those they love at these times, than being away from them. When my mother-in-law died, our two sons came with us to the temple service and to the cemetery. They weren't quiet and reserved all of the time, either. They stayed with us and were deeply moved one moment, and played around like kids the next. But they were included and this was important. We were showing them that we knew their grandma's death was just as important for them as it was for us and that we all needed to say good-bye together. There is a helpful finality about the cemetery and it can be a good way for children to say good-bye.

Children can bring grownups comfort at these times. At the cemetery I held Jesse in my arms and he kept wiping my eyes and telling me everything was okay. It was very soothing to have him near me. Dick and Joshua stood together, holding hands. Though it is difficult for all of us, grownups and children, to take leave of those we love, it is easier to do this together, sharing feelings, comfort, and courage.

Some parents have disagreed with me about wakes, saying it is not appropriate to bring young children. Parents know their own children and have a feeling for how they'd react, and so much depends on the parents' attitude. If a wake is a part of your tradition and you gain comfort from it, then you may wish to include your children.

When Sam was three years old his great-grandfather died. Sam wanted to know what would happen to him now that he had died. "Will he be put into the garbage?" Sam asked.

Children need accurate information. Even a three-year-old can be told that after a person dies, his body is put into a coffin ("a special box") that is buried in the ground. Some people choose to be cremated, and this, too, can be explained to the child.

Curiosity about details that seem morbid to us is natural for children. They may want to know what happens to the body in the grave, about bones or dead animals they may see on the road. We need to listen with respect and then give them information that will be helpful. Children are searching for information and truth. They are not being morbid; they are trying to figure out the world around them.

Families have different beliefs about life after death. One father wanted to know how we should go about explaining to children what takes place after death.

It is as important to help children build an understanding of death on a spiritual level as it is to help them come to terms with it in a personal and emotional way. I believe each parent should share with his children his own beliefs. He can share what comforts him and also listen to his children's views. Children often have their own ideas and thoughts about what lies ahead, and their thinking should be respected, never ridiculed. Children can often have profound insights into life and the universe, and they can teach us too.

It is valuable to explain to children that other people believe different things and describe some of these other beliefs. Children can accept that not everyone thinks alike about this. Eventually, they will decide for themselves what seems right to them.

One mother was concerned about her son's reaction to the death of his grandfather's dog. The son seemed to be revealing a fear of death and dying and said to his mother all day long, "I don't want to die!" The mother, instead of reassuring him, seemed to be taking on his fear. She, too, began feeling worried and anxious much of the time and felt unable to calm her son.

Parents and children are separate people. Parents help children when they reflect, understand, and sympathize with their children's feelings, not when they make the child's feelings their own. It is very important that when the issue of death arises, the parent's attitude be calm and accepting, not fearful. Here, the mother would be helpful if she showed her son that we can come to terms with death. She should let him know that she has accepted the fact that all people and animals do eventually die, but also that life is meaningful and chances are she and her son will have a long life to live together. When the son said, "I don't want to die," the mother could have calmly answered something like "I can understand that" or "I feel that way sometimes too." She could also discuss how the unknown quality of death can be scary to think about and she can share her thoughts about what happens after death. She can handle these issues in a comforting way. It is not helpful for the son if the mother becomes anxious along with him, as this can only add to his fears.

One night right before bedtime when Joshua was four, he asked me, "Do eyes die?" I didn't want to get into a conversation with him about death before his bedtime, thinking it might disturb his sleep, so I answered, "No." Of course, my answer was ridiculous and my son responded by saying, "Of course eyes die, Mom. They die when people die!"

What if Joshua had believed my answer? Then, indeed, he might have gone to sleep with something to worry about! He might have pondered all night about the fact that people die, but their eyes do not. It made me realize that it is best to give children truthful information, even before bedtime. Perhaps I might have been smarter to have said, "Let's discuss it tomorrow morning," if I really felt it was not a topic best discussed right before bedtime; but giving wrong information to children is hardly appropriate. I was thankful he corrected me and did not need to go to bed with confusions about this on his mind. I saw that it was my worry that Joshua couldn't handle a discussion of dying before his bedtime, not his.

When a person a child knows well or is close to dies, should the child be told the circumstances causing the person's death?
I believe children should be told how the person died—whether of an illness, accident, suicide, or old age. Sometimes a child may become angry at a parent, grandparent, sibling, or friend, and in her moment of anger might think, for example, "I wish my grandpa was dead!" Two minutes later the girl is once again happily playing with her grandfather, but if three weeks later the grandfather dies, she may feel that her thought caused his death. Young children can't distinguish very well between thoughts and actual events. It is therefore important for them to learn the real causes of a person's death so they will not blame themselves or harbor guilt feelings and scary thoughts.

A child may at some time encounter the death of another child. She may identify more strongly with another child than with an older person and be afraid that she, too, will die soon. She will need to know the real reason for the death, be it illness or accident, and she needs to be reassured that it is very unlikely the same thing will happen to her. She is probably experiencing a combination of feelings: sadness, anger, confusion, loss, abandonment, and perhaps some guilt that she was spared while the other child died. All these feelings need expression and clarification from an adult who will listen and provide comfort along with appropriate and truthful information about the causes of the death.

A mother had a miscarriage after six months of pregnancy and she and her husband had wanted to know how to explain this to their three-year-old daughter. They consulted two pediatricians who both said to tell the daughter it was all a mistake; they had thought the mother was pregnant, but found out later she wasn't. The parents followed this suggestion, but did not feel comfortable about giving inaccurate information.

Much later, they were together in a parents' group and they asked me if I knew a better way to have dealt with this. They were especially concerned because the mother was pregnant again. The questions this pregnancy was raising for their daughter made them want to make all the issues clearer for her.

Again, I emphasize that it is necessary to be truthful with young children. They need to understand what has really happened so they can process their emotions as well as the truthful information. I suggested that the parents tell her that there really had been a baby growing inside her mother; she had really been pregnant. They can explain that usually babies grow for nine months and then are born, but occasionally a baby stops growing and dies.

The child's parents went home and gave their daughter this explanation. She said to them, "That makes me very sad. It's a sad story." Her parents answered that it had been sad for them also. The girl talked on and off during the day about "the little baby who died." For the first time, her parents had been able to share the truth and their real feelings about this pregnancy, and she could share her feelings with them. The parents felt tremendous relief.

The girl had many questions about the new baby growing. Her parents explained that most likely they would have a healthy, full-term baby, but there was a small chance of another miscarriage. Throughout life, adults and children have to live with ambiguity; we cannot always know the outcome. Talking truthfully will help the child to feel optimistic, yet give her a realistic idea of the possibilities.

At his father's death, an extremely painful and sad event for the entire family, a five-year-old boy showed sadness and anger. For several months there was more than the normal amount of misbehavior on his part. The boy's mother was very understanding. She accepted her son's misbehavior as an expression of his deep hurt, loss, and confusion. She knew it would take this young child time to absorb and adjust to the death and the inevitable changes in the life of the family.

It is not uncommon for children to misbehave and act up, even to act silly, when someone close to them dies. Death can evoke strong feelings in children and strong confusions. They need time to readjust. It's helpful when parents understand that children are not being malicious or insensitive, but that they are adjusting to the new feelings and the changes in their young lives that a significant death will cause.

A young child experiencing the death of a parent (or sibling, grandparent, or best friend) often feels angry at the world or at God for letting this happen, and also may be angry at the person who died, thinking he abandoned him on purpose. It is important to help children express their anger so it is not bottled up inside.

The five-year-old boy cried when his father died, but afterward he also cried over things that normally wouldn't upset him. It was difficult for him to express all of his feelings at one time. His tears came out when no one expected them, over things that appeared to be insignificant. However, his mother understood and would help him out at these times by holding him and comforting him saying, "I know. We all miss Daddy so much. It's so hard."

Adults and children often harbor guilt feelings when someone they've been close to dies, thinking about the things they'd done or said in the past that might have hurt the person who died, and thinking about things they never said or did, but wished they had. It is helpful to get these kinds of feelings out in the open too. A grownup can recall with a child the fun and good, loving times he had with the person who died, and can also help the child remember times he was angry or annoyed at the person. The mother in the above situation could talk with her son about how he used to love it when his father made him pancakes on Sunday mornings, and how he hated it when his daddy would make him go to bed on time. Recalling the past like this accepts the reality of the past and the richness of life. Sharing memories and strong feelings together allows children to heal and go on to embrace life anew, while keeping the loved person alive in memory.

A mother said that her husband had died when her daughter was two. The daughter, now eight, mentions to her mother quite often that she feels cheated, because her brothers, who are several years older, got the chance to be with their father for more years than she did. The mother was not sure how to deal with her daughter's feelings.

The daughter is expressing her feelings of anger. Her brothers did get to live with their father for longer than she did and consequently had many more memories of him to savor. Her brothers were five and eight years old when their father died, and they had within them a much stronger vision of their father.

It would be helpful if the mother acknowledged her daughter's anger, her feeling cheated, and let her know that these feelings are acceptable. This might help to relieve them. The mother might also help her daughter to remember the kinds of things the daughter and father did together, to help her daughter focus also on some of the nice times and feelings she shared with her father, when he helped to care for her and play with her when she was a baby and toddler.

A mother explained that her son was two and a half years old when his father died. The death was sudden and unexpected, and the mother went into shock for several days. The son was left with a friend of his mother's and didn't see his mother again until about four days after his father's death, when his mother came out of shock. The son is now seven years old. His mother is surprised that her son remembers back that far and that he keeps on recalling "those scary days" when his father died and he didn't see his mother for four days.

When an event is very significant, a child's memory can be very keen, especially the memories of the feelings involved, even if not all of the specific events. The mother was in shock and couldn't help what had happened, but losing his father and being separated from his mother made a strong imprint on the child. His mother talks with him about what happened and he can understand now why she went into shock and why he was left with her friend. She thought that after a while he wouldn't need to talk about this anymore and is surprised at his persistence. When people experience such intense times in their lives, it is more often the case that they do need to talk about their feelings and the events sporadically throughout their lives. These kinds of feelings don't just get expressed and then put away forever. They keep popping up, and it is healthy and good that this should happen. This mother said that her son, though only seven years old, was a very "deep" person. Since his father's death, he had never seemed the same to her, but had an added quality of strength and depth.

Parents ask how to handle the death of a pet.
If a child's pet animal dies, the parent shouldn't hurry out immediately and buy a new one. The death of a pet may be a child's first

experience with death, and through it the child can be helped to learn that death is a normal part of life. It is valuable to give the child time to feel sad. The child may wish to bury the pet, and this is fine if it is possible. After the child's feelings of grief have been expressed and subsided, it would be fine to get a new pet if she wants one.

Children are often exposed to death and violence on TV. Much of the death on TV is fictional, but a good deal of it is real, in the news. Parents want to know how to help children (especially young ones) deal with this and whether they should limit a child's viewing of violent material.
Certainly parents should limit TV time, but most children will be exposed to some violence on TV, whether it is real or simulated. In the case of a show that is not real, young children can be told that the person is an actor or actress who has not really died, but will go home to his or her family; the person is just playing a part. If the action is portraying a true episode (the story of Lincoln, for instance), the parent can explain that the actor is not really dying, but that the real person in history died that way. Parents should shelter young children from some of the violence in the news, as it can be difficult to deal with, but these kinds of events are unfortunately part of our world and even young children will learn about some of them. We can let them know that these are very sad occurrences and that we are hoping to see a better, more peaceful world within their lifetimes.

CHAPTER 11

Independence and Interdependence

Setting the Stage for Children to Become Responsible Adults Who Will Live Cooperatively with Others

Children do not remain helpless infants for long. They soon grow into independent individuals, different from their parents in many ways, each following her or his own road toward the future. Parents can't create their children's destinies, but they can help them to move forward with confidence by encouraging self-reliance at all appropriate opportunities. Many ways to do this are discussed in this chapter. Parents can also foster an awareness of the spirit of cooperation that is needed among independent individuals, so children will learn to get along well with others at the same time that they develop personal strength. In a family, this shows up most clearly when it comes to household chores and responsibilities. This issue is therefore considered in several situations in this chapter.

Every day, a father would ask his three-year-old daughter what she had done in nursery school. Her answer was always the same: "I played." Her father was genuinely interested in her day and felt frustrated that she wouldn't tell more.

Children (and adults) often need time to digest experiences before they wish to talk about them. The father may have more success later on in the day, or he may find that she will bring up the really important events at some time of her own choosing. This is also quite often the case with older children returning from school or camp, or teenagers returning home from dates.

This father was able to share with the group how hard it is for him to accept that his daughter has a life completely apart from his. She is, in fact, a totally separate person, and throughout her life, though she will be sharing much with him, there will be things she'll be keeping completely to herself. Parents are like this, too. We share a good deal with our children, but not everything. Children benefit from an attitude that says "If you'd like to tell me such and such, I'd be glad to hear it." In this way, they see they can share with their parents what they are comfortable sharing, but are under no pressure to do so.

A girl of almost three did not like to spend any time playing alone. Her mother played all day with her and never got any time for herself. She thought maybe the girl was just unusually sociable and it would be cruel to force her to play more independently.

It's true that some children and adults have a greater need than others to socialize, but it is also healthy to enjoy some time alone. Sooner or later, this mother will resent never having any time to do her tasks or just relax, and the time spent with her daughter will become unpleasant for both. She needs to develop confidence that asking her daughter to play alone at times is fair and reasonable. A parent's attitude is usually sensed by a child. If the mother can feel comfortable making this request, knowing that the girl won't wither away with loneliness (she won't), then the child can begin to see that if Mother isn't concerned, then maybe it's actually okay to play alone. That doesn't mean she will love the idea right away, but it is a change she can manage.

Her mother can help her by providing a gentle transition. While they are together she can say, "Now we're going to play together, but after this story I will need time to do some other things." The mother can help the girl decide what she will play with while she's alone, and she can even get her started at it. Later, when the child becomes more comfortable with this arrangement, she can decide without her mother's help how she will use her time.

A father who was a doctor often brought home hospital equipment for his three-year-old daughter to play with. Several doctors he knew had been telling him that this wasn't a good thing to do. They remembered how their own parents had pushed them to be doctors and felt this man was falling into the same pattern. He wanted to know if bringing home stethoscopes and bandages for his child to play with was actually pushing her into a doctor's career.

Preschoolers engage in imaginative play where they try on many adult roles to figure out what this world is all about. This girl can feel close to her father as she shares in his world by playing doctor. Having real stethoscopes to use in her play is a great asset. I do not feel that this man was getting good advice from his friends. It would be sad if he were to shut her out of his world and not encourage her interest. What is important is if the father's attitude allows the child to choose her own interests in life. This father said, "Well, I actually wouldn't be unhappy if she were a doctor." That's fine, and if she shows an interest in medicine, she deserves his enthusiastic encouragement and support, just as she does if her interest is welding, law, or homemaking.

A mother tried to encourage her fifteen-year-old daughter to come to a diet workshop with her and met with adamant refusals. Then a friend of the mother's invited the girl to the workshop and received her delighted acceptance.

As children get older, they look for adult models other than their own parents. Though parents desire to be an influence on their growing children, and should be, in certain situations it is wise to let other grownups help out. It is good to encourage relationships with many adults throughout childhood. Teenagers will more likely turn to someone they've known throughout their growing years, whether grandparents, aunts, uncles, or family friends.

A woman and her husband were having a very difficult time giving their six-year-old son, Dan, responsibility appropriate to his age. For example, if he walked down the block to a friend's house, they would nervously watch him go, not trusting him to get there on his own. They didn't allow him to cross nearby quiet streets by himself, and in many other ways were failing to provide opportunities for him to develop self-confidence. What's more, Dan was aware that his friends were doing these things with the support and trust of their parents. How can parents begin to give up their fears?

It would be difficult for the parents to give up their hold overnight, but they can begin slowly to take steps to overcome their fears. They could start by letting their son go down their own block or across a quiet street to a friend's while they deliberately stay indoors. To allay their fears, they could ask him to call when he has arrived. After a few times, the parents will trust Dan's competence and gradually allow him to go greater distances on his own.

When it comes to crossing the street, the parents can make sure Dan knows the rules for safety and they can watch him cross until they are sure he is trustworthy. If, while observing him, they ever see him cross carelessly, then they should review with him the right way to cross, still letting him know they are confident he will remember. If he is still careless after several reminders, then they will know he is not yet ready for this particular privilege even though some of his friends are. They can let him know they understand how hard it is to wait, and just as soon as they feel he is ready, he will have these privileges too.

A general rule is that the child's readiness should determine his privileges. The parents' exaggerated concerns should not hold him back, and peer pressures should not push him forward before he is ready.

While the parents are helping Dan to branch out, they can deal with their own fears. They can tell themselves, each other, and their friends how hard this is for them, how afraid they are to see their son grow up and face the world alone. By acknowledging these feelings, they can learn to express their fears, but not act on them to the detriment of their son's development.

A mother allowed her three-and-a-half-year-old son to pour his own juice. At times he'd pour perfectly, but at other times he'd spill. Should she let him go ahead and do this anyway, or would it be better to wait until he can do it competently more of the time?

Children learn by doing. This child won't want to pour every time he has juice, but when he does want to, he should be given the chance. This way he will increase in coordination, skill, and confidence. The mother can help him by filling the container halfway or getting a smaller container. He will have spills, but children need to make mistakes, they learn from them just as we do. Parents should give their children trust and the message that it feels good to be responsible and capable. When a three-year-old spills juice, or an eight-year-old burns a scrambled egg, or a fourteen-year-old doesn't make the chicken just so, what he needs is our praise and encouragement for wanting to learn how to do these things and some help with how to proceed. Each time, he will become more adept.

Parents report the wonderful feeling of having their five-year-old bring them sandwiches he's made or their ten-year-old bringing them eggs and toast in bed. Dick and I enjoy sleeping an extra half-hour on Saturday morning while Jesse and Joshua are getting their own cereal. Children, too, feel good about learning, and proud when their parents acknowledge their growing steps.

One thing to keep in mind is that each child in the family needs chances to become responsible. I often hear that at five years a child was setting the table and pouring her own milk, but when her younger sister reached five, she was not being asked to do these things; the parent was still asking the older child. Remember to allow each child to begin to do what she can; every child needs plenty of chances to learn skills and develop confidence.

Sometimes young children become frustrated because they want to do something like zip a jacket, but just cannot get the zipper to hook. In these kinds of situations, how much should parents do?

It is most helpful for parents to just do the one part of the process that is at the moment too hard and then encourage the child to do the rest. In this particular case, the parent can connect the zipper and let the child zip it up. Then he can feel a sense of achievement. The parent can also set aside time to help him practice connecting the zipper, and then one day, behold, he will get it!

We should remember that there will be other days when he may want us to do the entire process, connect the zipper and zip it up, and that is fine. By giving children help when they want it, we fortify them to proceed on their own once again. Older children and adults are this way too. Most of us can cook, yet we enjoy going out to dinner and having someone else cook for us on occasion.

"I am having a hard time with my son because he's too independent," said a mother. What did she mean by this? For the first five years of his life, this mother had let him try to do most things on his own, and as a result he became extremely competent. At five years old he enjoyed making his own sandwiches, setting up projects for himself, and structuring his own time. In the past, this mother had had the time to encourage her son and also to help him clean up after his endeavors. Recently, the mother's life had changed. She had returned to school and had obligations of her own to fulfill. She had less time now and less patience to encourage her son's creativity, for this usually meant that she'd be needed to help out in some way with the cleanup. The mother felt bad about her new feelings of impatience.

It is certainly commendable that this mother had offered her son many opportunities for his growth and development, but now she had other needs that were equally important. This doesn't mean the mother's needs should replace the son's, but a balance of needs would be helpful. The mother could explain to her son that there were times and days she could allow him to set up projects and make his own sandwiches, since she'd be available to help in the cleanup, but that other days she had her own work to do and needed to make the sandwiches herself, and it would be necessary for him to get involved in less elaborate activities. Her son will still have many chances for his independence to be nurtured. By creating a balance of needs, she will stifle neither her son's needs nor her own.

Jared, nine, and his sister, Jennie, who was five, had been invited to a late movie with their friend and his mother. Since the show was too late for Jennie, their father said he'd take her to the afternoon show of the same movie in a few days. This was okay with Jennie, but Jared wanted to go to the afternoon show as well as the late one. His father said that he couldn't go to both shows but he could choose which he'd prefer. Jared began to have an all-out tantrum.

Jared's mother said she understood it would be nice for him to see the movie twice, but repeated that it wasn't possible and he needed to make a choice. She went on, "It can be very hard to make choices sometimes. Take a little while to think about it." Jared stormed out into the hall while his mother stood by supportively, again saying how hard it was to decide and to take his time thinking about what he wanted to do. In a few minutes Jared said, "I'll go to the night movie!" His mother said, "Great, that'll be fun for you to be out so much later than usual; that's a good decision."

Jared's mother had been annoyed by his behavior and felt tempted to cancel both movies, but knew that decision-making skills need to be learned and stood by Jared as he struggled with his choice.

It is good to give children practice making choices. It may surprise us to see how they will struggle to choose between the gum and the candy bar, or agonize over which friend to invite home or which book to buy. Even if the issue seems trivial to us, it can be important to the child. We help most by saying, "It's hard to decide, isn't it? Take a minute to think." These are the child's beginning steps at decision making. We must respect the effort and struggle involved in thinking things through and making a choice.

A twelve-year-old boy always asked his mother to remind him about hockey practice, and she did, but resentfully, as she felt he was old enough to remember the practice himself. One day she took a new approach. When her son asked her to remind him she replied, "I know it can be hard to remember on your own. But I know you. You'll find a good way to remind yourself." He did remember, but it was hard for the mother to make this change. Later, in her group, she wondered if she did the right thing. Was she asking too much of him?

It is almost always appropriate for parents to help their older children learn to take responsibility for themselves. This boy showed just how ready he was by, in fact, remembering the practice with ease. His mother can reinforce his competence by commenting how good he must feel now to do this by himself.

On the other hand, if he were having trouble getting there on time, she could have discussed various ways to remember things, like keeping a calendar, writing notes and leaving them somewhere obvious, or using an alarm clock. Parents can even help a child to set up these aids at first, but there is no need to be as directly involved in his routine as this woman had been.

In order to see that her nine-year-old son got his homework done, one mother took to organizing his evening routine. Her son wasn't happy with this arrangement and as a protest was doing less homework than before.

The mother decided to help develop her son's autonomy in the situation. She told him that from now on, as long as the TV was off and lights were out for bedtime by 9:30, she'd expect him on his own to decide when to get his homework done, when to watch TV, when to feed the cat, and when to do other things. If he needed help from her, she would be willing to give it to him, but she let him know that she felt he could do his own structuring and was capable of organizing his time properly now that he was getting older. The son seemed satisfied and said to his mother, "Are you a philosopher, Mommy?"

Another mother didn't organize her daughter's routine, but found herself constantly reminding Beth about her Hebrew school homework. The daughter resented these reminders.

I suggested that this mother leave the sphere of homework responsibility solely to her child. If her daughter ever neglected her work, then she'd receive the natural consequences of her action in Hebrew school. Her teacher could then work out the issue with her. It is often more effective for children to learn for themselves what the consequence of their actions will be than for parents to try to make sure those consequences don't occur.

The mother should inform Beth that she is changing by saying something like "I know you hate me to remind you of your homework, so I have decided not to do it anymore. It is really your job, and I know you'll get it done without my reminders." This way the mother gives her daughter something better than reminders—she gives her faith in her ability to remember and do her homework on time, and trust in her self-reliance. If children occasionally want parents to remind them and help get them started, they can, but more and more, as children get older, it is wise to offer them chances to help themselves.

A family was having terrible fights because the twelve-year-old son was consistently coming home after his curfew. If the father said to be home by 9:00, his son would come in at 9:15 and the father would be enraged.

Many parents find themselves stuck in battles of the minute. Instead of asking children to be home on the gong of nine or ten or midnight, like Cinderella, it can help to be more flexible, adjusting the time to the occasion. If the movie gets out at 8:30, the parent can expect him home *around* 9:00, and if he will be late for any reason, he should know to call home. A parent shouldn't be home worrying while the child is out having a good time. Parents deserve to enjoy their evening too.

Many parents have found that when they put trust in their children, they generally find the trust is well taken. If a child is home very near to the expected time, a matter of a few minutes shouldn't be cause to create a major scene. One mother recalled her teenage years when her parents would say to come home when a party or movie was over (within a reasonably acknowledged time) and that she and her brothers and sisters always did. There were no terrible scenes and they lived up to their parents' trust in them.

A mother shared the following experience involving her fifteen-year-old daughter, peer pressure, and trust. She and her husband had recently extended their daughter's privileges, allowing her to stay out later and go to more places, as long as she was with a group of friends. One evening, a family friend observed the girl smoking and immediately reported this to her father. Her parents were particularly upset because she'd always been a vehement antismoker, even leaving the room when her father smoked. They were very upset to hear that she would tell them one thing and do another. They thought about how to handle this and chose a very sensible approach.

After their daughter came home they waited a while and then went up to her room. The father was direct and let her know his friend had seen her. He said if she was going to smoke, he wanted to know about it, and he didn't like her pretending to hate smoke and then smoking on the sly. The daughter insisted that she didn't like smoking, but that her friends were making fun of her for not joining in and so she decided to take a few puffs.

Her parents now realized this wasn't a case of a breach of trust, but an issue of peer pressure. Her mother said that both she and her father had thought the daughter was ready for increased privileges and responsibilities and that's why they'd recently extended her curfew. They had thought she was able to withstand peer pressure and therefore were comfortable in extending the privileges. "After all," her mother went on, "what if this had been a more serious issue concerning drugs or drinking? Would you follow your peers or make your own decisions?" Her parents then said that they wanted her to take some time to think about whether she felt she was ready for extended privileges—which meant, according to their thinking, being able to withstand peer pressure—or if she'd rather they cut back temporarily on some of the new privileges. They asked her to think it over and, when she was ready, to come and let them know her decision.

About an hour later, the daughter came to her parents and said she wanted to maintain her new privileges and felt she'd rather keep them and stand up to peer pressure than lose her privileges. The parents said that was fine and they would trust her in this. Over the next few months, their daughter did prove to them that, in fact, she was handling things quite well. On several occasions where parties had involved heavy drinking, she stuck to soft drinks, and she reported feeling good about her strength.

Parents need to set limits for their teenagers, just as they need to for their younger children. This helps them feel secure. The boundaries, however, do need to be extended more and more for teenagers as they show they are ready to take on increased responsibilities. Parents will need to allow their teenagers to go more places and stay out later, but they should increase these privileges only as their teenagers reveal they can handle them.

Also, even though teenagers need opportunities to do things on their own and to learn from their experiences and mistakes (as younger children do too), parents are wise to help them avoid plunging into certain situations unadvised. Parents can discuss facts about sex, smoking, drugs, and drinking with their teenagers to help them make better decisions for themselves. If our teenagers ever do take paths that lead to problems, we, as parents, should be there to help them pick up and start again.

Some adults regret that when they were growing up they were burdened with household chores and baby-sitting responsibilities. They felt cheated out of their childhood, not getting enough play

time. Others say that they were never expected to do anything and they felt robbed of a good opportunity to learn responsibility. Parents discuss these viewpoints and wonder how much they should ask their children to do at home.

Most parents agree that children need ample time to play and be children, and many parents observe that children of all ages are very interested in their own world of friends, play, and school. Housework is just not on their minds. I feel that children benefit nontheless from contributing to the household of which they are important members. They needn't have so many chores that there is little time left for play, but a few simple jobs will develop their sense of responsibility. If the chores are varied, then they will have the opportunity to learn many of the skills that make a household function well.

Parents can gear responsibilities to the child's abilities. Even a young child can begin learning to put his toys away, sponge off a table, or cut a cucumber with a dull knife. As children get older, they can recognize certain obligations on their own, such as putting their own clothes into the hamper, hanging up their coats, putting their toys away, and seeing to it that they brush their teeth. In addition to these, it is reasonable to ask for help with jobs that affect the entire household, like hanging laundry or sweeping floors. Techniques like making charts of jobs that rotate at regular intervals work well in some families, while other parents find that a more casual approach works best. For example, if a parent is cooking, he may ask one child to set the table and another to come and peel the carrots. When children are asked nicely, they usually respond well.

Children enjoy doing jobs more when their parents work together with them. If a parent is raking the yard and the child helps too, they get to enjoy each other's company as they accomplish the job. Other jobs, like taking out the garbage, are best done alone. It is good to learn to work well both independently and cooperatively.

Children generally prefer to have a say in deciding their own jobs. Individual preferences can be honored when possible. It is helpful for both fathers and mothers to share in housework, for then children will see that the household is the responsibility of all who live in it. Some functions are more pleasant than others, but even the unpleasant ones need to be done. The home is everyone's to enjoy and participate in and care for in some way.

On Saturday mornings a mother would gather her four children together and tell them each which chore she expected them to do that morning. Every Saturday morning each family member helped out with some of the housework. The children always did their assigned jobs, but not always with great cooperation.

One Saturday the mother gathered her children and included them in the decision-making process. She asked them to help decide which chore each of them was to do. There was some brief friction since some of the children wanted to choose the same chore, but soon each child had chosen some job he or she found satisfactory. The mother reported that the jobs got done with a great spirit of cooperation.

She also found charts to be effective. Another Saturday morning she put up a chart with all the jobs listed on it (and pictured too, so the younger children could understand it). She chose the job she would do, did it, and checked off that it was done. Her children followed suit. Cooperation without words or nagging!

It is very helpful to allow children to share in decisions concerning them. When they don't feel that all the orders are coming from the parents, they're usually more willing to cooperate.

Ann, age six, was required to set the table every night, and each evening the mother and daughter found themselves fighting about it. The mother wanted to know what would ease these confrontations.

The mother should consider that perhaps Ann is not yet ready for this kind of daily job. Perhaps there can be more flexibility in her routine. The mother could let Ann know that her help setting the table is welcome and appreciated, but not rigidly required. If the mother wants her to have a chore every day, perhaps Ann could have a choice as to which chore she'd like to do on a given day. If the mother feels strongly about having Ann set the table, then perhaps she could make this a warm special time for her and her daughter, when they listen to music and talk together as each of them does her evening job. It would be helpful at times to reflect the girl's feelings, as by saying, "I know there are some nights you enjoy setting the table and some nights you really feel it's a drag. I can understand that. I don't always enjoy having to do all of my jobs. But the job needs to be done."

The mother could also talk with her daughter away from the actual situation about her rationale for assigning this chore, explaining that everyone in the family needs to help out in some way, to help the family as a unit. Once Ann sees that the request is not arbitrary, that her help is actually needed, she may be much more willing to comply. Ann can learn to see that doing one's share can make a person feel good.

An eight-year-old was responsible for returning his bike to the garage each evening and he almost always remembered to do so, but

every now and then he forgot. His mother wondered if it was her obligation to remind him at these times or if she should insist that he assume this responsibility on his own and suffer the consequences of a stolen bike if that ever happened.

We do need to teach our children to become responsible, and one way to do this is to give them particular jobs. Children should not, however, be expected to assume certain responsibilities entirely on their own. Parents often need to supervise.

This boy seems to be doing a fine job, with lapses few and far between. His parents can let him know they are proud of how well he is taking care of his bicycle. They can also do a quick doublecheck each night and if ever they notice his bike still outside, just quietly remind him to put it away. Everyone would suffer if the boy's bike were stolen, and to look for trouble does not make sense. Parents can continue to give children more and more chances to take on responsibilities as they grow, but should also be prepared to offer assistance and supervision when it is needed. Adults, too, have lapses on occasion and usually appreciate a helpful reminder, but not a spiteful "I told you so."

A mother and her eight-year-old daughter had an ongoing conflict over a messy shelf in the girl's room. The mother often nagged and got angry at her daughter about this. The girl was a collector, coming home quite often with random, useless, and broken objects that got dumped on this shelf. Her mother was disgusted by the girl's disinclination to keep things neat. "She's a regular packrat," she said.

In every home the values are different. In another home the mother might keep her own shelves messy and would not care about her daughter's. Orderliness was valued by this mother, and that is fine, but an eight-year-old should have some say about the condition of her room. This seems like a good situation for compromise.

I suggested that the mother calmly discuss with her daughter her own feelings about order, at the same time listening to her daughter's feelings about her room. The mother could ask the daughter to think about a compromise that might satisfy them both, and also the mother could offer some suggestions. Perhaps once a week the girl could sort the objects out, saving the special items and throwing away the rest. Or, instead of using her shelf for her collections, she might decorate a "junk" box to put things in, out of sight. The issue had become such a heated one that neither mother nor daughter could consider it clearly while facing the shelf. Talking about it reasonably, out of the room, at a quiet moment, they are sure to arrive at a fair and sensible solution.

Each evening a mother found herself yelling at her five-year-old son. She would ask him to put his toys away and he wouldn't, so she'd begin to scream about how he never does it.

The mother was emphasizing the negative by saying to her son that he *never* put his toys away. If a parent tells a child that he never cleans up, he'll probably believe it and continue to leave his toys all around. It's better to show positive expectations and say somethings like "I expect you to put your toys away" or "It's time to put your toys away and I know you can do a good job of it."

A five-year-old may still need a parent to help out. The parent can say, "It's time to put the toys away now. How about you doing the blocks and me doing the cars?" Or "How would you like to work this out? I'll help. Which toys shall I put away and which ones will you do?" Singing or chanting along something like "Oh, we're putting the toys away now" can make a chore more fun. Afterward, the parent should appreciate the child's efforts with a statement like "We worked hard, but we did it" or "You really know where each toy belongs" or "I knew you'd be a big help."

If the child still isn't cooperating, working neither with the parent nor on his own, the parent can then express annoyance. "This makes me very annoyed. I expect you to put your toys away. I feel like not getting you more things until I see you taking care of what you already have." Note that she is not actually threatening not to buy toys, but stating her *feeling* of annoyance in a strong way. Her son is likely to get the point about how upset his mother feels, and this may be a good incentive to earn his cooperation.

Holly, an eleven-year-old girl, had an extremely messy room. She wouldn't make her bed or pick up her toys and would leave crumbs and half-finished glasses of milk around. Her mother called her a slob and told her she was lazy, which didn't help, and then she would clean up Holly's mess herself.

When children are labeled, they tend to believe they really are what their parent calls them. Once Holly becomes convinced that she is, in fact, a lazy slob, then she's got a great excuse never to do anything!

Holly's mother needs to communicate to her daughter that she is a fine person so that Holly will see herself in a positive way and not as a lazy slob. Then her mother needs to discuss Holly's responsibility for her room. Holly's bedroom is part of the household; leaving crumbs around is unsanitary and affects the entire family. The mother might agree to some sort of compromise—for example, that the daughter may leave some of her books or clothes lying around but may not create a complete disaster area in her room.

The mother should also stop doing everything for her daughter, as this takes away the opportunity for Holly to improve. Instead, the mother should show both in words and in attitude that she knows Holly can be cooperative and will be. She might have to help her daughter learn to structure her time better to fit in these jobs, and she might even need to show her how to clean, but she must let Holly know that this is her job. She might say, "These are your responsibilities now and I know you'll take care of them. It'll give you a good feeling to be doing these things on your own." Even if Holly does not attend to these matters immediately, the mother should not rush in to do it. If the mother is getting angry, she should still not do the job, but say something like "I expect you to cooperate! I get mad when you don't. I need the job to be done!" This tells Holly that her mother is mad but that she is still expected to do the job on her own.

If none of these methods succeed in changing Holly's ways, her mother may want to back up her words with action. She can explain once again that she will no longer assume responsibilities that Holly can handle and now she needs to make a new rule: Before Holly may go outside to play on Saturdays, she will have to put her room in reasonable order. This is not the same as punishment, in which the mother might say, "You have to stay inside for three Saturdays." Instead, this rule give Holly the chance to play, but insists that her responsibilities to the household be met as well. When a child assumes a cooperative and responsible attitude toward her required tasks, then it can be left to her discretion when to do them (before or after dinner, playtime, or TV). If she is unable to get things done on her own, then the parent may have to do this type of structuring for her.

Holly's mother mentioned that her daughter was good about her schoolwork and personal hygiene. She began to take notice of this and let her know how nice she looked and how good it was to see her taking care of herself so well. This kind of positive reinforcement, giving attention to the areas in which her daughter was displaying responsibility, will help Holly see that she can also do this for her room. When we consider children capable of being responsible, fine human beings and give them opportunities to demonstrate these qualities, they will live up to our positive expectations.

Parents discuss allowances and helping children to understand more about money and managing it.

Many parents give weekly allowances that increase as children get older, and let their children know that the allowance can be used for immediate pleasures or saved for future purchases. They see the allowance as an opportunity to manage money, get an idea of how much things cost, and begin to balance short-range needs with long-range ones.

Some parents say that they pay their children for doing household chores because they believe chores are work and it's a good feeling to be paid for the work one does. They feel working and then earning contribute to a child's sense of responsibility and achievement. Other parents disagree, believing that everyone in the home should do his or her chores to contribute to family living and that the payment should be the good feeling derived from knowing one has done one's share. These parents may, instead, encourage their children to find paid work experiences outside the home like lawn mowing or baby-sitting. In either case, I believe it is important that throughout childhood children have some money of their own to spend as they wish.

One day Susan and her son, Sam, were at the supermarket, and Susan noticed Sam fiddling with the candy near the checkout counter. She thought she had succeeded in distracting him, but later, in the car, she saw him unwrapping a candy bar. Sam's instant remark at being seen was "You weren't supposed to look" (showing that he was well aware he had done something wrong).

Susan was upset by this but realized that Sam was expressing frustration at having no way to get what he wanted. She said, "It's time you had an allowance, Sam, so you can buy candy when you see some you want to have, provided I agree that it's a good time for eating candy."

Susan's response was creative and direct. She had let Sam know that items from stores had to be bought, not just be taken, but she did not label Sam a stealer or make him feel that he was a thief. Susan did not approve of Sam's theft, but she understood by his action that he was feeling a need to make his own decisions, at times, about what he wanted. From then on, if he wanted some candy she didn't want him to have just then, she'd suggest they return on Saturday when he got his allowance, and Sam, having some control, was satisfied by this response.

A mother wanted to allow her fourteen-year-old daughter to choose her own clothes, but felt that she consistently came home with high-priced items that were a strain on the family's budget. The mother wondered if she should shop for her.

The mother can choose the price range and let the girl select the clothes within it that she likes best. Children need opportunities to make choices that concern them, but not in a way that sacrifices the feelings and needs of other family members.

I'd like to share with you my philosophy on independence and interdependence.

Independence and interdependence are closely connected. Each person is unique and needs to express his individuality, contributing his special flavor to the world. At the same time, each person needs to realize that all other human beings are expressing their natures and making their individual imprints. Along with personal development, there must be cooperation among people who value and respect each other's special beauty and individuality, and who want to pool resources to create a good world. As children grow toward self-fulfillment, parents can emphasize *cooperative effort* so that each child can blossom and also live and work in harmony with the other people in his life. Parents can encourage children to think globally, toward planetary as well as personal fulfillment. They can inspire them to apply their creative intelligence to making a more beautiful world that will express the love, cooperation, intelligence, and good will of the individuals in it.

CHAPTER 12

Parents' Feelings

It's Not Easy Being a Parent, Though Parenting Is Filled with Joy

Parenting is a difficult job, with lots of responsibilities and demands. Parenting is also filled with joy, in the love we receive from our children, in the privilege of sharing their energy and laughter, and in observing the ever-wondrous process of their growth. Parents, too, are growing in maturity, and their parenting is an aspect of that process. Understanding the anger, guilt, sadness, and anxiety we feel can contribute as much to our self-awareness as the ability to savor our pleasure. Many of these feelings are common to the experience of parenting, which is why parents benefit so much from sharing their concerns. This chapter presents the parents' side of the picture—how it really feels, day to day, to be a parent. I also present here some Parent Awareness "success stories"—the experiences of parents who have changed happily from generally negative to predominantly positive parenting techniques.

A father wanted to know if being a good parent means sacrificing oneself for one's children. He found that on certain evenings he was not in the mood to plunge right in and play after work. He needed time to relax first but wasn't sure if he is entitled to unwind or if it is better to ignore his needs for the sake of the children.

The hours from five to seven are difficult ones in many homes. Children are getting tired, and they need dinner. If one adult has been with the children all day, he or she is likely also to feel tired, hungry, and tense. If another is returning home from a long workday, he or she, too, will want to unwind.

How can everyone's needs best be met in this situation? Ignoring one's own needs to meet another's may work on occasion, but in the long run the sacrificer feels martyred and the children feel guilty yet still unsatisfied. Certainly there will be times when parents need to make sacrifices for their children, but, overall, family harmony is best served by creating a balance in meeting the needs of children and parents.

In this family, the children were three and six. The father would always say hello and hug and kiss them when he returned from work, but then he wanted some time alone. Compromises can be reached. He could explain to the children that sometimes he comes home tired and likes some time to refresh himself before playing with them. The mother could explain that she needs time to get dinner going. The children can learn that at that time of the day they will have to do things on their own, and afterward they will get attention from their parents again. At this age, they might need some help getting set up with an activity, but so long as they are getting enough attention from each of their parents overall, they can adjust to the idea that this hour of the day will be reserved for individual quiet time.

A mother asked, "What do you do when a child asks you nicely to read her a story and you were just about to have tea and some time for your own thoughts?"

Parenting involves a constant juggling of needs. The important thing is to meet whoever's need is most pressing at that time. Sometimes it will be the parent's need and other times the child's. In this situation, if the mother judged that her child was perfectly capable of playing on her own for longer, then she could say that she would read to her daughter later, after her tea and quiet time. If, on the other hand, the mother saw that her daughter really needed attention very badly, more than she herself needed tea and relaxation, then it would be best to play first and have tea later.

A mother discussed her preferences and strengths. She enjoyed reading to her children, talking with them, and watching them at play. She did not like active play outdoors. Her four-year-old son was constantly requesting that she play ball with him. The mother was starting to feel guilty for not wanting to meet his request.

Like our children, we are all different. One parent has a more cerebral nature and loves to share activities such as reading and exchanging thoughts. Another parent is more physically inclined and loves to ski or skate with her children and has boundless physical energy. Other parents are strongest in emotional areas and find it easy to comfort and soothe a child. We all have some capacities in each area—mental, physical, and emotional—but we combine them in different degrees. We need to learn to accept our natures and build on our strengths.

I believe it would be valuable for this mother to let her children know what she really does enjoy and also let them know what she doesn't like as much. Yet, weighing her son's need, too, she might aim for a compromise. Her four-year-old really wanted her to play outside with him, especially in the hours before his older sisters got home from school. If she would play ball for five or ten minutes at a time, even every few days, his wish might be satisfied. She would be letting him know that they could enjoy this kind of playing together sometimes, but in general she preferred other activities. Sometimes parents do need to make compromises, but they still needn't feel guilty for their preferences. Just as we love each child for being a special, unique individual, our children love us for being the unique blend of qualities that we are.

Many parents realize that it is good to make time for their own needs, and yet they still feel guilty when they do. One mother described her situation. She had a two-and-a-half-year-old with whom she spent a good deal of time. She had been married for six years before having her daughter and was used to a certain amount of time with just her husband, as well as time for herself alone. The mother structured her life so that she worked two days a week (out of desire, in her case, not financial need), played tennis with her husband two hours on Sunday, and usually went out alone one evening each week. The rest of the time she was at home. A regular baby-sitter came on the days she worked. In addition, her daughter was in a play group three mornings a week with two other children. Each mother watched the group one morning a week. The mother felt that this schedule was a good one for her, and yet she fretted about taking time away from her daughter. She knew she couldn't be with her daughter all of the time and that realistically she wasn't going to change her life to do so, but still the gnawing guilt remained.

She was also troubled by the rigidity of her routine. If a friend would ask her to go shopping for an afternoon, the mother would feel that one extra afternoon away from her daughter would be the last straw. If she felt like having a late candlelight dinner alone with her husband, that, too, was too much; she felt that happy families always eat together. Yet the quality of her marriage was suffering from her inability to be flexible or spontaneous and her overconcern with her daughter.

Guilt can be draining; it robs us of energy. While the mother was at work or taking time for leisure, her daughter was in excellent care, and this is essential. Children, even young ones, need to develop lives away from their parents, and this schedule provided the child with opportunities to do so. Children learn attitudes from their parents. If the mother continues to feel guilty every time she leaves her daughter, her daughter may start to feel guilty as she gets older and wants to do more things with her friends. Parents can help to make the family a meeting ground where its members take time to be together and then have satisfying activities apart.

Parents, too, need to make sure they have chances to experience life without a child clinging to them, where they are for a time their own complete person, in their own mental and emotional space. This is crucial to renewing energy for parenting endeavors. It is so important to feel good about taking time to fulfill ourselves as individuals. The mother in the above situation needs to stop feeling guilty and begin feeling good. Fortunately, this is an attitude that can be learned.

A father expressed a different perspective. His work schedule was very demanding and he wanted more time to spend with his three-and-a-half-year-old daughter.

Many other parents, men and women, experience this pressure. Sometimes it's possible to rearrange one's work schedule to provide for more family time, and sometimes it isn't. When we can't, then we have to make the time we do have with our children be quality time as much as possible. Even so, a parent can get into a bind if he divides his life just between his work and his child. This father did want more time to be with his daughter, but recognized that he also needed time for himself, his wife, his friends, and leisure pursuits.

We never create a workable balance that will be suitable forever. We will always be in the process of creating and maintaining a healthy balance between our parenting role and our individual needs. When we're needing more time with our children, we'll know it, and when we're needing more time for ourselves, we'll know it too. Each of us has different needs and must strive to create the balance that works well at a given time.

A mother told how she took her daughter someplace special for the day. They both had a great time, but when they got home, Tiffany was mad because it was bedtime and said, "I had a lousy day." Her mother was devastated and felt that after trying so hard to give Tiffany a pleasant time, she hadn't done well at all, and she apologized for being so strict about bedtime. Tiffany was aware she had struck her mother where it hurt.

Children often try to employ guilt for their benefit with statements like "I hate you" or "You hate me." They hope that if they can make the parent feel bad about a rule or limit, then it will be changed.

It is not healthy for parents to grovel before their children. Then parents lose respect for themselves, and children gain a scary type of power. They really don't want to control their parents like this and shouldn't be allowed to do so.

This girl knew well how to manipulate her mother. Instead of allowing her daughter to attack her, the mother could have said, "Instead of your complaints, I'd like to hear a thank-you for our nice day together." After trying hard to please a child, it is infuriating indeed to receive only crankiness, and it is good to let the child know we expect gratitude.

In other cases, when a child says, "I hate you," the parent can accept the child's anger and say, "You're angry with me now." When a child says, "I had a rotten day," or "You hate me," a parent might say, "I set a limit you don't like so you're feeling that I hate you. The rule is necessary, however, and I love you."

A father was disappointed at first when his plan to take his son for an ice cream after school as a surprise treat fell through. Robbie didn't want to go out, but preferred to go straight home. After talking with his son, the father understood his reasons and no longer felt disappointed that the day didn't work out as planned.

It's good to be aware that what a parent may feel will be a special treat for a child may not always be appreciated. This doesn't mean we shouldn't ever plan outings, but we should also be prepared not to be upset if our idea was not something the child considered terrific at the time.

Some parents say they go crazy when their children talk to them in a demanding tone.

Parents enjoy being treated courteously. When a parent is not asked politely, it is hard to listen and want to help out. Parents can let their children know by saying, "This is how I would like to be asked," and demonstrating the request in the tone of voice and using the words the parent would like the child to imitate. This helps children learn to ask for things in a way that makes people feel good about giving.

A father was finding his five-year-old daughter quite annoying lately. If she was upset about something, she'd tell him how she

felt over and over again. He wanted to listen once, but didn't have the patience for a siege. He wondered if his feelings were appropriate or if he should be more patient. Sometimes he'd get so frustrated he'd say, "That's enough already!" or "Leave me alone!"

At times like these a parent can let his child know that he understands how upset she is and that he is glad she came to tell him. Then, the parent can try to stop the child's repetition by saying something like "As I continue my reading, I'll be thinking about how annoyed that made you." This way, the parent accepts the child's feelings but discourages the repetitive expression in a supportive way. This might not always stop the child; on occasion a parent does need to say something like "That's enough for now!" or "I've heard you; now go do something else," as children sometimes have a way of ignoring our understanding remarks and continuing anyway.

One morning during breakfast a three-year-old boy was crying so forcefully that his mother couldn't stand it. She didn't know why he was crying and he wouldn't tell her. She told him to take his bowl of cereal and eat in a different room until he calmed down. A few minutes later, hearing no more crying, the mother went in search of her son. She discovered him eating in the bathroom, looking forlorn. Seeing her son like this made her feel guilty. She began to cry and took him in her arms. She said to me, "When I saw him like that I felt what a terrible mother I was to send him off to eat alone." Did the mother really do something terrible?

Parents have needs that must be respected, too. The mother could not tolerate his crying and she was afraid she might blow up at him for it. She didn't do anything hurtful, and in fact he did calm down once alone. Setting a limit, as she did, can be a helpful safety valve for both of them.

A mother was finding that around the time when she was menstruating she'd be very moody and do a good deal of screaming at her children. She felt her moodiness lasted for too many days. What could she do to diminish her irritability?

Severe premenstrual tension is a reality for many women. It helps a lot to know that it's the cause of a bad mood and that as sure as the mood comes, it will go away again. I advised this woman to be extra kind to herself at these times—relaxing, perhaps getting some extra child care, or planning a special treat like taking herself out to lunch She should let her family know, too, that she needs special considera tion.

I also suggested a way for this woman to keep her irritation from getting out of hand. When she finds herself screaming for nothing, she can learn to go into another room and cool off. To help calm herself down, she can close her eyes for a few seconds, while breathing deeply. I do this when I am quite upset, and I like to tell myself that with each breath, I am taking in some fresh energy from the universe and that each breathe will make me feel calmer.

For eleven days, four-year-old Debby had to take a certain medicine. The mother believed the medication was causing her daughter to be especially crabby and she found herself responding back to Debby with irritation. She just couldn't stand the fussiness and more than once she said, "Get away from me." At the same time, she was worried about Debby's health and felt very guilty about her unsympathetic reactions. Now that the illness was over, she was afraid that she had permanently harmed their relationship during this time.

I would advise a parent in this situation always to ask the doctor whether the medication is responsible for this effect. If the prescription could be the cause of extra crabbiness but can't be changed, the situation will just have to be accepted. Children are often irritable and restless anyway when they are sick, both as a result of not feeling well and from staying indoors all day. It is normal for parents to resent the extra demands on them at these times. It's hard for a parent to be cooped up inside, too, and it's a good idea to try and take a break by asking a friend or baby-sitter to come over for a few hours.

Parents can also provide safe outlets for their resentful feelings. When the child is out of earshot, the parent can say quietly to herself, "I can't stand it when you're sick" or "If I need to read you one more story, I'll scream out loud." This can bring relief and make it easier to provide the comfort and special attention the child needs to get better.

A parent can also share some of her feelings with her sick child. "We're both feeling tired and crabby from being stuck in the house so long. I can hardly wait till you're all better!" This gives the child's feelings consideration too. If the bad feelings are allowed expression, it will make it easier to comment on the good moments they do have: "I like playing this game with you" or "I'm rocking you to help you feel better. It's good to be holding each other."

I felt this mother was being very hard on herself for her behavior during Debby's illness. Life with children will have its unpleasant moments and we can't expect ourselves always to be the parents we'd like to be. No damage is going to be done to a solid parent-child relationship because of a few bad days. I asked the mother to tell me one good thing that had happened to her and her daughter since the illness and she laughingly said, "Oh, a lot!" and shared several.

It's the whole tone of our relationship that is important. We can't torture ourselves over each little situation. Let it be over and done with. Sometimes it is appropriate to apologize to a child for something we've done or said, but we don't have to agonize over it. If in general we handle things positively, our children will have happy childhoods, and we will experience pleasant parenting. Nonetheless, we won't always respond positively, and we can relax about this, accepting our humanity.

Parents sometimes feel totally responsible for a child's personality. A child is easily upset, and they worry that something they did has caused her to become so sensitive. Another child is at ease playing with one friend at a time but has trouble fitting into groups, and the parents think this is their fault.

Each child who comes into the world is already a special, unique person. One is more high-strung, another more easygoing. Often her personality will change over time. A child who has trouble in groups will need our best thought to help her adapt to living effectively with that characteristic. Blaming ourselves for our children's personalities misuses our energy and does not help them at all.

During her third pregnancy, a woman had a terrifying dream for two nights in a row. She dreamed that her oldest son had died and she was joyful as she watched the wake and funeral. The dream troubled her deeply. She didn't understand how she could dream such an evil thing.

Parents, as well as children, benefit from separating reality from fantasy. This mother loved her son dearly and would have been heartbroken if he had really died, but parents are people with all kinds of feelings. Dreams can mean many things. This woman's unconscious could have been expressing anger at her son, or anger at something her uncle did ten years ago. She had mentioned to me feeling overwhelmed at times by her responsibilities, and perhaps the dream was an expression of this. In reality most parents accept their responsibilities appropriately, yet in fantasy most of them nurture urges to be once again carefree, to come and go as they please. This mother was going to have yet another child to care for soon. It would be natural for her unconscious to express some rebellion at all this responsibility. It has nothing to do with the reality of her love for her child.

Parents almost always love their children, but many find that they do not always like them. A parent may be having an especially hard time with a certain child for a few days, even weeks. A tone of voice or specific behavior may be difficult to tolerate. At these times parents can get the feeling that they just do not like that child. Sometimes the parent is so furious that he or she even hates the child for a time. Are these feelings normal?

Most parents experience these feelings at some time, and they need not feel guilty when they do. As long as these feelings are not shared directly with the child, they do no harm. It is not helpful to tell a child that we hate her or don't like her. It is, however, valuable to let her know in a constructive way how her behavior is affecting us. We might say, "When you act like this, I don't enjoy being around you." Then we should go on to state our positive expectations; for example: "I expect you to talk to me in a quieter voice." A concrete description of the behavior we'd like to see will provide the encouragement and support the child needs to change.

It also helps at these times to remember the things we especially like about this child, and let her know these are appreciated. We can avoid getting stuck on the temporary annoying behavior if we make efforts to remember that it is not the whole picture.

A mother reported that she had tried positive methods but was still often angry. She was afraid she just didn't have the patience to use positive techniques.

Expressing anger constructively *is* using a positive method. Anger is a normal and valid emotion. When it does not find appropriate expression, it builds up and usually has much worse effects than when we acknowledge it. Using positive methods means learning to use anger constructively. A positive parent is not one who is forever patient, but one who expresses her honest feelings in helpful ways.

I encourage parents to express their true feelings—to be pleasant and calm when they are feeling good, and to express annoyance or anger when they are angry. When parents express their own feelings truthfully, children, too, become comfortable with all kinds of feelings. It actually feels good to be able to express what we're really feeling. When anger is expressed in positive ways, it relieves tension without the guilt that follows a hurtful display of violent feelings.

One muggy night when I was hot and tired, Joshua made me good and mad. His friend David was sleeping over and just before bed, David accidentally broke Joshua's sunglasses. Joshua asked me to fix them. I told him I wasn't sure I'd be able to, but I'd try. He said, "I want you to fix them, shitty ass!"

I had to work hard not to call him names back. I was in no mood to be insulted. My feelings were hurt and I was furious. I shouted, "I do not want to be called such names ever. It makes me so mad to hear that, that I feel like smashing a wall. I also feel like crying, my feelings are so hurt. You can be mad about your sunglasses, but my feelings are not to be hurt. When my feelings are hurt, I don't even feel like trying to fix your sunglasses!" Joshua had tears in his eyes when I was done. I said I'd like him to hug me to make me feel better. He did, and both of us felt much better.

This incident reminded me that, of the many ways to approach a situation, the one we choose is closely connected to how we are feeling at that moment.

Joshua had been experimenting a lot with name calling for the past few days. Sometimes ignoring this kind of behavior works well. At other times it's helpful to humor the child by repeating what he has said in a playful way so he can hear how ridiculous it sounds. Had I been in a more playful mood, I might have said teasingly, "I want you to fix them, shitty ass!" so he could hear how awful it sounded. Had I been in a more rational mood, I might have responded more calmly with "When I'm called names, I can't help you out at all. You can be mad, but you'll need to find a nicer way to express it." Parents will, however, respond according to their moods, and because I was tired, hot, and crabby, I was easily offended. I responded very emotionally, even more so because his friend was present. I had also let him know that it was embarrassing to be called names in front of people.

Parents ask about losing their cool. Is it terrible, or can it serve a good purpose to blow up occasionally?

All parents are going to lose their temper sometimes. This can serve the healthy purpose of revealing that no one is perfect and when people get very angry the world doesn't fall apart; we can pick up and go on from there. I do urge parents, even when they are losing their cool, to try very hard to refrain from hurting a child physically, by hitting, or emotionally, by name calling. We can learn not to do these things.

Once everyone is calmer, it is very helpful for parents to speak with the child about the incident. Parents can let the child know how unpleasant it was when the child wasn't cooperating and that it also wasn't enjoyable to yell that loud or say the things they said. They can discuss how much nicer it is for everyone in the family when children cooperate and parents are in a happy mood. Talking like this with children gives them the opportunity to reflect on the situation and it is hoped, to try to act more cooperatively in the future. It is also reassuring to say at times, "Even when I am angry, I still love you."

Crying is another response that parents sometimes have when they lose their patience. This is normal and we can feel comfortable with it. It too, can serve a healthy purpose. Children can see that their parents are fully human, even fragile sometimes. Children cry pretty often when things don't go right for them. Every so often this is going to happen to a parent as well. Most parents say that their children come right over to them, apologize, give them a big hug, and immediately become cooperative. A child will feel proud to know that she can bring comfort at a time like this. Certainly we should not use crying as a method to get children to cooperate, but when we do cry, we need not worry that we have damaged our authority.

In my family there are times when everyone is getting on each other's nerves. We sometimes declare a family "freak-out time," and all yell together. This clears the air and it's fun. Sometimes, a structured freak-out can prevent things from getting truly out of hand later.

Parents sometimes worry that once their children are a certain age they won't be able to adjust to positive methods. One mother beat her daughter with a belt whenever she got mad at her. She knew that she and her daughter had trouble communicating; they couldn't talk to each other or enjoy being together. The mother earnestly wanted to learn to live with her daughter in a loving way, but she was also afraid that it was too late to alter things since her daughter was already ten.

It is never too late to change our lives for the better. We are never too old to learn, change, and grow. Parents and children are flexible. Parents can learn to use positive approaches at any time in their lives. It will take effort, time, and commitment, but the effort is well worth it. Parents and their children still have many years to live together, even after the children are grown. Also, children brought up with positive approaches by their parents are more likely to use these same positive approaches with their own children, so making the change has effects that will carry far into the future.

This mother was eager for positive suggestions, and the members of her group offered many. They felt that the first step was for her to stop hitting her daughter, and then to set aside special times to be with her. They suggested that she try to talk in a pleasant tone and also begin to chat with her about many things so they could start sharing ideas. She was urged to begin using positive touching right away, hugging her daughter or holding her around the shoulder as they talked.

As the weeks went by, the mother reported a lot of changes. The first night she left the group, she threw away her belt. She started to tell her daughter some of the things she liked and appreciated about her and began to think about the good things, not just what was going wrong. She told her daughter she loved her and started reaching out to hug her. They even sat in a chair and rocked together. She slapped her daughter once the first week, but still a great change was occurring. They talked together about the fact that things had not been pleasant for them and that she was learning new ways. Her daughter was naturally wary at first but soon responded to this new love, and things did really get better.

All the old ways will not be changed in a few weeks. Trust takes time to develop. Each day, however, the mother will build confidence that she can relate in positive ways, and each day her daughter will believe more and more that what is happening is really how things will be. The mother explained that she'd still be getting angry at times and would be setting certain limits, but in helpful ways. Children will test us to see if we are serious about our new commitments, so it is critical to demonstrate both that we intend to stick to the new ways and that limits will still be set.

This mother's situation brings up the issue of child abuse. As emphasized earlier, I believe that all hitting is abusive, for it harms a child's body and self-esteem. Degrees of abuse do vary, however. The parent who disciplines her child with an occasional spanking is hurting her child, to be sure, but the parent who subjects her child to repeated and intense beatings risks much deeper psychological damage and more serious physical harm, possibly death.

Child abuse occurs in all socioeconomic groups. The causes vary. The abuse may originate in the parent's own childhood experience (she is repeating what was done to her) or her present life situation or a faulty understanding of discipline (thinking that hitting is a useful tool, when actually it is not). Sometimes the abuse is due to an unconscious connection the parent makes between a particular child and someone—perhaps a hated sibling or despised former teacher— in her own past. No matter what has led to the situation of repeated abuse, once a parent is stuck in the hurtful pattern it is often hard to stop, because she just does not know better methods. New patterns need to replace old ones. Parents can learn how to spend time playing with a child, to reach out for a kiss, to talk in a pleasant tone, to express anger constructively. These tools are a tremendous resource.

Quite often, abuse occurs because a parent has unrealistic expectations. She may think her two-year-old is capable of cleaning her own room, and then become extremely angry with the child when she cannot. Learning about the stages of child development is one way to avoid child abuse. The parent who knows what to expect at what ages will be spared overexpectations and their frequent companion—exaggerated anger.

The parent's own life is relevant too. When parents are happy with their lives, pursuing interests and friendships, then it is easier also to enjoy their children. The mother in this situation had revealed to her group that her life was lonely and unsatisfying. Group members made many good suggestions to her about how to spend her time more fruitfully. She was in the habit of hardly leaving her house; her daughter was her main contact with the world. With her group's encouragement, she began to branch out, taking courses, going places, visiting friends. She had found that when using negative methods she felt exhausted at the end of the day. Using positive approaches gave her more energy to devote to other aspects of her life, and as she became more involved outside her home, good feelings from these other pursuits entered into her parenting. A circling effect of positive energy was created.

Other parents who abuse or neglect children may be markedly successful in their job or career, yet still have difficulty with their parenting.

It is my hope that we will not look down on the abusive parent but carry the strength of a positive way of life to the public consciousness more and more. To begin to treat children in positive ways, a parent needs first to know *what* the positive ways are. *Wanting* to change is half of the battle; the other half is *learning* the better ways to relate. Positive skills need to be made available to all parents. Otherwise, how will a parent who is repeating harmful patterns know how to change? For many parents, it is valuable to undergo some form of counseling or psychotherapy to explore the roots of their parenting difficulties; but all parents need to know the positive techniques. With the new skills, dramatic changes can occur, and in much less time than we'd ordinarily think.

A mother spent most of her time cleaning the house, but no one was happy living there. She was very tense and often blew up and beat her children for minor transgressions. She joined a Parent Awareness group to try to improve her home life, and shortly after the group began, she related this incident. One day she was beating her daughter severely with a belt. The daughter was sobbing. At this moment, the comments she had been hearing in her group started to come together in her mind; things clicked. She stopped hitting, and began to cry too. She sat down to talk with her daughter about their relationship. For the first time, she was able to hear her daughter's side of things.

The girl told her mother that she never gave any time to her or her brother, never played with them or helped with schoolwork. The mother was startled. "Why, I'm here every afternoon when you come home from school!" she said. The daughter replied, "Yes, but you're always too busy for us."

The mother then thought about her own childhood and remembered that her mother had always been cleaning and had never spent any time with her or her brothers and sisters. This woman saw that for years she'd been treating her children like robots, clothing and feeding them, sending them off to school or out to play. I had been asking the parents in her group what they liked about themselves as parents, and this mother had felt that there was nothing good she could say.

She began slowly to change her ways. She used to take her children for an ice cream only because she had felt it was her obligation as a mother to do something nice occasionally. She really didn't enjoy it. The day after this scene, she took them for an ice cream and had a good time. Her daughter accidentally knocked the spoon out of her mother's hand. Previously, she would've slapped her and called her a jerk. This time, she joked about eating the ice cream without a spoon and played a game, pretending to steal the children's spoons for herself. Once she relaxed a bit, she saw that her children were people with personalities she could enjoy. She realized that her anger had become a habit and not a true expression of feeling. She stopped forcing the children to eat dinner and go to bed early, remembering as a child how she was forced to go to bed before she was really tired.

Changing these old patterns was beginning to make for a happy home. She liked herself for making these changes. She was excited by her new desire to become a loving and understanding mother and she expressed optimism and hope for the future. Each new change and the joys they were ushering in gave her new energy to keep up the attempts.

A mother was feeling angry at her husband. He wasn't home, so she felt she couldn't resolve her feelings until later. While she and her daughter were working on a baking project, the girl broke an egg on the table and the mother yelled at her. As soon as she had called her "clumsy," the mother started to cry. She felt terrible about saying hurtful things to her daughter and was ashamed that she had misplaced the anger meant for her husband.

Many parents are concerned with the fact that they often direct anger at their children when they're not really mad at them at all. The parent is unhappy, worried, or angry about something that has nothing to do with the child, but she hasn't worked out her feelings in adequate ways, so they are fresh and raw. Then, if a child makes a minor mistake, the parent blows up and lets out all the built-up tension.

A parent's life is more complicated than the life of an adult who doesn't live with children. Children are vulnerable, and when they are around it's so easy to make them our scapegoats. Everyone will lose her or his temper at times, but I feel that parents have a responsibility to realize this possibility and take some precautionary measures.

It is very helpful for parents to let their children know when they are upset, unhappy, or particularly angry. Children can be quite understanding. Parents can even say what is specifically bothering them if they feel the child is mature enough for this information. If the child isn't, the parent can simply say, "Today I'm angry about something and it has nothing to do with you," or "I'm upset today so don't be surprised if I'm somewhat crabby." It's helpful for parents to tell a child that these feelings have not been caused by her, for quite often she will assume that they were. Children, too, know what it's like to have a bad day, and when they are given helpful information they can show surprising consideration.

Parents can try to tune in to their own feelings and take some time each day for self-examination. A parent can ask herself if there is something that she's upset about, angry about, or unhappy with that might interfere with her parental responses. If there is, she could try to direct the feelings toward the appropriate people so that they don't get stored up and released toward her child.

Sometimes it will not be appropriate for her to express the feelings toward their rightful target. This woman did need to talk things out with her husband, but she could not do so until later. At times like this, she can just go into a room alone and write an angry letter (to rip up later or not) or talk out or cry about her feelings to herself. She could say inside her mind or softly aloud (so the daughter won't hear) things like "I'm so angry" or "How will I have a pleasant afternoon?" or whatever phrases she feels could give her some relief. Then she might have less anger stored up and better control of the afternoon until she can be with her husband later and work through the feelings with him.

A mother had been learning to use positive methods of child rearing and approached her husband about using them too. He felt, however, that the old ways were fine and was not interested in changing his style. The mother continued to use the positive approaches and often criticized her husband for his negative ways of handling things. Parenting together was getting tense. Were there any suggestions for resolving this important issue?

I suggested to this mother that she continue using positive ways, but refrain from condemning her husband's methods. Let her be a model for him; in time he will see that the positive ways work and that she clearly enjoys her parenting more than before.

The mother tried this tack and noticed that once she had stopped criticizing her husband, the atmosphere immediately improved. In not too long a while, she noticed he was also turning to the new ways and seeming to get more pleasure from parenting. Still, she said nothing, for fear of putting him on the defensive. One day, he approached her and said, "I'm having a hard time right now keeping my cool. I suppose you've noticed I've been handling things in different ways. I'm trying to keep it up. You'd better go in there and take care of this situation, because the way I'm feeling I'd ruin it and blow up." The mother went in to take care of the immediate issue, and here was the start of effective teamwork.

An eight-year-old boy was invited to play at his friend's house pretty close to dinnertime. His father felt he shouldn't go, while his mother felt it would be okay to go until supper was ready. She criticized her husband for his position. Parents ask how to handle situations in which one parent is at odds with the other, and what I think about quarreling in front of children.

Children do not benefit from watching one parent belittle the other, but they do learn from watching a respectful discussion of differences. In a case like this one, it is best to take a few minutes to discuss the issue before giving a final reply. Sometimes when one parent has already stepped into the situation, it is best to let him or her continue and discuss the differing points of view later.

Whether a particular issue is appropriate to discuss in front of children is a matter of judgment. Disagreement, even quarreling, is not bad per se. Parents are individuals and will not always agree. Certain kinds of devastating quarrels are not appropriate to conduct in front of children, and some issues (including some that involve the children themselves) are not appropriate for them to hear. On the other hand, trying to hide all signs of disagreement is unrealistic and does not help children learn to deal with conflict.

It helps to point out that the quarreling is not the child's fault, as children will often worry what they did to cause the argument. Parents can explain that they still love each other and that adults who love each other do argue at times, just as parents and children do.

One mother told us that her relationship with her boyfriend had improved dramatically by using the methods she was learning in Parent Awareness. She had applied the techniques to this relationship in the following ways: She made a point to set aside special time to be with him. She had learned to consciously affirm him, letting him know what she liked and appreciated about him. She was focusing more attention on the good aspects of their life

together, rather than its problems. When she became angry, she would no longer shriek or turn to sarcasm, but express her anger directly. She had realized that her boyfriend was not always aware of her needs or expectations, but when she was clear and specific about them, he would be surprisingly cooperative. Warm affection and a pleasant tone of voice were going a long way too. Best of all, she was seeing him picking up on the positive methods and spontaneously changing himself in ways she'd been nagging about for years.

This book is for parents, so I have dwelt on how parents relate to children; but this woman made explicit for us the fact that we are really talking about human interaction in all its manifestations. Parent Awareness techniques can be applied to all relationships to enrich them and make a better world.

A father commented that he hardly ever discussed his feelings with his children or even with his wife. He mused, "Wouldn't it be helpful for me to open up so I could then help my children express feelings?" He wondered how to begin.

He could begin anywhere! If he were enjoying reading, he might look up and say, "I'm really enjoying reading this book," and perhaps go on to talk about it. If he were playing with his son, he might tell his son, "I'm having a great time playing catch with you." If he were angry or annoyed, he could express these feelings, too. If he saw his two children squabbling, he might say, "When you fight like that, I feel annoyed. I expect you to find something better to do." At the end of the day he might share his feelings about the day's events. He could begin to communicate to his wife and children his good feelings for them, his love and appreciation. They will be so glad he did!

One father had an unhappy childhood and had no pleasant memories to share. One of the most painful things was that his father was hardly ever home. Now he saw himself doing the same things, working longer hours than he needed, in order to stay away from his family. He had joined the group when he realized he was repeating a destructive pattern, and he asked for help learning to enjoy his family.

Our own childhoods influence our present parenting in many ways. It is very important to review our childhood experience and sort out what was helpful for us as we grew up and what was not. The purpose of this is not to assign blame; all parents (ourselves included) do the best they can with the knowledge available to them at the time. When we do this kind of exploring and sifting, we often find that we have been repeating something we didn't like when we were children, out of habit.

Some of the things group members have found to be negative were being hit, being called names, not getting the chance to express their feelings, not receiving much physical affection, being talked down to and often criticized, and becoming stifled by overprotection. Some of the positive memories were family outings, warm affection from their parents, a parent with a good sense of humor, being reasoned with and not hit, parents who played with them and took interest in their activities, and encouragement toward independence. One mother recalled the time her father, who was not often physically affectionate, placed a gentle hand on her forehead to soothe her when she was sick. Parents recall their own childhoods with strong emotions, some painful, some joyful.

My suggestion is to cherish the good from our past and attempt to keep this up in our family life, while working hard to discard what was negative. By thinking about our childhood, we can make conscious the influences that guide us and make intelligent choices about how to live our own lives.

This father's childhood experience was generally miserable, but by looking hard at it he was finally able to rediscover a few good things. He recalled a time that his father had taken him on a long walk and told him an amusing, inventive story as they walked along. This was an isolated good memory, but it proved helpful to search for it; a walk with his children could be a good beginning of a better relationship with them.

A father asked, "What difference will it make if we use positive methods? It's a dog-eat-dog world out there. Does it really matter what I do in my own home?"

One of the greatest agents for social change is consciousness-raising. Many people are deeply committed to the process of learning to understand themselves and each other better, seeking to better their relationships on every level, wanting the skills and awareness to get along with others in positive and humane ways, and they see this knowledge as the basic tool for worldwide change. I see the family as a consciousness-raising group in which each person learns the creative art of relating to others in positive ways, and I see this as fundamental to making the world more humane.

I believe that when we deal positively with our children, we send off a spark of light that reaches into our communities. When many of us do this together, we create a force of light and love, of strength and beauty and peace that will attract others to it. We can create a loving world with loving people, one by one, beginning in our own homes. We need to use loving and creative methods to do this, and we can, because they are available to us.

Parenting is a privilege. Let us use it and not abuse it. Together we can make it possible for the positive ways of relating to be passed on from us to our children. It is my vision and hope that they will then continue on to our grandchildren and great-grandchildren. This will be a beautiful legacy, the potential for peaceful, creative, and joyous family living for all the future generations of children on planet Earth.

Most parents readily agree that parenting is not easy; it's a difficult and demanding job. I would like to share some general thoughts on how to make life easier for ourselves.

A cooperative, community spirit can help a lot to ease the burdens of parenthood. Everyone needs an occasional vacation. Parents can trade an afternoon off or an occasional weekend. We can relax away from our children if we know they are in the care of friends we trust. It's important to get chances to be alone, without our children. We need this for our physical, mental, and emotional recharging.

Parents also help one another by providing a sympathetic ear. A parent can usually hear another's frustrations with empathy and respect. He or she knows firsthand of the sleepless nights with a sick child, the difficulty of getting time alone, the bedtime that goes on and on, the tantrums over trifles. Talking out our feelings about these events is therapeutic.

Parents can be a valuable support to one another as they learn to use the positive approaches. This happens in Parent Awareness groups, but I believe it is also something parents can do for each other informally outside a structured group. By brainstorming constructive alternatives, we help each other and also treat the daily issues of child raising with respect. When we look upon day-to-day situations as experiences in human development that deserve our intelligent and thoughtful responses, we are acknowledging that good parenting requires skill as well as intuition. Each parent knows his own children best and needs to intuit from his knowledge a good response; but he also needs to combine his intuition with parenting skills. When parents openly share their daily issues and search together for creative alternatives, they supply valuable encouragement to each other.

Parents can also share their pride at seeing their children grow. They have seen their own children pass through the developmental stages and can share a deep understanding and appreciation of others' joy at this process. Parents bring the happiness more out into the open when they share it with others. The more parents can acknowledge their joy, the more they can treasure it.

Parenting requires tremendous energy. We benefit from finding ways to use our energy to its best advantage. For example, if a mother is usually tired out at five P.M., while at nine P.M. (once the children are put to bed) she gets a second wind, then she could use the good energy she has at nine to make a casserole to heat up the next day at five, and lighten the workload at dinnertime. By using energy when it is most available, we can make it work best for us at these times.

We can also help ourselves by thinking about the fact that we, too, were once children. We got dirty, came home late, tested the limits, fought with our friends and siblings, got angry at our parents, had adventures. A parent will always be more relaxed when he can hold on to the child within himself. We can also help each other in this regard, reminding one another that each of us was a kid once too.

I encourage parents to review their family experiences at the end of each day or week and consider what worked well and what did not. We can learn something every day from the situations that occur and how we handle them. Taking time to review helps us learn from our experiences, good and bad, and use our knowledge for the future. Similarly, it is helpful to think every now and then about the nature of our relationships to each of our children, taking a look at what is going well and where our problems lie. We can appreciate what is going well and consider positive alternatives for those aspects that need improvement.

My last suggestion for making life easier is perhaps the most important of all: Keep a sense of humor if at all possible. The situation is probably not as serious as we think, and if we can keep a humorous distance, our troubles will recede. Humor is often the key to maintaining sanity amid the most trying situations. Humor provides balance and equilibrium and makes our home a pleasant place for children and adults to grow and feel fulfilled.

Epilogue

What's the value of a good childhood?

Some parents feel that good parenting will pave the way for their children to have untroubled adult lives. Looking around, they see adults choosing careers or partners they wind up not liking and making other important decisions that end in unhappiness. They hope that by giving their children positive childhoods and the chance to get in tune with themselves earlier, these later difficulties will be avoided.

Parents also say that they hope their children will never need psychotherapy. They think that seeking this type of help would mean that they had not provided such a good experience after all.

Other parents fear that in spite of a happy childhood, their children will choose life styles and careers that they, the parents, cannot approve. They feel that then the good childhood years will have all been wasted.

We need to consider these feelings. Is it realistic to assume that our children will have smooth adult lives without struggle or hard times? Most adults face some situations that are difficult, and often they emerge from these experiences stronger and wiser. The best we can hope is that if we give our children good childhoods, they will have the necessary resources to face the difficult and sometimes unforeseen events in their lives.

Growth and development do not end with the teen years. Adults seek various forms of individual or group therapy as a tool for self-exploration. In therapy people can sort out their pasts and explore their present needs, feelings, capabilities, and hopes. They can begin to focus their resources toward creating their futures. I believe that therapy should be viewed as a positive means of self-exploration, not as a negative endeavor.

Parents must also realize that their children are separate people whose choice of life style and career might be quite different from their own. Ultimately their children will have to choose for themselves. Parents can hope that their love for their children will enable them to accept whatever route in life the children select. This is a powerful goal, to be a source of affirmation for our children, no matter what road they decide to travel.

Good childhoods are never wasted. Parents benefit from them too; by offering our children a good experience of growing up, we also give ourselves a good experience of parenting. This means that a large part of our own lives, as well as our children's lives, is spent positively. This is of value in itself. We do not need to justify good parenting by the specific end product.

We live each day in the present. Let us work day by day to create a good present and trust our children to create their own meaningful adult lives when they are grown.

Summary of Parent Awareness Techniques

This summary is for reference when you need to be refreshed or reminded of a particular approach. It contains information on what is helpful and what is harmful in discipline, and discusses ways to further family harmony. I suggest reading straight through once, and then using the material as a support in your attempts at positive approaches toward dealing with your children.

BASIC POINTS: GETTING FAMILIAR WITH DISCIPLINE

What Is Discipline?

1. Discipline is a process whereby children learn to make parental standards their own. It is a slow, gradual process that extends throughout childhood. The goal of discipline is the creation of a strong and reliable conscience in a child.

2. A discipline situation that occurs in our homes is not a battle that we seek to win. Our responsibility is to help form our children's characters, not to prove that we are stronger.

3. Parents are not needed in every situation. Some incidents are very important and demand our attention, and some are best ignored.

4. Parents sometimes create major confrontations over little nothings. Ask yourself: Is it worth this hassle? Does it really matter if a child has one cookie or two cookies, goes to bed at 8:15 instead of 8:10? Don't waste your time and your child's energy on trivia.

5. Sometimes parents don't handle a situation soon enough. Then the misbehavior gets way out of hand and the parent's anger, which was slowly building up, comes out in a sudden torrent. Set the limit on the child's misbehavior before it has gone too far, and try to express your anger before it turns to rage.

6. Learn to take a few seconds to think before rushing into a situation. As long as nothing dangerous is happening, there is usually a little time to spare. Think: What do I want to accomplish here? or What would be a positive response? Then you will be better prepared to handle the situation.

7. Parents want to be able to stop their children's misbehavior whenever it occurs, but in fact there will always be some things they won't be able to control no matter what methods, positive or negative, they use. This is a reality of life with children.

8. Children even need some chances to get away with inappropriate behavior. Most parents can remember how good it felt to get away with some things when they were children.

9. When a child persists in a misbehavior that the parents are trying to stop, they can let the child know that they disapprove. The displeasure will register and create mild feelings of guilt, which will help the child to do better next time.

10. Parents can let their children know that they don't expect cooperation in every single instance, but that cooperation does feel better and they would like a reasonable percentage. This is realistic, and children are relieved to know they are not expected to be perfect. Grownups themselves would not appreciate someone hovering over them to comment on every move and indiscretion.

11. Children do need their parents to set the limits. If a child is acting inappropriately and can't control himself, he feels uncomfortable. Children feel safer when parents define the boundaries of what is and what is not acceptable.

12. Children will not always like the rules. To show their displeasure they might stomp their feet, stick out their tongues, fuss, cry, or say to their parents, "You hate me." The parent can accept the child's feeling while sticking to the limit, saying, "I see you don't like this rule, but it has to be this way," or "In fact, I do love you, but I need to make this rule."

13. Sometimes a child will misbehave to get her parent's attention. Then, when the parent does direct attention to her, she gets negative attention, disapproval and anger. It's helpful for parents to make sure they are giving their children ample positive time doing enjoyable things together, so that children won't need to act up to get attention.

14. Children misbehave for many other reasons:
- To "test the limits"—to see if the parent really will follow through.
- Because they're feeling jealous, angry, tired, hungry, overstimulated, understimulated, confused, or frightened.
- Because of troubling circumstances such as a death or divorce.
- Because their consciences are not yet strong enough to provide

them with the control needed to prevent inappropriate behavior. Conscience development takes time.

• Because they are in a more difficult stage and are behaving according to the characteristics normal for that stage (like a two-year-old who is rebellious or a four-year-old who is demanding).

15. Parents sometimes feel that their children's misbehavior is a judgment on them. This is not so. Children are separate from us, and we shouldn't take their behavior personally or allow ourselves to be judged by others for it.

16. Different families have different standards, rules, and values. What one family says yes to, another family forbids. All families, however, can handle discipline situations with the same humane methods.

17. There are always several positive ways to approach a discipline issue. One parent might use humor, another might offer a choice, while yet another parent would express anger in a helpful way. Each parent can aim to use a variety of approaches.

18. Using positive approaches won't eliminate problems. Life with children means a certain number of conflicts, usually each day. Positive approaches *do* help us to live through and handle the stressful times with more ease and dignity. It is important for parents to show that there are positive ways to deal with conflicts and that using them can create harmony once again.

Adopting a Positive Style

1. Parents are human. No one will be able to use positive approaches all of the time, but the more a parent uses positive methods, the better off the family will be. We can aim to use positive alternatives most of the time.

2. Parenting is more fulfilling when positive methods are used. Negative methods drain energy. Slapping and yelling leave parents feeling irritable and drained of energy. When parents use positive methods, they feel better about themselves and they have more energy to devote to aspects of their lives other than their parenting.

3. Parents will "lose their cool" at times. This can even be good, for it shows children that their parents aren't perfect any more than they are. When parents can express their raging feelings in ways that are not hurtful, then they offer a positive model for resolving conflict and showing strong feelings.

4. Parents should not feel bad for having used negative methods in the past. They've been following tradition. More is known today, however, about what provides a healthy, supportive growth environment for children. Parents now have new options, and it's never too late to start using them.

5. It's hard to use methods we haven't learned from our own child rearing. It's hard to change old methods for new ways. It takes time, effort, and commitment. But it's worth it!

6. If we bring up our children with positive methods, they can keep up the use of positive methods when they themselves become parents. Our actions can be effective far into the future.

7. Don't feel judged by others who aren't using positive methods, and don't be influenced by people who aren't using positive methods.

8. Influence and teach others to use positive approaches. Be a positive model for others.

9. Help to make life on earth more fulfilling, pleasant, and loving. Spread the good word. Let's embrace the positive and uplifting methods of our age.

THIRTY-SIX POSITIVE APPROACHES TO DISCIPLINE

Verbal Methods

1. State your expectations. It is helpful for parents to let children know what they expect. Too often parents assume a child knows what the parent wants and the child doesn't. Be direct and clear in letting your children know what you expect of them.

2. Be encouraging. It is helpful to use encouraging phrases that show you are confident that children can live up to your expectations. Examples of positive ways to phrase your expectations are: "It would be helpful if . . ."; "I have confidence that . . ."; "I expect you to . . ."; "I know you can . . ."

3. Appreciate improvements. Let children know that you notice and appreciate their efforts when they correct a misbehavior and show they are able to cooperate.

4. Spend a great deal of time praising, acknowledging, and appreciating a child's desirable behavior. This encourages and reinforces it.

5. Parents can help to change unacceptable behavior by making environmental changes:
- If the children are bored, help them to set up constructive activities (modeling dough, water play, games, etc.).
- If the environment has become too stimulating and active, redirect the children to a quiet activity.
- If the children are hungry, feed them; if they're tired, adjust sleep schedules.
- Sometimes children don't cooperate when they can't manipulate their environment; they feel frustrated and helpless. Parents can

adjust the environment to meet the child's level by arranging coat hooks where children can reach them, placing stools near high sinks, allowing children to pour their own drinks from a half-filled container, etc. Try to make your living space into an environment in which all family members can feel at home.

• Parents can set aside a place for messy activities, such as one small table where children know it's okay for them to paint and paste.

6. Prepare children for changes and transitions. They will cooperate better if they've had time to adjust. For example: "In ten minutes we'll be leaving for the park, so start to put your toys away"; "In two weeks we're going to visit Grandpa. Let's think of what you'll need to bring along."

7. Consider the effect of any emotional stresses (divorce, a new school, etc.) on the children's behavior and give them plenty of opportunity to work through their feelings in appropriate ways.

8. Keep in mind the age and stage capabilities of children and what they are emotionally ready to handle. Try not to ask too much or too little of a child. Quite often, parents believe a toddler or young child can handle more than he really can. When there is a recurring conflict over the same situation, it could indicate that the child is not capable of what you are asking. Being familiar with the developmental stages can keep your expectations realistic.

9. Distract. Don't mention the child's misbehavior, but direct his attention elsewhere.

10. Avoid asking a toddler questions that encourage a "no" answer and a possible attack of rebelliousness. Instead of asking, "Do you want to put your shoes on?" be affirmative, and say, "It's time to get your shoes on now."

11. Be clear and emphatic when you need to be. Say, "You must wear your winter jacket this morning. There is no choice in this matter."

12. Stay simple. Don't make a long speech when a stern glance or brief "Cut it out" is all that is needed.

13. State the limit impersonally. "Walls are not for writing on" is better than "You may not write on walls." This puts the focus on the rule, not the child.

14. Offer alternatives. Children need to know what they can do, not just what they cannot do. For example: "The chair is not for jumping on. You can jump on the floor" or "Your sister is not for hitting. Hit this pillow instead."

15. Bend your rules for special occasions. If bedtime is usually 8:30 and a special TV show is on until later or a family friend is visiting, you can extend the bedtime hour.

16. Give the reasons for your rules and limits.

17. Be prepared to repeat the limit, even several times, as children can't be expected to jump to command.

18. Give children the chance to express their feelings about a situation before expecting them to try and resolve it.

19. Allow a child in fantasy what he can't be allowed in reality: "You wish you were grown-up and could go to bed much later, but now it's really your bedtime."

20. Teach your child to use words instead of hits, kicks, or bites when he is angry: "You are angry at your brother, but he is not for hitting. Use words to tell him you are mad at him."

21. When your child needs a more forceful outlet than words for his anger and aggression, encourage him to hit a pillow, and help him verbalize his angry feelings as he does so.

22. Give a warning. Warn children of the effect their behavior is having upon you: "Right now I am still a pleasant daddy, but in a few minutes, if this keeps up, you'll have an angry father to deal with."

23. Tell your child you are angry when you are. Giving your honest disapproval lets your child understand the consequences of his behavior, and also he will feel more secure when you respond in an honest way with your feelings.

24. Use statements that express: "When you cooperate with me, then I want to cooperate with you." For example: "If you cooperate and let me have a quiet cup of tea with my friend, then I will feel like cooperating with your request to have your friend spend the night."

25. When you are in the middle of an argument you realize you don't even care about, erase the scene and start again. Leave the room, come back, and pretend the conflict never even happened.

26. Offer choices: "You have a choice. You can play ball outside, or stay inside and pick something else to do." A choice is clear-cut. The parent must be prepared to follow through. If the child remains indoors and continues to throw the ball, the parent needs to take the ball away saying, "You decided to stay inside; go do something else." Choices help children become more responsible for their actions.

27. Tell children how their behavior is affecting you, and then leave them to think of a way to remedy the situation on their own. Instead of saying, "Please turn down the radio so I can hear," a parent can sometimes say, "I can't hear on the telephone with the radio so loud," and let the child figure out what needs to be done, whether it's closing doors, turning down the volume, or taking the radio to another room.

28. Give children some control. As children get older, they need some flexibility: "You can do your homework whenever you want to, as long as it's done before you watch TV."

29. Begin your request with "as soon as": "As soon as you put your toys away, you can go to your friend's house" or "As soon as you brush your teeth, I'll read you a story."

30. Use role reversal, in which parent and child pretend to be each other. You can reverse roles just for the fun of it at times and also in discipline situations. Children feel powerful playing the adult role, and then return to being the child refreshed. (Never force a child to reverse roles; only do this if he is willing.) When the child becomes the parent for a short time, he is not on the spot. This gives him a few extra moments to think the issue through. By playing the parent, he gets to set the limit, and he will often listen to it better when he can state it himself. Switching roles lightens the tone, too. Even very young children can appreciate the humor of a parent pretending to be a fussing child.

31. Be humorous. Humor can be a great aid in solving conflicts, whenever you are up to it. Children of all ages appreciate humor at their level.

32. Use a gamelike approach often. If a child is resisting putting his pajamas on, his mother can say, "I'll close my eyes and spin around three times, and then you'll have your pajamas on." This approach is often more effective than getting angry.

33. Put some requests in writing. When children begin to read, occasionally having a request in writing can make it easier to accept: "Dear Jason, You said your clothes would be left in the hamper, not on the floor. How about it? Love, Dad." The child can be encouraged to write back.

34. Make a deal! "You can stay up until nine o'clock tonight if you play quietly in your room while we have dinner with our company. Otherwise, you'll need to go to bed at your regular time. Is it a deal?"

35. From time to time, bribe. Occasionally, it's a reasonable way of making a situation easier for ourselves: "If you are pleasant and cooperative while I go to the supermarket, I'll buy you an ice cream after" or "If you go to bed on time tonight so that I can enjoy my company, you'll find a surprise in your shoe tomorrow."

36. Approach issues as problems to solve. Parents can encourage children to think of ways to solve a problem, and often the children will come up with excellent, original solutions. If not, the parents can offer possible solutions themselves, and include the children in the process of deciding from among them. It's good to discuss all of the alternatives thoroughly and try to agree on a solution acceptable to all. Parents can rely on this approach more and more as their children grow older. It's much easier for children to comply with a decision if they helped to make it and their needs were genuinely respected in the process. When parents use this technique routinely, they begin to see children turning to problem solving more and more on their own as a way to work out issues with their friends. They are developing the important skills of self-reliance and creative approaches to problems.

When Words Are Not Enough . . .
Take Positive Action

1. When parents are not succeeding with words alone, they need to accompany their words with helpful action. This is not the same as punishment, with its emphasis on having children pay for their misbehavior. Parents need to stop thinking in terms of punishment and work toward helpful action steps. When we take action, we show children that we will take the necessary steps to teach them what is appropriate, and we will do so in a teaching and supportive way. Our actions should be taken with an eye to helping children understand better the importance of our limits and rules, and building up their own self-control. Parental action is helpful when:
- It is taken in a supportive spirit.
- It is as closely connected as possible with the misbehavior so the child can learn from it.
- It lasts only until the child demonstrates that he is once again ready to handle the situation appropriately, not for a predetermined length of time.

2. Some appropriate kinds of action for a parent to take are:
- *Removing an object the child is misusing, until she is ready to have it back and use it appropriately.* This is more sensible than saying, "No squirt gun until tomorrow." It makes good use of the child's inner timetable. Our goal is to help our children follow our rules *as soon as they are able to.* If the child's control returns sooner than tomorrow, so much the better.
- *Temporarily removing or altering a privilege, until the child can handle it responsibly.* A ten-year-old comes home from school each day, drops her lunch box and school items in the living room, and races outdoors to play. Her mother makes a rule: "No going outside until your belongings are put in the proper place."
- *Removing a child from a situation in which he is acting up.* This can mean leaving a store where he is behaving disruptively or, at home, sending him to play in his room until he can be pleasant company for the rest of the family.
- *Holding a child to prevent disruptive behavior, using the minimum force necessary to accomplish this.* If a child is kicking a kitchen cabinet and has refused to be redirected, the parent would need to take action by holding him so he won't wreck the cabinet. Holding a child is protective. The parent is not hurting the child, and he is stopped from acting dangerously or disruptively.
- *Physically guiding a child from one place to another.* A two-year-old who doesn't want to come inside for dinner gets carried in by a parent who is firm and in control. (She could be "flown in"

airplane-style if the parent is in the mood.) When children are out of control, they benefit from having their parent stay calm and authoritative. This reassures children. The parent uses physical force to carry the child, but is not hurtful.

• *Following through on the statement "When you don't cooperate with me, then I don't feel like cooperating with you" by acting in accordance with your mood.* If the room is still a mess, say, "Your toys are still not put away and I'm feeling quite worn out about it. I'll read to you later when my good mood returns."

3. When the damage is done, taking action means focusing on a solution. If a child has thrown all her toys about in a rage, the parent can express displeasure and then take helpful action by cleaning it up together. Blaming or punishing her is not helpful; working toward a remedy is the best use of everyone's energy.

The Do's and Don'ts of Anger

1. DO use language that is helpful. Words like "furious," "mad," "unhappy," "disappointed," "angry," "displeased," "annoyed," and "irritated" describe feelings and are helpful words.

2. DO use anger to express feelings, values, needs, and expectations. Statements like "I am furious," "This displeases me," "I'm unhappy about this," "I expect you to put your shoes away," "Our walls are not for ruining," said firmly and angrily to children, let them know clearly and strongly how parents feel and teach them the rules.

3. DO match the expression of anger to true feelings. If you are only mildly annoyed, you can say, "I'm a bit annoyed," or "This is making me slightly irritated." If you are very angry, let the child know: "I'm very mad about this" or "This has made me very angry."

4. DO express helpful *wishful* anger when an expression of angry feelings is not enough. Wishful anger helps parents gain more relief for their feelings and gives children an extra incentive to correct their behavior. A mother might say, "I am so angry that you are banging the wall with your truck that I feel like saying no trucks in the house ever again!" This is a helpful statement of wishful anger. The mother is not saying the child can never use his trucks again, but only that she *feels* like saying, "No trucks."

5. DON'T use harmful wishful anger. "I am so angry I feel like killing you," "I'd like to break your neck," and "I could bang your head against the wall" are statements of wishful anger that are harmful and scary. Parents should never threaten violence or physical injury. A child's sense of fantasy and reality is too fragile to understand that his parent is not going to do these things.

6. DO think to *yourself* thoughts like "I feel like killing that kid" or "I'd like to break his arm," if you need to. It's normal to have these kinds of thoughts, and it gives relief to admit them to yourself.

7. DO say a phrase like "I'd like to break her neck" over and over *mentally.* This is a harmless way to give these thoughts expression and it keeps them off the tip of your tongue as you deal with the situation in a positive way.

8. DO take a moment to mumble these intense feelings quietly aloud, out of the child's hearing range, when thinking them silently is not enough to give relief.

9. DO turn to another adult and say, "I'd like to kill that kid," to get relief. Again, the child shouldn't hear this.

10. DO take to heart the Parent Awareness teaching that people (adults and children) are not for hurting. Parents are always trying to teach their children not to bite or hit or kick. Parents need to demonstrate self-control too.

11. DO go to another room when your anger is so great you may lose control. You can approach the child a bit later, once you have cooled off.

12. DO hit a pillow if you need to hit. This may sound strange. It isn't. Hitting a pillow is a therapeutic technique to get off intense momentary anger. The pillow isn't hurt. When children are hit, their bodies and self-images are damaged. Many children need to hit pillows themselves sometimes. They'll be able to understand a parent's need to do this on occasion also.

13. DON'T let anger get bottled up and stored. Sometimes, after the situation has been resolved, the parent is left still feeling mad about it. A parent who has spent an hour hassling with a child at bedtime may have handled the child and the situation very well, but after the child is asleep he may still be fuming and unable to relax and enjoy the evening. The parent can find expression for his feelings by saying them to himself, a friend, or his spouse. For example, he may say, "What a drag that bedtime scene was. What a lousy hassle. I could've killed that kid!" Do it out of the child's hearing. If the parent is still so mad, he may hit a pillow for a few seconds while saying the angry feelings. Why carry around leftover anger? Expressing angry feelings relieves them.

14. DO try to direct your anger toward the people and situations that deserve it, and DON'T let it all get dumped on your children. It's appropriate for parents to warn their children when they are feeling angry and upset, and likely to be grouchy. Admit to them that you are angry, but reassure them that your anger is not directed at them. Sharing with our children that we're upset can also help to relieve the feelings.

NEGATIVE METHODS OF DISCIPLINE THAT NEED TO BE ELIMINATED

Negative Verbal Methods

1. *Sarcasm.* It cuts children down and hurts emotionally.

2. *Hurtful teasing or excessive kidding around.* Most parents do kid their children sometimes, but too much of it makes a child feel powerless.

3. *Calling names.* When parents call children "rotten," "bad," "stupid," "naughty," or "bratty," children begin to believe these labels and can develop a poor self-image. Parental disapproval should be aimed at the child's behavior, not his character. Your child is still a good person, even when he is doing something you cannot approve. Say, "I don't like what you are doing," not "Your are a bad boy."

4. *Judgmental praise*—telling children that they are "good" in a judgmental way, meaning "well-behaved." *This can make children feel they are loved only when they behave perfectly.* It *is* fine to tell children that they are "so good" in a loving, affectionate way.

5. *Making statements of negative expectation.* "Why can't you ever" (get along together, listen, act nicely), "You'll always be" (lazy, late, a slob), "You'll never" (learn, be careful, get it right)—these are statements that demonstrate to children our lack of faith in them. This can cause them to think, "If my mother says I'll never be able to, she must know what she's talking about"—and then live up to the parent's negative expectations.

6. *Being wishy-washy or vague.* "You can write on the wall a little" is confusing, as is "Be good." Make your rules and limits clear.

7. *Concentrating attention on misbehavior.* When a parent is always pointing out and reprimanding unacceptable behavior, this causes the child to focus more on it too, and he may, in fact, increase it.

8. *Rubbing it in.* Once a child already feels bad for something he has done, don't keep dwelling on the matter.

9. *Threats.* When a parent says, "If you do it one more time, "I'll . . . ," the child may find it hard to resist. Threats are like dares; they egg children on.

10. *Looking for the culprit.* It's better to expend energy solving a problem than finding out who caused it and blaming that child.

11. *Encouraging competition* between children by holding one up to another as an example of good behavior.

Punishments and a Punishing Attitude

1. All the old phrases like "I'm going to punish you," "You're going to be punished," and "You're on punishment" are negative statements. Punishment sets the parent up against the child and this is not good. Instead, parents need to show they are for their child and will guide him forward, supportively.

2. Sometimes, parents need to take action to stop a misbehavior, but this action should *not* be:

- Given in a spirit of revenge, as by saying, "I'll show you!"
- Done in a way that has nothing to do with the misbehavior, as when TV privileges are revoked for using a squirt gun in the house.
- Excessive, for too long, or for a rigid, set length of time. If the child who is misusing his squirt gun is deprived of using it for three weeks, he will use much more of that time feeling resentful than learning a rule and the reason for it.

Humiliation

Washing children's mouths out with soap, standing children in corners, depriving children of meals, and putting them to bed in the daytime are old-fashioned methods that humiliate and pain children and do not treat them with respect as human beings.

Physical Attacks

All hitting, hair-pulling, pinching, belting, spanking, and slapping are bad. It is incorrect to hit, whether we hit a child two times or ten times. Hitting is inappropriate whether we use light or hard strokes. Hitting is wrong whether we hit a child infrequently or often, use a hand or a stick. Hitting in *any* form is a harmful method. We need to do away with physical punishments completely, because they:

- Hurt.
- Offer a poor model for handling conflict.
- Create resentment.
- Do not teach correct rules or standards.
- Can give a child a poor body image.
- Make a child feel powerless and unworthy.
- Can make a child feel that his debt is paid and he is free to repeat the misbehavior.
- Do not help to develop the child's own self-control.
- Do not treat a child with respect.
- Make parents feel like bullies.

• Perpetuate a double standard that needs to end. Adults are now protected by the laws of our land from physical harm. Children, too, deserve and need full legal protection from any harm to their bodies. Children cannot lobby for themselves. As adults, we are the ones who need to make sure that the laws of our land defend children.

FURTHERING FAMILY HARMONY

Special Time

1. Every day, try to spend some *special time* alone with each of your children and let each know this is your special time with her or him. Give the child your total attention during this time.

2. Many parents lead busy lives and schedule all kinds of activities, but forget to leave some time to spend enjoyably, purposefully, and in a relaxed manner with their children. Even five to thirty minutes each day can go a long way to cement a good rapport.

3. Don't be folding laundry or going to the bank during special time, and don't let it be an occasion for conflict or fault finding. Let this be pleasant time together.

4. Use special times to do things with the child that he wants to do and that you can enjoy doing with him. Children usually have ideas about how they'd like to spend their special times with you, and you can make suggestions as well. Some ways to spend special time are:

• Talking with and listening to each child.
• Watching as the child plays and showing an interest in what he is doing. As he builds with blocks, you might comment, "I like your tower," or "You're working so hard on that castle."
• Doing something together, like reading a story, doing a puzzle, baking cookies, building a treehouse, playing catch.
• Going on an outing together, to a restaurant, museum, library, playground, or ball game.

5. *Tell* your child that the special times you spend with him are both meaningful and enjoyable for you. Tell him either during the special time or after, your thoughts: "I'm enjoying reading to you now" or "I loved our walk together yesterday." Knowing that you like to be with him helps a child feel good about himself, and he may not be aware of your feelings on these occasions unless you tell him. As you tell him, a kiss or touch on the shoulder adds warmth. When a child hears positive feelings shared directly with him this way, he is likely to return positive thoughts and affection to you in a similar way.

6. Even older children and teenagers need special times with their parents.

7. It's nice for grandparents and aunts and uncles to spend some special time with children and tell them some of the things they like about them and some of the things they enjoy doing with them. Parents can encourage their children to tell these relatives what they like about them and what they enjoy doing together. This extends harmony through the extended family.

8. Have family times when everyone joins together to talk and do things. Also arrange times when a few members of the family have special times with each other. For example, two children can have special time with a parent while the other two children are out visiting friends. At these times, too, remember to let the children know how much these experiences mean to you.

9. Siblings can enjoy special times without their parents, just being kids together, playing and doing things on their own.

10. In addition to the special times parents set aside for their children, parents can transform ordinary moments into special times:

- If a parent is doing the dishes while his children are playing a superhero game, the parent can join in as a superhero who's doing the dishes, talking and planning the plots along with his children.
- There are many daily opportunities in which parents can affirm their children through words and touch. If a father is having coffee while his son is doing homework next to him, the father might say, "It's very nice to have you here next to me," and lean over and touch his son on the shoulder. A mother might say to her children at breakfast, "It's good being with you. I'm enjoying having breakfast together," and give them a hug or kiss. Those simple words, It's nice being with you," can contribute much toward a child's sense of self-worth.

Be Affectionate and Appreciative

1. Let your children know the things you like and appreciate about them. Point out to each child his strengths and fine characteristics. He or she will be very happy that you noticed. "I love your smile," "I appreciate your way of helping others," "I like your sense of fun," "I love the gentle care you give your hamster," and "You have a wonderful way with numbers and math" are comments that make children feel good.

2. It's nice on occasion to put your appreciations in writing, too.

3. Appreciate your children totally for being the special people they are, not for their achievements. Certainly, it's good to appreciate our children's accomplishments, but they deserve to be loved for who they are, not just what they do.

4. Be physically demonstrative with your children, with boys and girls of all ages. Be warm and loving and kind. Children need hugs and kisses. Try holding your child's hand or massaging your child's back at times, too.

5. Say, "I love you." Our children need to hear these words from us, often.

6. Occasionally tell your children some of the things you like about yourself. Share some of the things you enjoy doing, alone and with them. Often people find it hard to say positive things about themselves and others. When parents do so, they are teaching children that it's valuable to express positive feelings. When family members express positive feelings freely, everyone feels better about each other and himself. Children hear a lot of complaints ("I have a terrible headache," "What a lousy day!") and criticism. Appreciations like "I'm enjoying this book," "That was a great bike ride," or "One thing I like about myself is that I have a lot of energy" set a positive tone for the entire household.

7. Let your children know that you enjoy being a parent. Let each child know you are glad he or she is your child. Share with your children what gives you pleasure and joy from being a parent: "I love watching you grow and change. It's great for me to be your father." "I love reading to you at night. I'm glad I'm your mother and get to enjoy this." "Being a parent is wonderful for me. I love it when I get to live through the special times, seeing your first tooth fall out, watching you walk off to first grade for the first time on your own." Children will swell with good feelings inside when they hear their parents expressing their pleasure in parenthood.

8. Sometimes ask children to think about and share some of the things they like about themselves and what they enjoy doing, and ask them to tell you some of the things they like about you as well. If it is hard for them to express these thoughts, you can help out: "I bet you like the way you've just learned how to tie your shoes so well" or "I know you really enjoy playing with your dollhouse people" or "I bet one thing you like about me is the way I read to you." After getting your assistance for a while, your children will soon be able to express positive feelings on their own. You will be surprised and delighted to hear their spontaneous appreciations.

9. Parents can encourage good feelings between siblings. It is important to help brothers and sisters express angry and jealous feelings, but parents can also help them to value each other. Parents can comment to children on the benefits of having siblings and point out the ways they enjoy each other. At dinner, while all the children are present, the parents might say, "What do you like about each other? Let's go around the table and take turns saying what each of you likes about the others." Parents also need to foster a cooperative spirit among their children, not a competitive one. They can encourage sisters and brothers to help each other out at times, play together, and be affectionate with one another.

10. People in a family are different from one another. Don't expect children to be just like you or each other. Value each child's individual interests and needs.

11. I encourage fathers to be actively involved in parenting—to diaper babies, feed and bathe them, tuck them in at night, and be physically affectionate. I ask fathers to continue active fathering as their children grow older, to go on taking care of them in every way, when they are sick and when they are well, playing together, showing interest in their activities, setting limits in positive ways. I urge fathers to be kind, gentle, and affectionate with their sons and daughters of all ages.

Be Considerate

1. Speak with your children in a pleasant way as much of the time as possible. Raising your voice and yelling should be saved for when you really need it.

2. Don't know all the answers, and don't be condescending. Speak with children in a natural way, as you would with anyone else. If parents always sound wise and understanding, it can get deathly boring. Humor is a good way to vary your tone. Using a gamelike approach is another good variation. Children love games and appreciate it when parents can have fun along with them. When children and parents can laugh, share their imaginations, and goof off together, the discipline and conflict are in better perspective.

3. Make requests with a cooperative attitude, not a bossy, demanding one. Children learn from their parents how to relate to others. When you model pleasantness, warmth, and consideration, they will learn positive ways to relate to you and others.

4. Don't pounce on children when they come home from school with negative remarks like "You forgot to take out the garbage!" First say, "Hello. It's nice to see you. How was your day?" Let children return home to a pleasant atmosphere.

5. Be a sounding board. Listen to your children's feelings about how things are going. Share with them your own feelings about the things you do. You can do this as you are together around the house and also sometimes at more formal family discussions.

6. Often children do want to share their thoughts and experiences, but not immediately. A child may need some time after school for the day's events to gel. Later, he is ready to tell all about the day. You can communicate that you would like to hear about it, if and when he would like to talk about it.

7. Children often have different ideas about things than their parents. Don't put children down for disagreeing with you on an issue. You might say, "You feel one way, I feel another," or "That's your way of looking at it; here's mine." Respect children's rights to their own feelings and ideas.

8. Children and parents are separate people. Children will share much of what they think and do with their parents and also keep some part of their experiences to themselves. Value your child's right to privacy.

9. Let your children know that you are a complete person, with good days and bad days, good and bad moods, just like they are. Let your children know that you aren't perfect. Don't expect your children to be perfect either!

10. Be realistic. Talk to your children about the fact that each person (young or old) has certain strengths and limitations. Help your children to accept the limitations alongside of the strengths. People are better off when they view themselves realistically and are comfortable with their total selves.

11. Do not identify children with labels like "bully," "lazy," "clumsy," "irresponsible." Labeling damages a child's self-esteem and creates negative expectations to live up to. If you already see a child through a negative label like "bully," you can change this by:

• Changing your view to see him as a good person, not a "bully."
• Giving him opportunities to act positively.
• Helping him to act positively.

12. At the end of the day, sometimes go over with children some of the nice events of their day, to help them think about pleasant things before settling down for the night.

13. Don't let conflicts go unresolved after a fight. Try to discuss things later when you are both calm. Try not to let a child take off for school or go to bed with bitter feelings still between you. If you cannot agree just then, you can say, "We love each other and we are good friends. Later on, we'll work out a solution to our problem."

Enjoy Yourself!

1. Parenting has pleasures and satisfactions. So many of the joys are at once simple and profound, like the feelings parents experience when they see their child peacefully asleep, looking so beautiful and angelic, or when they kiss a child's warm cheek, or hear a child say, "I love you," or watch the many ways their child keeps on changing and growing. As much as possible, parents can focus their attention on these wonderful aspects of parenting, cherish them, and remember them. They make parenting worth it, and help to balance out the rougher going that parenting involves as well.

2. Put positive energy into your parenting! The more good feelings you put into your parenting, the more blessings and pleasures you'll get from it. Let's all follow the powerful positive path of parenting day by day and leave it as a legacy to our children and all future children on earth.

Saf Lerman is also the author of the *Parent Awareness Group Experience Leader's Manual* and the Parent Awareness Booklet Series (fourteen booklets on positive approaches to family life). Persons and organizations interested in obtaining these program materials or in finding out more about the Parent Awareness program itself can write to Saf Lerman, Publisher, P.O. Box 293, Newton Centre, Massachusetts 02159.

Index

About Dying: An Open Family Book for Parents and Children Together (Stein), 168
About Handicaps: An Open Family Book for Parents and Children Together (Stein), 126
Achievement, sense of, 124
Adjusters (or bribes), 45–46
Adolescence, 53, 68–71
Adopted children, divorce and, 155–56
Adult companion, treating child as, 163–64
Adult models (other than parents), 182
Affectionate, being, 232–34
Afraid of being left alone, 119–21
Afternoon nap, 61–62
Ages and stages (growth and change), 52–71; adolescence, 68–71; afternoon nap, 61–62; aggressive behavior, 65–66; disruptive behavior (setting limits), 64–65; early-rising phase, 62; Erikson's scheme, 53–54; four-year-olds, 63–66; giving up bottles and pacifiers, 58–59; handling responsibility, 62–63; hitting and biting, 56–57; life stages, 52–55; messy eater, 63–64; mood changes, 64; one-year-olds, 55–58; preschool programs, 60–61; school-age behavior expectations, 67; sharing with others, 59; "slow" child, 63; talking back, 65–66; toilet training, 57–58; two-year-olds, 54–63
Aggression, 65–66, 75
Allowances and money management, 193–94

Anger, 3, 7, 11, 13, 14, 15, 18, 19, 20, 27, 34, 43, 48, 56, 60, 65, 67, 80, 83, 92–98, 99, 102, 138, 154, 156–57, 175, 176, 177–78, 200, 205, 207, 212; at children (built-up tension), 209–10; do's and don'ts of, 227–29; expressing, 94–95, 98; as a habit, 209; momentary feelings of, 95–96; mothers verbalization of, 5; positive methods, 94–95, 204; ways to handle, 31
Anxiety, 58, 109, 122, 124, 155, 174, 175
Apology, mother's, 99
Appreciation, learning, 106–7
Appreciative, being, 232–34
Apprehension, minimizing, 121–22
Approval, 12
Attention, 14, 42, 50, 63
Authority, 10
Autonomy, sense of, 53

Baby Sister for Frances, A (Hoban), 74
Baby-sitters, 121
"Bad," calling child, 3
Bad dreams, 130–31, 132
Balance, family's, 11, 64
Bedtime, 47–51, 175
Bed-wetting, 66–67
Before You Were a Baby (Showers), 136
Behavior: difference between good child and, 3; ignoring, 9, 11; *See also* types of behavior
Bernstein, Joanne, 168
Birth control, 150
Biting and hitting, 56–57
Body language, 25, 44
Boredom, 42

Bottles, when to give up, 58–59
Boys and Girls Book About Divorce, The (Gardner), 155
Boys and Sex (Pomeroy), 151
Bribes, 45–46
Brightman, Alan, 126–27
Brown, Margaret Wise, 98
Bullis, Glenna E., 54

Capabilities, concentrating on, 108
Car trips, 45–46
Child abuse, 29, 207
Child Behavior from Birth to Ten (Ilg and Ames), 54, 142
Child custody, divorced parents and, 158–59
Child from Five to Ten, The (Gesell, Ilg and Ames), 54
Childhood influences (on parents), 212–13
Childhood and Society (Erikson), 53
Childproofing the home, 2
Child rearing, positive ways of, 210–11
Choices, making, 185
Civil rights movement, 28
Clothes, selecting, 194
Clumsiness, 111
Clumsy label, 112
Coffin, 173–74
Comparisons, 86
Confidence: self-image and, 116–18; showing, 20
Confrontation, 2
Conscience, development of, 2–3
Consciousness-raising, 213–14
Considerate, being, 234–35
Control, losing, 27
Cool, losing one's, 205–6
Cooperation, 77, 78, 82, 86, 88; *See also* Independence and interdependence
Copulation, children imitating, 142
Coutant, Helen, 168
Cremation, 173–74
Criticism (that puts down child's efforts), 113
Crying, 8, 37, 84, 93, 113, 201, 206; as healing, 101–102; when parent leaves, 122
Curious George Goes to the Hospital (Rey), 130

Daily life, 34–51; adjusters (or bribes), 45–46; bedtime, 47–51; car trips, 45–46; dinnertime and eating issues, 34–38; fantasy and reality, 41–42; five-year-olds, 37–38, 44–45, 48–49;
four-year-olds, 41–44, 46–47, 49–51; fun and games and humor, 47; inquisitive (irritating) questions, 44–45; lies, 41–42; name calling, 44; "one more" requests, 46–47; personal care situations, 47; pestering child, 42–43; play situations, 39–42; pleasant morning experience, 38; quarrels, 39–40; shopping, 44–45; six-year-olds, 38–41; swear words, 34–38; three-year-olds, 36–37, 48; two-year-olds, 45–46
Dark room, fear of, 130
Death, children and, 167–79; anxiety and fear, 174–75; bedtime, 175; cheated feelings, 177–78; discussing the topic, 167–68; fears, fantasies, and feelings, 168–70; "gone on vacation" story, 172–73; grief, 170; life after death beliefs, 174; misbehavior, 176–77; miscarriage, 176; parent's openness (or lack of it), 170–72; pets, 178–79; recalling "those scary days," 178; television, 179; telling real cause of death, 175–76; wake, funeral, and cemetery, 173–74
Decisions, including children in, 85–86
Demanding tone, talking in, 200
Depriving a child (for punishment), 16–17
Descriptive praise, 115–16
Diapering, 57
Dining room table, playing at, 42–43
Dinnertime and eating issues: battles, 34–38; behavior, 8–9, 36; messy eater, 63–64; setting the table fights, 190
Disappointment, feelings of, 93–94, 200
Disapproval, 9, 12, 23
Discipline, 1–33, 207; assertive self-defense, 6–7; basic points of, 219–21; eleven-year-olds, 22–24; feet on dinner table, 8–9; five-year-olds, 9–11; four-year-olds, 8–9; hitting children, 3–7, 15–16, 24–31; inclination to retaliate, 11; learning positive parenting, 29–30; lighting matches and, 13; negative methods (that need to be eliminated), 229–30; nine-year-olds, 20–21; not listening attitude, 4–5; nuisance child, 13–14, 22; Parent Awareness groups and, 31–33; positive style, 22, 25, 221–22, 226–27; punishment, 16–22; reversing roles, 7–8; rock throwing, 20–21; setting limits, 9–16; seven-

year-olds, 13–20; six-year-olds, 11–13; slapping, 11–12, 25, 29; spanking, 2–3, 5, 8, 11–12, 26, 28; "tell the truth and not lie" confrontation, 22–23; three-year-olds, 4–8; toddlers, 1–2; two-year-olds, 2–4; verbal methods of, 222–25
Disposable Parent, The (Roman and Haddad), 155
Distraction, 2
Divorce Is a Grown Up Problem (Sinberg), 155
Divorce and single parenthood, 153–66; adjustments, 153–55, 158; change in relationship (with other parent), 160–61; child as an adult companion, 163–64; custody and caring for children, 158–59; ex-husband and adopted children, 155–56; father visit, 156–57; joint custody, 162; missing one parent feeling, 158; pent-up feelings and talking things over, 162–63; preference for weekend parent, 160; remarriage, 164; talking things out, 164–66; unresponsive father, 157–58
Doctor visits, fear of, 127–28
Dogs barking, fear of, 125–26
Dolls, 73, 84
Dream, of death, 203
Dressing himself, 38

Early-rising phase, 62
Eating issues, see Dinnertime and eating issues
Elkind, David, 54
Energy (for parenting endeavors), 198–99
Erikson, Erik, 53–54
Explaining Divorce to Children (ed. Grollman), 155

"Facts of life," 136–37
Family harmony, how to further, 231–32
Fantasy and reality, 5, 41–42
Fears, 44, 119–33; bad dreams, 130–31, 132; barking dogs, 125–26; being handicapped, 126–27; confronting, 124; dark room, 130; death and, 168–70, 174–75; doctor visit, 127–28; eleven-year-olds, 123; four-year-olds, 119–21, 125; left alone, 119–22; of a new school, 123; nine-year-olds, 131–32; separation, 122–23; seven-year-olds, 126–27; six-year-

olds, 128–30; three-year-olds, 124–26, 130–31; tonsillectomies, 128–30; understanding danger and, 132–33; when company arrives, 123–24
Feelings: adult model for, 92; of children, 91–103; crying as healing, 101–102; expressing, 100, 212; hearing out, 98–99; parents', 196–215; parents divorce, 153–55; reflecting, 102; separating children from, 91; sexual, 148–49; sharing, 102, 126; See also types of feelings
Feet on the dinner table, 8–9
Fights and fighting: and taking object away, 19–20; setting the table, 190; sibling, 80–82, 83; See also Hitting
Firm stand, taking, 10
First Snow (Coutant), 168
Flexibility, 48, 49, 198
Funerals, 173
Fussiness, 93

Gardner, Dr. Richard A., 155
Getting along (brother and sister), 86–87
Ginott, Haim, 102
Girls and Sex (Pomeroy), 151
Gregg, Elizabeth M., 43
Groaning, 15–16
Grollman, Earl A., 155
Gruenberg, Sidonie Matsner, 136
Guilt, 3, 87–88, 198, 200, 201, 202
Gullo, Stephen, 168

Haddad, William, 155
Hitting, 3–7, 15–16, 24–31; and biting, 56–57; commitment not to hit, 29–30; feeling of power from, 25; and name calling, 5–6; and pinching, 81; reasons to give up, 24–28; teaching child assertive self-defense, 6–7; wanting to hit feeling, 30–31
Hitting back, 7
Hoban, Russell, 74
Homework, 186; child's self-esteem and, 114
Homosexuality, 140, 143–44
Horseplay (at bedtime), 85–86
Hospital Story, A (Stein), 130
Hostility: redirecting, 73; toward parent of same sex, 147–48
Housecleaning and time with children, 208–9
Hugging and kissing, 104–5, 147
Humiliation, 27, 230

Humor, 9, 12, 36, 39, 47, 60
Hurt feelings (of mother), 199–200

"I'll show you" attitude (of parents), 18
Imagination, 53
Independence and interdependence,
67, 70, 76, 180–95; adult models (other
than parents), 182; allowances and
money management, 193–94;
clothes, selecting, 194; decision
sharing, 189–90; digesting
experiences and talking about them,
180–81; eight-year-olds, 190–91;
eleven-year-olds, 192–93; five-year-
olds, 192; frustration and parents
help, 184; homework and son's
autonomy, 186; learning by doing,
183–84; mother's impatience,
184–85; nine-year-olds, 185, 186;
orderliness, 191–93; parents' trust,
187; peer pressure and trust, 187–88;
philosophy on, 195; playtime and
responsibilities, 188–89; practice
making choices, 185; pushing child
into doctor's career, 181–82;
reminders, 185–86, 187, 190–91;
responsibility appropriate to age,
182–83; room order, 191; setting the
table fights, 190; six-year-olds,
182–83, 190; teenagers, 182, 187–88,
194; three-year-olds, 180–82, 183–84;
time alone, 181; twelve-year-olds,
185–86, 187; unbought items in
store, 194
Individuality: preferences, 84–85; reinforcement of, 89; sense of, 53
Infant and Child in the Culture of Today
(Gesell and Ilg), 54
Inquisitive (irritating) questions, 44–45

Jealousy, 75–76, 79, 81, 115, 164
Joint custody parenthood, 162

Kidding, self-image and, 112

Leaving the room (and coming back for
a fresh start), 48
Life after death beliefs, 174
Lighting matches, 13, 163
Like Me (Brightman), 126–27
Loneliness, 100–1
Love, 27, 61, 73, 75, 86, 97, 158, 205;
and approval, 12; and liking children,
204; divorced parents and, 164;

expressing, 104–5; self-appreciation
and, 106–7
Lying, 17–19, 22, 41–42

Making Babies (Stein), 139
Masturbation, 145–46
Matches, playing with, 13, 163
Menstruation, 139, 149–50; and
screaming at children, 201–2
Milk, refusing to drink, 36–37
Miscarriage, 176
Mood changes, 64
My Dentist (Rockwell), 127
My Doctor (Rockwell), 127
My Grandson Lew (Zolotow), 168

Nail biting, 92
Name calling, 44, 79, 83–84, 112–13, 204–5
Naughty, calling child, 3
Needs: juggling of, 197; of parents, 201
Negative feelings, 25
Negative labeling, self-image and,
111–12
New baby, adjusting to, 72–75
New school, boy's fear of, 123
Nightmares, 92
"Not listening" attitude, 4–5
Nudity, 135–36
Nuisance situations, 13–14, 22

Oedipal stage, 146–48, 155; feelings,
96–97; wishes, 148–49
"One more," requests for, 46–47
Orderliness, 191–93

Pacifiers, when to give up, 58–59
Parent awareness training: ages and
stages (growth and change), 52–71;
daily life, 34–51; death, 167–79;
discipline, 1–33; divorce and single
parenthood, 153–66; fears, 119–33;
feelings, 91–103, 196, 215;
independence and
interdependence, 180–95; self-
image, 104–18; sex identity and
education, 134–52; sibling issues,
72–90; summary of techniques,
219–36
Parenting: enjoying, 235–36; and
making life easier, 214–15
Parents Book About Divorce, The
(Gardner), 155
Personal-care routines, 47
Personality: ages and stages of, 52–55;
parent's feeling of responsibility
for, 203

Pestering, 42–43
Pet, death of, 178–79
Physical attacks, 230–31
Pinching, 81, 83, 115
Play, 39–42, 53, 56–57, 124; alone, 77–78; at dining room table, 43; for facing fears, 120; parents' feelings and, 197–98; sibling, 76–78
Playmates, 42–43
Pleasant morning experience, importance of, 38
Pomeroy, Wardell B., 151
Positive suggestions, change and, 206–8
Posture, self-image and, 111–12
Power plays, 83
Power struggle, 66
Preadolescence, 68–69
Preschool programs, 60–61
Problem solving, three-year-old's way, 5–6
Punishing attitude, 17, 230
Punishments, alternatives to, 16–22

Quarrels, 20, 39–40; one parent at odds with the other, 211; sibling, 78–80

Reality, see Fantasy and reality
Rebelliousness, 59–60
Regression, preschooler, 76
Rejection, 97, 100
Relationships, 211–12
Reminders, 185–86, 187; and lapses of responsibility, 190–91
Resentment, 38
Responsibility, handling, 62–63
Retaliation, parent's inclination for, 11
Rey, Margaret and H. A., 130
Rivalry, sibling, 84, 88–90
Rocks, throwing, 20–21
Rockwell, Harlow, 127
Role reversal, 7–8, 36
Roman, Mel, 155
Runaway Bunny (Brown), 98

Sacrifice (for one's children), 196–97
Sadness, feelings of, 99–100
Sarcasm, 38, 96, 97
School-age, behavior expectations, 67
Self-appreciation, 106–7
Self-confidence, 67
Self-control, 2, 3, 7, 23
Self-defense, 6–7
Self-esteem, 3, 25, 101
Self-image, 3, 25, 59; building, 104–18;

confidence and, 116–18; criticism, 113; descriptive praise, 115–16; kidding and, 112; labeling a child, 110–12; love and affection, 104–5; mother's way of seeing child, 109–10; name calling, 112–13; teachers and, 113–15; time factor, 108–9
Self-worth, 25, 107–8
Separation, fear of, 122–23
Setting a limit, 60, 201; ability to follow through, 10–11; for cooperation, 12–13; in courteous ways, 15; discipline and, 9–16; on disruptive behavior, 64–65; on groaning (without hitting), 15–16; nuisance situations, 13–14; too harshly, 9–10
Sex identity and education, 134–52; accurate explanations, 141; birth control, 150; body exploration, 142–43; bringing subject up, 137–38; direct answers, 138–39, 140, 146; eight-year-olds, 139–40; embarrassment (of parents), 140–41; "facts of life," 136–37; four-year-olds, 146–48; homosexuality, 143–44; involvement before marriage, 151–52; masturbation, 145–46, 150; menstruation, 139, 149–50; Oedipal stage, 146–48, 149; parents nudity (in front of children), 135–36; preschool-age children, 141–42; seven-year-olds, 138–39; six-year-olds, 137–38, 141, 142; stereotypes, 144; teenagers and, 149–52; ten-year-olds, 140; use of words, 138
Sharing with others, 59; decisions, 189–90; feelings, 103
Sheffield, Margaret, 136
Showers, Paul and Kay, 136
Shy, identifying a child as, 110
Sibling issues, 72–90; adjusting to new baby, 72–75; bedtime, 85–86; comparisons, 86; eight-year-olds, 80, 84; father's behavior and, 83; fights, 80–82, 83; five-year-olds, 77–78, 82, 83, 84–85; four-year-olds, 75–76, 84–85, 87–88; getting along, 86–87; horseplay (at bedtime), 85–86; individual preferences, 84–85; jealousy, 75–76; name calling, 83–84; nine-year-olds, 85–86; parents spending more time with one child, 87–88; playing alone, 77–78; playing together, 76–77; pretending to be a

Sibling issues (*continued*)
  baby, 76; quarrels, 78–80; rivalry, 84, 88–90; seven-year-olds, 82, 85–86, 87; six-year-olds, 76–77; tattletales, 82–83; teaching to help each other, 88; ten-year-olds, 86; thirteen-year-olds, 86–87; three-year-olds, 76, 86–87; twelve-year-olds, 83–84
Sinberg, Janet, 155
Single parenthood, *see* Divorce and single parenthood, 166
Slapping, 11–12, 25
"Slow" child, 63
Snacks, 45
Spanking, 2–3, 5, 8, 11–12, 26, 28, 59, 207; toddlers, 2; two-year-olds, 2–3
Stein, Sara Bonnett, 74, 126, 130, 136, 139, 168
Stereotypes, sex-role, 144
Storytelling and lying, parents and, 42
Supervision, 63
Swearing, 38–39, 99, 112–13, 138
Sympathetic Understanding of the Child: Birth to Sixteen, A (Elkind), 54

Talking About Divorce (Grollman), 155
"Talking back," 65–66
Tantrums, 48, 49, 55–56, 92, 95, 106
Tattle-tales, 82–83
Teachers, child's self-image and, 113–15
Teaching attitude, 17, 21
Teenagers: independence and interdependence, 182, 187–88, 194; sex identity and education, 149–52; value systems, 71

Television, death and violence on, 179
"Tell the truth and not lie" confrontation, 22–23
Tenth Good Thing About Barney, The (Viorst), 168
That New Baby (Stein), 74
Threat to leave home, 97–98
Time, self-image and, 108–9
Time alone, 181
Toddlers, disciplining, 1–2
Toilet-training, 57–58
Tonsillectomies, 128–30
Toothbrushing, 47
Trust, 187–88, 207
Trustworthiness, developing, 23
Truthfulness, 85

Unsympathetic reactions to child, 202–3
Upset feeling, child's repetition of, 201

Viorst, Judith, 168

Wake and funeral, 173
Water, fear of, 124–25
What to Do "When There's Nothing to Do" (Gregg), 43
When People Die (Bernstein and Gullo), 168
Where Do Babies Come From? (Sheffield), 136
"Whiner" label, 110
Wonderful Story of How You Were Born, The (Gruenberg), 136
Work schedule, time with children and, 199